S0-BRV-130

The Flower Teachers:
Stories for a New Generation

Candace Jesse Stout
Associate Professor of Art Education

The Ohio State University
Columbus, Ohio

The National Art Education Association

2002

For Sam, George, Bud, Connie and Carol

About the National Art Education Association

The National Art Education Association is the world's largest professional art education association and a leader in educational research, policy, and practice for art education. NAEA's mission is to advance art education through professional development, service, advancement of knowledge, and leadership.

Membership (approximately 40,000) includes elementary and secondary art teachers (and middle and senior high students in the National Art Honor Society programs), artists, administrators, museum educators, arts council staff, and university professors from throughout the United States and several foreign countries. It also includes publishers, manufacturers and suppliers of art materials, parents, students, retired art educators, and others concerned about quality art education in our schools.

The Association publishes several journals, papers, and flyers on art education; holds an annual convention; conducts research; sponsors a teacher awards program; develops standards on student learning, school programs and teacher preparation; and cosponsors workshops, seminars and institutes on art education. For further information, contact our web site at www.naea-reston.org.

© 2002 National Art Education Association
1916 Association Drive
Reston, VA 20191

Order No. 276
ISBN 1-890160-21-0

Table of Contents

Acknowledgements

The Flower Teachers: Stories for a New Generation grew out of a three year research project which I began in 1999 and completed in the spring of 2002. It is part of what scholars in qualitative research like Barone and Eisner (1997) call arts-based educational research, exhibiting a spectrum of design elements ranging from expressive language and storytelling to the promotion of empathy. The focus here is phenomenological, probing the essence of the career experiences of a group of veteran art teachers who began teaching in the late 1960s and early 1970s and continue to teach as the new century unfolds. For more than a quarter of a century, they have worked to build the schools and the visual arts programs we have today.

In the spring of 1999, thirty teachers working in elementary, middle, and high school classrooms from Montana to Massachusetts, became part of what I call the Flower Teachers' Project. Over a six-month period, they committed their time and energy to completing open-ended interviews, which in the end, generated some 600 pages of text. From their reflections, I have woven a collective story of what they have seen and experienced, and after decades in the classroom, the sense they have made of it all.

There are many to whom I am grateful for sustaining me in this project and for helping to bring this book to fruition. First there is my husband Sam, the anthropologist who offered critical advice and who came to know the stories of the Flower Teachers as well as I do.

And there are, of course, the Flower Teachers themselves. To this moment, I am amazed at my good fortune in collecting a group of teachers with such sterling credentials and stalwart commitment. [See Chapter 10 for abbreviated autobiographies.] Each of them dedicated hours to completing lengthy interviews, and afterward, over two years, responded patiently to additional queries for clarification and more information. They have sent to me words of encouragement and I to them. We have exchanged holiday cards and myriad e-mails. We have shared digital jokes and groused about national elections. We commiserated over the September 11th tragedy. And over the past three years, those who could attend have met at the National Art Education Association conferences where we have talked about the progress of the project. Though I knew only one of these teachers before my research began, and though they had no knowledge of each another, we have formed friendships that will endure.

I am grateful to Elliot Eisner, Professor of Education and Art at Stanford University, for his willingness to provide critical commentary on my early manuscript and to lend encouragement when I most needed it. I am also appreciative to Terry Barrett, Professor of Art Education at The Ohio State University, for pinpointing an essential line of inquiry that added perspective to the project.

I must acknowledge the people who took part in a pilot study for the project. First, there is Peter Herborn, a retired social studies teacher from the public schools of Columbia, Missouri. Pete is one of the most politically savvy and historically astute teachers I know. Years ago when I taught high school, I learned from him the necessity of teacher advocacy and of participation in organizations like the National Education Association, the American Federation of Teachers, and the National Art Education Association. Throughout the spring and summer of 1997, Pete spent several months in the cardiology ward of the University of Missouri Hospitals where he waited for a heart transplant. During that time I became a regular visitor. We spent hours just talking, and inevitably that talk moved to teaching, to trends, issues, school reforms, things both political and personal about our many years in the schools. It was from those conversations that I honed many of my interview questions for the Flower Teachers' Project. And I am happy to say that Pete received his new heart and is living a happy and healthy life. Jerry and Sandy Fernbacher who have dedicated their lives to teaching in the Cincinnati schools also took part in my pilot study; I thank them too.

From the University of Georgia, I received a Senior Faculty Research Grant which supplemented my computing needs for the project. From The Ohio State University, I am grateful to our Art Education Department's graduate associate Prashant Bansal who scanned the photographs of the participants. Finally, I wish to thank the National Art Education Association for having faith in the project.

The Flower Teachers' Project has been arduous and all consuming, and it has been the most rewarding work of my research and writing life. Following are several notes sent to me by the teachers during the summers of 2000-01. They have been displayed prominently in my office, inspiring me along the way.

"It is not very often that a teacher is called upon to reflect on his or her career. This has been an opportunity to examine what I do for a living, and upon reflection, I think I've done pretty well over the years. It also focused my attention on some negative images, memories of trying to maintain a standard of excellence amid an educational community that misunderstands why we teach the arts in the first place." (Gerald Vilenski, Plainwell, Michigan)

"I hope your summer is going well and you are making progress on your book. You certainly chose an interesting subject. I have pictured you sitting and listening to tapes and becoming friends with so many fascinating people from across the country. I am looking forward to sharing their stories." (Sharon Henneborn, East Windsor, New Jersey)

"I guess the best way to describe this interview is that it was a catharsis of sorts. That's what kept me going. This was a lot more work than I originally thought it would be. I considered my answers carefully and that took time. I laughed and shed some tears and thought about some issues that I don't face every day." (Carolyn Skeen, Oak Ridge, Tennessee)

"I am struck by the richness of what is my own personal story as an art educator. I feel that I have been fortunate to have had so much variety of experience. Struggling with honest answers to these questions has caused me to ask what is most important? What really counts? and What is it that I can offer now?" (Nancy Zadra, Missoula, Montana)

Project Participants and Schools
(as of September, 2000)

Candace Alexander, Church Hill, TN, Church Hill/McPheeter's
Bend Elementary Schools

Lora Barrett, Holyoke, MA, Holyoke Magnet Middle School for Arts

Martyna Bellessis, Bloomington, IN, University Elementary School

Phyllis, Bosco, Tallahassee, FL, Florida State University Elementary School

Suzanne Greene, Houston, TX, Spring Branch Middle School

Yvonne Greene, Slaton, TX, West Ward Elementary School

Sharon Henneborn, East Windsor, NJ, Ethel McKnight Middle School

Barbara Hirokawa, Littleton, CO, Columbine High School

Jane Hollingsworth, Gainesville, GA, Gainesville Middle School

Bonnie Keyser, Covington, VA, Alleghany High School

Susan Kropa, Mt. Pleasant, IA, Lincoln/Salem Elementary Schools

Lurline Lapolla, New Canaan, CT, Saxe Middle School

Carrol Morgan, King George, VA, King George Middle School

Joan Newcomer, Owings Mills, MD, McDonogh Elementary School

Mark Phillips, Quarryville, PA, George A. Smith Middle School

Sonia Pratt, Oakland, MD, Southern Garrett High School

Sudee Sanders, Cherry Hill, NJ, Cherry Hill Schools

Lloyd Sensat, Boutte, LA, Hahnville High School

Marie Shack, Wilmington, MA, Wilmington High School

Jeannie Siegler, Missoula, MT , Loyola High School

Carolyn Skeen, Oak Ridge, TN, Linden Elementary School

John Skrabalak, Altoona, PA, Altoona Area High School

Cherie St. Pierre, Kenmore, NY, Charles A. Lindbergh Elementary School

Kathleen Thompson, Ellijay, GA, Gilmer Middle School

Gerald Vilenski, Plainwell, MI, Starr/Cooper Elementary School

Carol Wellein, Monkton, MD, St. James Academy (K-12)

Ken Wilkie, Princeton, NJ, Riverside Elementary School

Judy Williams, Shelbyville, TN, Southside Primary School

Anita Winfrey, Collinsville, VA, Irisburg/Stanleytown Elementary School

Nancy Zadra, Missoula, MT, Missoula County Public Schools

Reproduced with permission.

The Eleventh Day (2001), created by students of Spring Branch Middle School, Houston, Texas under the direction of art specialists Suzanne Greene and David Butler. This 30' x 12' black and white mural was painted with house paint on two canvas drop clothes, all supplies were donated.

Teacher Commentary

The tragedy of September 11, 2001 moved a group of middle school art students in Houston, Texas, to exercise their freedom of expression, to speak loudly, vividly with their paintbrushes in the language of art. From their efforts emerged a 12 x 30 foot canvas.

Hanging in our art rooms at Spring Branch Middle School in Houston, Texas is a poster of Picasso's *Guernica*. The "experimental" mass fire bombing in 1937 of the Basque town of Guernica moved Picasso to paint one of the world's great art treasures and one of the most shocking "documents" of the horrors of war. It was this poster that brought one of our art students to ask, "Can we do something like this in honor of Sept 11?" So, inspired by *Guernica*, SBMS art students spoke the language of art with their thoughts, feelings, hopes, and dreams and spent two months working on their response to our nation's tragedy.

After over 200 individual paintings were finished, my partner in Art, Suzy Greene and I chose over 20 images to be "collaged" into a "Picasso-like" composition. Shades of black, white, and gray house paint, brushes and canvas were donated by a local business. Beginning October 11, over 40 art students in teams of 8-12 met before and after school to work on the mural on a front hallway floor. During the course of four weeks, values lightened and grew dark, lines appeared and disappeared, images morphed, merged, and transformed into a unique language of art. It was as if the spirit of Picasso were with us, as the painting took on a life of it's own, filled with the vitality of American children. One month later, we were finished.

David Butler, Art Specialist, Spring Branch Middle School

Chapter 1
For Better and For Worse

We shall not cease from exploration
And the end of all our exploring
Will be to arrive where we started
And know the place for the first time.
T. S. Eliot, "Little Gidding," from *Four Quartets*, 1942

Introduction

A generation of teachers is about to empty their desks, pack their belongings, and close the doors of their classrooms for the last time. These are the veteran teachers who, from the 1960s through today, have dedicated over 30 years of their lives to teaching the visual arts in elementary and secondary classrooms across the nation. As one century ends and a new one begins, they are on the brink of retirement. These are the teachers who were educated and came of age in the 1960s, and who first opened the doors of their classrooms in the late 60s and early 70s. I call them the "Flower Teachers," for they were part of that youth generation, donning their bell-bottoms and mini-skirts at 6:00 a.m. and humming the tunes of Simon and Garfunkel as they drove to school in their Volkswagen Beetles. Conservatively, each of these individuals has logged in some 60,000 hours of classroom instruction; collectively, they have touched the lives of thousands of children. They are a waning generation of teaching professionals who, more than any before, have experienced a fast and furious flow of trends, issues, and reform movements in public education. They thrived on books like Postman & Weingartner's *Teaching As a Subversive Activity* (1969), Lowenfeld's *Creative and Mental Growth* (1957), Bel Kaufman's *Up the Down Staircase* (1965), and Alvin Toffler's *Future Shock* (1971). They were intrigued by the idealism in *Summerhill* (1960), A. S. Neill's radical approach to child rearing. And when they entered their first classrooms, they witnessed firsthand the devastating effects of inequality, poverty, neglect, things they had only read about in the impassioned books of Jonathan Kozol, John Holt, Richard Wright, and Paulo Freire. These were the young teachers who deconstructed classroom walls, ushering in a new era of humanistic, open education. They were the vanguard faculty who welcomed racial integration and stood waiting as school buses boarded their students, carrying some to the suburbs, some to the projects of the inner city. They were the teachers who convinced the school boards, administrators, and parents of the essential need for the arts in the core curriculum of a school. They are the faculty who fought the hard-won battle for a multicultural curriculum. It was their commitment and effort that introduced African-American, Native-American, Asian, Hispanic, and female voices into the arts in our public schools. They have taught in times of sadness and turmoil, through loss in Vietnam, assassinations of political and spiritual leaders, the introduction of drugs and violence into the schools, and now the ultimate brutality of the Eleventh Day of September. They have taught, too, in times of prosperity, of innovation and hope. In their classrooms, children saw humankind launch into space and walk on the moon. They have seen unprecedented advancement in science and technology and have experienced the proliferation of new schools, instructional materials, and means. Now, at the opening of a new century, as seasoned veterans and master teachers, they are experiencing the wonder of the World Wide Web and the social, pedagogical, and technological complexities that come with it. For this generation, the sweep of the educational pendulum has been long, deep, and pronounced. At the close of the Twentieth Century, they are part of the capstone generation, a culmination and summary of the philosophy and practice of an era of American education. At the opening of the Twenty-first Century, they are nearing retirement, but before they bid their farewells, there must be some summary, some meaning assigned to the richness of their individual and collective experiences. Most important, there must be some lessons to learn from these veteran teachers about children and life in our schools, about teaching and learning in a rapidly changing society, and not least of all, about these formative years in the field of art education.

The Flower Teachers: Stories for a New Generation is based on the experiences of 30 of these people who, in times of social upheaval and political change, decided to become art teachers and who committed themselves along the way to staying in that profession, for better and for worse, for more than a quarter of a century. Though their discipline is art, their experiences document the history and uncover insights relevant to teachers of this generation in every discipline. The stories here are not about perilous risk, gallant rescues, or dangerous liaisons. The narratives show no stunning climax or startling conclusions. They are not the stories of high profile pursuits. Instead, they tell about fervently dedicated and tenacious people who are united under a common ethos, mutual goals, and a passion for the visual arts. There are those who believe that every age or generation is inspired by what may be called its inevitable idea. The stories here are all about the inevitable ideas and ideals of the Flower Teachers and what they have given to a generation of children in our schools.

This book is based on an in-depth, on-going research study, the Flower Teachers Project, which I developed over a three year period. The focus is on the social history of this generation of visual arts teachers and the pedagogical issues, trials, and tribulations with which they have wrestled over the past quarter of a century. The ultimate goal of the project is to try to understand the essence of these teachers' experiences, to impart personal and professional understanding of what it has been like to teach, both in general terms and in the visual arts, and to interact with students, parents, and administrators throughout one of the most radically changing eras in American education.

Uncovering the Story
Volunteering hours of their time to collaborate in this project are 30 visual arts teachers working in rural, suburban, and urban centers, elementary through high school, in 17 states from Massachusetts to Montana. Their experiences extend from Peace Corps service in Sierra Leone, to frontier efforts in desegregating the nation's classrooms, to surviving the tragedy and promoting the healing at Columbine High School. Through written and taped interviews, they provided in-depth, reflective descriptions of their teaching experiences over the last four and five decades. Remarkable in the whole of their interviews is authenticity. The tone is not confessional; rather it is truth-speaking. Within a body of open-ended questions, participants told their own stories, thus describing and summarizing experiences, encapsulating philosophy and practice, and ultimately offering their own interpretations of significant people, events, trends, and issues that have characterized and affected their long tenure in the schools. Finally, they made recommendations, gave advice, and offered predictions for art education and for the general scope of American education for the century to come.

In writing this book, what I have tried to do is extract the most savory material, the nectar if you will, from all that the Flower Teachers have related to me in the project as a whole. The wealth of information they provided came in varied forms. Some were purely expository, straightforward accounts of times, events, or instructional approaches. Depending on the question, some were terse or in the form of prioritized lists. It came as no surprise, however, that at the very heart of all that was said were the threads of stories, woven within the contexts of time, place, and personality. After all, *The Flower Teachers* is a book about lifetime experience, and in the idea of contemporary education researchers "experience is the stories people live" (Clandinin & Connelly, 1994, p. 415). The teachers in this study are experts in recognizing the value and the integrity of experience itself. They are acutely aware of the progressions and hallmarks in their professional lives and, when asked, are keen in narrating the sequence and flow, the past, present, and future, of their times in the classroom. Essentially, it is the stories of these people that bring us as close as we might come to a sympathetic understanding of their growth and change, their routines and epiphanies, and of their feelings and understandings about their lifetime of endeavor. "Stories such as these, lived and told, educate the self and others, including the young and those, such as researchers, who are new to their communities" (Clandinin & Connelly, 1994, p. 415).

As author of this book, I find myself playing two roles that are braided together by one compelling goal. In undertaking this search for the meaning and significance of these teachers' experiences, my hope has been to uncover a story that has been hiding in plain sight—inconspicuous, yet perpetually growing and unfolding. In doing so, I work as both researcher and biographer. As researcher, I bring together a group of people and ask them to tell their stories. From their narratives, my charge is to study their words, to find out what is actually there and what is not, and ultimately, identify the themes and patterns, the inevitable ideas if you will, that unite these individuals in their common cause. As a biographer, I select, sort, order, and mold. I accentuate and downplay. From the thoughts, feelings, and described events, I endeavor to cull out the compelling, to gain insights, and reconstruct, through clear and interesting writing, the collective essence of my subjects. Intertwined within this reconstruction are primary texts, that is, the actual quotes of the teachers as they were stated in their interviews. Likewise, there are composites, the consolidation of teachers' words and ideas. In some instances, I use the latter to protect the anonymity of individuals; in others, it is done for efficiency.

I have written this book in the context of my own personal experience, as a part of this generation, having begun my career in 1968, and having taught elementary through high school over an expanse of three decades. In essence, in sorting through the data and studying the complex layers of these teachers' stories, I have drawn on my own interpretive framework, and at the same time, I have striven to dovetail my interpretation with as much empirical data as possible from the teachers themselves. From the project's inception, my intent has been not to judge the teachers and their perspectives, though I recognize that this is never wholly possible. Rather, my focus has been on relating their experiences, their truths as they see them. They may not be my truths or yours, but they are the heart of what these teachers have lived and understood from their years in the classroom.

In providing commentary, I have worked carefully not to undermine the narrative character of the teachers' stories. Early in the writing of this book, I completed a chapter called *Cultivating the Project*. It explains what motivated the Flower Teachers' Project, the strategies for finding participants, the methods of collecting their stories, and the inspiration that kept the project thriving throughout three years of research and writing. The researcher's voice inside of me dictated that this chapter should follow the Introduction. An ulterior voice, the writer within, convinced me otherwise, maintaining that this is not a research monograph and I must be careful not to undermine the narrative character of the teachers' stories. What is most interesting here are the people and the magnetism of their individual and collective stories. They pull us in, suspend us in their telling. They help us understand, trust, and believe. So as not to interrupt the flow and integrity of the narrative, I have explained the project's cultivation in the Epilogue.

The value of this project lies in the educational insights these experienced individuals can provide. Their theories, practice, and critical observations are credentialed by years of on-going study in art and education, by graduate degrees and hours of post baccalaureate work, and by decades of classroom presence. Their stories are characterized by both optimism and dejection. Their perceptions, advice, and admonitions are worth critical reflection by contemporary and future teachers in every discipline, as well as all others interested in understanding and bettering teaching and learning in our schools.

Chapter 2 defines the context of this special generation of teachers, describing their college years and those formative times when they came of age. In their own terms, it explains the circumstances that made them the kind of teachers they are.

Chapter 2
A Common Spirit

We are stardust,
We are golden,
And we've got to get ourselves
Back to the garden.
Joni Mitchell, *Woodstock*, 1969

What made them who they are?
These were times of great lust for life, magical, wonderful times. The
intensity of the 60s created great friendships. Growing up in that era led us
to believe that we could make the world a better place.
Lloyd Sensat, Jr., Hahnville High School, Boutte, Louisiana

I knew it then as I know it now, the experiences of this group of teachers are
framed and decided by a special set of circumstances. Despite the diversity
in family and upbringing among these 30 people, in studying their interviews, I discovered a complex of basic values that permeates their thoughts
and motivates their ideas and practice. In essence, there is among them a
common spirit. From their own perspectives, there was something about
being a youth, about being educated and coming of age in the 1960s and
early 70s that patterned this generation of art teachers.

For the most part, they were the first of the Baby Boomers, born of parents
who came of age during the Great Depression and the Second World War.
They were nurtured by the post-war notions of accountability, productivity,
and possibility. In childhood they tuned into Captain Kangaroo, Howdy
Doody and Buffalo Bob. They shared TV dinners with Ozzie and Harriet,
David and Rick, and gave cautious consideration to the paragon of *Father
Knows Best*. With the opening of their first newspaper came *Peanuts*, the
antics of Snoopy, Lucy, and Charley Brown. Brought up on the philosophy
of Benjamin Spock's *The Common Sense Book of Baby and Child Care*
(1946), made literate through readings of *Dick and Jane* (Kismaric &
Heiferman, 1996), and entertained with the animated stories of *Alice in
Wonderland* (Carroll, 1953) and *Peter Pan* (Barrie, 1956), for many,
childhood was characterized by a mellow idealism. But there were other
narratives too, some more cynical and grim. Sometimes in the evenings

when adults had their time, fathers and uncles shared stories of World War II and of serving in the bitter cold of Korea. Parents and older siblings watched newscasts about Khrushchev, Senator McCarthy, and Mao Tsetung. In school, in a class play called *The Diary of a Young Girl* (Frank, 1952), they learned from a Jewish teenager about The Holocaust. Not infrequently, between recess and reading, right in the middle of learning about the Iron Curtain and communists, they crouched under desks in designated drills, just in case of attack from something call an "H-bomb." And there was a disease called polio, so the school nurse came around and they waited in fretful lines for the vaccine in her needle. All was not well everywhere.

As elementary and junior high school students, they were generally accepting, even docile— products of an orderly institution marked by benign authority and clear-cut expectations. Somewhere in the early days of it all they read in *The Weekly Reader* about a satellite with Cyrillic lettering and an emblem of a hammer and sickle. In October of 1957, Sputnik I had been launched into orbit and they found themselves unceremoniously ushered into the race for space and technology. Science and math books got thicker and foreign languages became "musts." Curricula took a fundamental turn to basics and essentials. Somewhere in the rush of Cold War competition, the childhood times for stories and music and watercolor painting were lost from the days spent in the post-Sputnik classroom.

The vigor of childhood in the 1950s and early 60s was a peculiar amalgam of "happy days" on the surface and premonitions of a difficult reality underneath. While filmstrips at school and features in *Look* and *Life* boasted of expanding scientific, medical, and technological progress, Huntley and Brinkley's evening news reflected a disconcerting lag in humanity. There were poverty and distress, inequality in the job market, in the courthouse, polling place, schools, and more. Early on in 1954, when this generation was in the primary grades, the Supreme Court made a crucial decision, *Brown vs. Board of Education of Topeka, Kansas*, declaring "Separate educational facilities are inherently unequal," and a year later schools were to be integrated with "all deliberate speed" (1954, 347 U. S. 483). Shortly after, from somewhere in the middle of Alabama came another act, symbolic but powerfully catalytic. In 1955, a black woman named Rosa Parks took a bus ride, and with the simple word "No!" laid bare the reality behind the life of white picket fences.

Stretching into adolescence, they were at the leading edge of the "youth generation," discovering Elvis, voices from Motown, and hootenannies on *The Ed Sullivan Show*. In the crowded school auditoriums that were the hallmark of their post-war generation, in 1963, they gathered with class-mates to share the hopes of Martin Luther King, Jr. in his "I Have a Dream" speech. In that same year, there was strife in the streets, Rachel Carson's warnings of environmental devastation, and on a horrible November day, the assassination of President John F. Kennedy. In the words of singer Don McLean, for many in this generation, it was "the day the music died" (1971). For a while, they had Camelot and prom nights with Beach Boys and *Help!* from the Beatles. The death of a President opened a glaring window on a new truth.

Before they knew it, high school had ended. In the fall, they ran barefoot among the flowers of college campuses, reading books like *Siddartha* (Hesse, 1951), *Jonathan Livingston Seagull* (Bach, 1970), *Catch-22* (Heller, 1961), *The Autobiography of Malcolm X* (Malcolm X, 1965), *Soul on Ice* (Cleaver, 1968), and *Bury My Heart at Wounded Knee* (Brown, 1970). They consumed films like *Easy Rider* and *The Graduate*. They took courses in "new math," painting and drawing, biology, and poetry. They signed waiting lists for trendy classes like "Philosophy of Protest" and "Warhol's World." There was also something called ROTC (Reserve Officer Training Corps), required specifically for young men. In the after hours, they began the tradition of big concerts, making famous a little farming town called Woodstock in New York. Throughout these years, they shared with thousands the musical philosophies of the Beatles, Carol King, Joan Baez, Cat Stevens, Bob Dillon and the raucous rock of Janis Joplin, Jimi Hendrix, and The Doors. They read *Rolling Stone*, laughed at Rown & Martin, applauded the Eagle's landing in the Sea of Tranquility, and cheered the brash antics of Mohammed Ali. They joined the Women's Movement and supported the March on Washington. Just as these were high times of excitement, joy, and effective change, so were they chaotic, revolutionary, and sometimes violent. When the boys became eighteen-year-old men, there were 1-A draft cards for "death lotto" and unscheduled excursions to Vietnam. There was the Tet offensive of 1968, the murders of Robert F. Kennedy, Martin Luther King, Jr., the deaths of students at Kent State in 1970, and Watergate. Castro was rattling swords in Cuba. Starva-tion and ethnic strife besieged people in places like Biafra, Uganda, and South Africa. The sky rained, the thunder rattled, and something called "reform" was hanging in the air. Encapsulated in songs like "Come Together," "Give Peace a Chance," and "Imagine," a generation of young people had begun their transformation into vehement social consciousness, calling for peace and flowers to replace weapons, asking for a more humane world and communal caring from all.

In the midst of it all, the youth generation, dubbed broadly by the media as the "flower children," graduated from college. Symbolized, perhaps, in the rebellious nature of Benjamin Braddock in *The Graduate*, many turned from the traditional career path to what was fondly called the "white knight" professions. Some joined the Peace Corps, travelling to Mexico, Latin America, and Africa to help people in impoverished lands. Some signed up with VISTA and various church-related organizations to aid the needy at home. Inspired by the values in *Silent Spring* (Carson, 1962), the Sierra Club, and Greenpeace, many became instrumental in the "green scene" and were there for the first celebration of Earth Day on a beautiful spring morning in 1970. Many went to serve in Southeast Asia—both willing and not. Quite a few became counselors, nurses, doctors, and lawyers. And from this generation of youth, there was a dedicated group of individuals who signed new contracts to become teachers, because they believed in human potential, held tight to the possibilities for change, and were committed to the ideals of heroes like John and Robert Kennedy and Martin Luther King, Jr.

So this is the thing that happened with us . . . .
Among those youth who signed up to teach during these seminal and transitory times were the people whose experiences form the heart of this book. As part of what contemporary researchers call the "grand tour questions" guiding this project, there was one that set the stage, delving into what it was that made these teachers who they are today. The question posed to them was this:

> During your formative years in the 1960s and early 1970s, in secondary school or college, what were some of your experiences, who were the people, what were the events that shaped your attitudes, values, basic assumptions, and philosophy about life and about teaching? In other words, what, in particular, was it about being a youth and being educated in the 1960s or early 70s that made you the kind of person and the kind of teacher that you are?

For those familiar with the times, the overarching themes emerging from their responses should have a familiar ring. However, what provided the most telling insights into the indelible hallmarks of this generation are the vehement particularities of their individual reflections. Below are the accounts of several of the teachers.

Ken Wilkie
It's as if the whole society was going through a period of adolescence.

> So this is the thing that happened with us. . . . Where were we when Kennedy was assassinated? That's the frame of reference. I was in the seventh grade in music class. It was three months after the March on Washington with Dr. Martin Luther King. It seemed

like this . . . it was the point where you're coming of age, becoming aware of things and here was a world that was extremely dramatic for a kid developing awareness.

Adolescence is always a challenging time, a time when you're going to question values and wonder where you're going, and here we had on television, in the streets, everywhere around you, a world that was changing, that was being challenged. It's as if the whole society was going through a period of adolescence. And so it was a very exciting time to be this age. I often think that people about ten years older then us are kind of jealous of the excitement of our lives, of going to demonstrations, going to the rock concerts, being a vital part of political activities on campus. And then the experimentation with drugs and sex, all the things that are kind of tied together with that image of the 60s

So what this did was make me look at the role of education—the teacher as somebody who was part of changing the world, of making change, and helping others to see it. We weren't just out for ourselves. We weren't just going to get a job and make money. That was looked upon as selfish and not full enough, not noble enough. You know, people talk about going into the Peace Corps. I remember I had friends who said this and they had *nothing* to offer in terms of services or skills. They just wanted to go *do* something. This is that sort of exotic ideal of going off and having a genuine effect, being a hero to somebody. Being a hero to yourself, maybe. And I think that kind of steers you into teaching, to be some place where you can make changes, where you can make a difference in people's lives. And it's very exciting.

Carrol E. Morgan
It was one big alternative life styles experience, and it was the greatest education I could have had in the arts.

There were extraordinary events taking place in Richmond, Virginia, while I was attending college. From the first day, I loved R. P. I., living in the Richmond "Fan District" and being part of one of the most exciting art colleges in America during the 1960s. It was one big alternative life styles experience, and it was the greatest education I could have had in the arts.

As for the city itself, Richmond was fighting against racial integration of public facilities. Broad Street, the main east-west corridor was traditionally (bizarrely) segregated by black businesses and pedestrians on one side and white businesses and pedestrians on the other, facing each other but never crossing over. On one infamous day, my photography teacher sent my class downtown to take pictures of what he thought might be historical events. Black people were crossing Broad Street and going into Woolworth's Department Store to sit down at the lunch counter. We grabbed our cameras and arrived just in time to see police with dogs trying to prevent the sit-in. One of my classmates took THE PICTURE of a police dog attacking an elderly black woman. He sold his roll of film on the spot to a professional journalist and the famous photo appeared nationwide.

I knew it was wrong to treat people like second-class citizens— more like non-persons. I began to deliberately sit at integrated lunch counters and take a seat next to black people on public buses. Those earliest days of integration in Richmond had a profound effect on me. Remembering the bigotry I had seen in those early years, I vowed that I would never consider people of any color less than equal. I have struggled throughout my teaching career with the effects of segregation and integration. Generations of people have believed, and still believe, in the stereotypes of black culture. My black students and their parents still have to face prejudice, injustice, and harassment, even if it is silent. Is it getting better or worse? I see some of both, and the greatest roadblocks have been removed by integration of public schools, but that only reflects the degree of integration that exists in local communities. Equal opportunity for minorities has made many lives better, but I still see the little behaviors and words that belie true equality of respect. I sympathize with my minority students and the hazardous path they tread—the silent mistrust of others and the wondering if all things *are* equal for them. Many of my black former students are the parents of my current students, and I can only trust that their warm hugs and handshakes speak well for my efforts to treat all of my students with love and respect.

Bonnie Keyser
I knew that I was the first person in my family to graduate from college and that I had better not screw it up.

I remember in the 60s how important family was. We would go to church on Sundays and then go visiting friends' homes. Dad worked in a factory and Mom was a housewife. None of my friends had working moms. Wow! What a change! My teachers and parents were very influential through secondary school and college. I remember a week before graduation at Madison College when we marched and had a "sit in" against the war in Vietnam in front of the school cafeteria. As the campus police started taking names of the protestors, I left before mine was taken. I knew that I was the first person in my family to graduate from college and that I had better not screw it up. One of my roommates was not so lucky. She was not allowed to participate in graduation and it was very upsetting. I felt bad because I had not stayed with the group but I could not let my family down. The value of family stays with me today.

John Skrabalak
I had anxiety attacks every Thursday when I had to go on mandatory ROTC drill practices.

I was a different kind of student in high school. I was a passive rebel. I was the first to own a Jimi Hendrix album and was thrown out of a school dance for trying to play one of his songs. I was awarded "love beads" at my Senior Awards Banquet. In college, I joined the S. D. S. and worked for Senator Eugene McCarthy for President. I went on peace marches and sit in's. I had anxiety attacks every Thursday when I had to go on mandatory ROTC drill practices. ROTC was mandatory for every male freshman to take. I hated war and still do. God blessed me with a high draft number. As a result, I always thought I had to be a good art teacher as a thank-you to God. I was devastated over the Kent State Massacre. At the time, I was on the college yearbook art staff. The art staff designed a controversial yearbook as our response to Kent State. It turned out so controversial that the whole art staff was fired. I have always had a rebel spirit in me. As a result of so many of my youthful experiences, I am a staunch advocate for the rights and personal choices of students.

Jeannie Siegler
My Crossroads and Peace Corps experiences in Africa during that time put problems in the U. S. in a different perspective for me.

Being young during the 60s and 70s certainly allowed more personal freedom and choices than occurred in the depression and war eras of our parents. My formative years of high school and college in the South found women still trying to fit traditional rolls of dependency, but also exploring independence in limited ways.

A lot of questioning and rebellion was going on in the late 60s and early 70s Some of it I related to, some I did not.

My Crossroads and Peace Corps experiences in Africa during the 60s and 70s put problems in the U. S. in a different perspective for me. I often think back to my first teaching experience as a Peace Corps volunteer in Sierra Leone, West Africa. Presently Sierra Leone is a country devastated by the civil strife of the last decades. In 1968, classroom facilities and materials were scarce. I tell my students almost every year that in my first classroom I would have loved to have had just the papers that are in our scrap box. But natural resources abounded in Sierra Leone and we were able to make clay in much the same manner local people built their homes. As a class we had to improvise and create with whatever we could find. To this day, optimism, perseverance, and collective coopera-tion have been my keys to making something out of nothing. That definitely comes from my Peace Corps experience.

Joan Newcomer
All the books that I had read in college like Autobiography of Malcolm X, Crisis in Black and White, and Eldridge Clever's Soul on Ice made me real sensitive to acts of prejudicial thinking.

"Don't trust anyone over 30." During those times, this was a popular saying. Throughout those formative years in the 60s and 70s, youth were questioning the values of the older generation. As an art student in college at the time, I was taught by instructors who also questioned many of our society's values. "Make love, not war." I remember reading our newspaper, *The Diamondback*, when I was at the University of Maryland. Besides trying to catch photos of nude streakers, there were always articles dealing with trust, and peace, and consciousness-raising. Many young people considered themselves hippies and moved into houses they called communes. I wasn't quite that radical, but I did reject a lot of the values that were so important to the older generation at that time. Many did not want to go to Vietnam, so they went to Canada rather than have to be drafted. There were stories about nasty college professors who would tell their students that if they did not perform well, they could send them off to die in Vietnam. Folk singers like Bob Dylan, Peter, Paul, and Mary, and Joan Baez had a lot of effect on the attitudes that were formed at the time. I felt that their messages were truthful ones. There was a good deal of mistrust of politicians and people in power. Long-haired students would be discriminated against by police or people who distrusted them because they were different. There was a general attitude among the youth of wanting to be free and happy, and not wanting to be tied down by material things. The Women's Movement at the time also had a big effect on the way I began to think. I was not a burn-your-bra and throw away your make-up person, but I was influenced by them. How did all of this affect the way I teach? This and all the books that I had read in college like *Autobiography of Malcolm X* (1965), *Crisis in Black and White* (Silberman, 1964), and Eldridge Clever's *Soul on Ice* (1968) made me real sensitive to acts of prejudicial thinking. Due to the Women's Movement, I am extremely sensitive to gender discrimination. John Dewey's philosophy of "learning by doing"—the ideals of activism— were vitally influential.

Marie Shack
When parents bemoan their boys, I tell them John's story and tell them not to worry.

I met John as my blind date for my college senior prom in 1968. He had come from a year in a hospital recuperating from wounds suffered in Vietnam. He had a body cast that covered his whole right leg and his torso. After the prom, he stayed for graduation and it really was love at first sight. He had started out at Boston College and was the last one cut from the basketball team, so he went off to join the Marine Corps. At first, he was stationed in Washington as a Presidential guard but kept getting into trouble and eventually was sent to Vietnam. Upon his return from duty, John re-entered B. C. in September 1968 under a veteran's benefits program. We were married the year following our prom date in 1969. I can still remember thinking that this man will never walk right again …and that it didn't matter. During the 70s these were hard times for Vietnam Vets, not appreciated and considered morons or government lackeys. My usually mild mannered husband picketed against the anti-war pickets at B. C. He now has a B.A. from B. C., an MBA from B. C. and a law degree from Suffolk University. He was president of the Rotary and of the Board of Directors of the WMCA. When parents bemoan their boys, I tell them John's story and tell them not to worry.

Jane Hollingsworth
At the beginning of my career, I was idealistic enough to believe I could open up the world of art to my students and they would change the world through artistic expression.

The mood of the 60s when I was a student was one of idealism and rebellion against the status quo. The 60s enabled me to be comfortable with disagreement and conflict. When I was a student at the University of Georgia, I had an art education professor who was totally anti-establishment. He recommended that we read books like *The Little Prince* (Saint-Exupèry, 1943) and Tom Wolfe's *Kandy Kolored Tangerine Flake Streamline Baby* (1965). I was a rule-follower and I was religious but I soaked up the culture for which the 60s became famous. When I would go home during the breaks, I would bait my parents with what I perceived as non-conformist, intellectual statements. The mood of protest so typical of the 60s carried over into my teaching at the beginning of my career. I must have been an instrumentalist because I felt that artistic expression had to have a purpose. Francisco Goya's painting, *The Third of May*, 1808, became the quintessential example of what I thought art should be. It epitomized the anti-war movement of the 1960s. Art changes people's ideas and beliefs. At the beginning of my career, I was idealistic enough to believe I could open up the world of art to my students and they would change the world through artistic expression.

Phyllis Bosco
In looking back, teaching and making art came naturally.

I was fortunate to grow up in a house that encouraged love of the arts and education. One set of my grandparents was from the Ukraine and the other from Sicily. My parents, raised during the depression, were extremely poor and without much formal education. However, they always seemed to realize—and insisted their children realize—the value of continued learning and personal expression. Although English was not her first language, my mother quickly learned the language and was able to compete with her classmates. She instilled in my brother and me her own value of education. No matter what his occupation, my father was always drawing and painting. As a girl, I remember teaching Grandfather the alphabet and getting into my father's oil paints and mixing them with water. In looking back, teaching and making art came naturally.

Yvonne Greene

I emerged from that period a political liberal, an environmentalist, a non-rabid feminist, an increasingly confident teacher and surprised myself by becoming an enthusiastic mother.

Civil rights turbulence far away in "those southern states," the Nixon-Kennedy debate, the Cuban Missile Crisis, the race riots in Detroit and other major cities, and the terrible series of assassinations— these are the social/political events of my youth that stand out like black & white flashes from Huntley-Brinkley news casts. It was during my student teaching experience in an elementary school classroom when word arrived that President Kennedy had been shot. With each frightening and horrible event during the decade when I was in my twenties, I felt my adolescent confidence, that all was right with us here in America, erode. My husband spent the first 10 years that I knew him dreading the threat of the draft to serve in the Vietnam War. He was never drafted.

I observed the hippie generation as an outsider, a quasi-adult. I wasn't quite sure what the dawning of Aquarius actually meant, but the refrain was constantly in the air. Staff development at my early art education conferences in those years featured psychedelic light shows, colorful sculptural environments and theater-inspired happenings. I emerged from that period a political liberal, an environmentalist, a non-rabid feminist, an increasingly confident teacher, and surprised myself by becoming an enthusiastic mother.

Carolyn Skeen

It was an exciting time and I feel sad when I remember the optimism and the hope that prevailed before Vietnam escalated.

College was a revelation for me. Suddenly there were others around me who liked learning. There were other young women who actually wanted to finish college and have careers. It was OK to be politically liberal. When Kennedy was elected President it seemed as though the United States was headed in wonderful new directions. It was an exciting time and I feel sad when I remember the optimism and the hope that prevailed before Vietnam escalated.

Lora Barrett

On our Catholic campuses, we built a sense of community, which I believe has had a tremendous impact on the way I try to build that same sense of community and belonging for the students I teach and for the colleagues I work with.

During the 60s and 70s, I was in Catholic schools for both high school and college where there was an emphasis on finding ways to work for our fellow man, building a sense of community and belonging, and including rather than excluding. "Peace, love, dove" was the way of action on the Catholic campuses where I found myself. I did volunteer community work; raised money for orphanages in Vietnam; collected food for black churches in the South. Where on other college campuses there might be protests against the war, we held candlelight vigils and services and prayed for the safety of the troops and for peace. On our campuses, we built a sense of community, which I believe has had a tremendous impact on the way I try to build that same sense of community and belonging for the students I teach and for the colleagues I work with.

Their Inevitable Ideas

Among the most essential elements that a researcher looks for in a collection of stories are themes, those recurring ideas that weave consistently throughout participants' narrative responses. Through the aggregate of their stories and the measure of their words, the themes in these teachers' responses concerning the formative events in their youth fell naturally into two categories, which I see as *public* and *private*.

First, pervading the narratives were public themes, those communal events that ineluctably touched everyone. It comes as no surprise that the war in Vietnam, the draft, and violence—local and global—dominated. Few days passed for those young people without breaking news of intense conflict, disorder, and loss. In the words of Gerald Vilenski,

I graduated from high school in 1969, and because it was the height of the conflict in Vietnam, of social and political upheaval, it had a profound effect on my approach to education as well as life in general. Looking back, I find that, like so many students of that era, I did well in spite of the system I found myself in.

War, the support of it, the opposition to it, and the fear of it were, directly or indirectly, constant companions to the youth of these times. "The reality of the times was Vietnam. When I graduated from college, my draft board said I would be in the army in one week if I didn't join something—I joined the airforce," wrote Lloyd Sensat. For many, the war intervened in relationships. For Nancy Zadra, "The Vietnam War had a grueling influence on my early teaching years. Every day I dreaded going home and checking the mailbox, as we knew a government envelope would arrive for my husband. This unremitting stress marked the beginning of the end of our marriage."

For Marie Shack, the hardships that her Marine Corps husband suffered from the war united them both under a common theme of survival and pride in overcoming adversity.

Discord, fear, and violence were not confined to the Vietnam War. Pervasive in their writings was the horror of what they lumped together as "the assassinations," referring, of course, to the public murders of John and Bobby Kennedy and Martin Luther King Jr. For Martyna Bellessis, "I was a huge fan of JFK and attended his first big rally in Chicago. I carried his signs, marched in the parade, and guzzled beer at headquarters. When he was assassinated, politics died for me." Carolyn Skeen, too, reveals the poignance of the murder of a President:

> When Kennedy was shot I was actually at my old elementary school. I was supposed to observe students as an assignment for an education class. As I walked down the hall, the same creaky wooden floors I had walked down thousands of times as a child, I heard cheering. They were cheering because President Kennedy had been shot. Teachers were allowing the cheering to continue. That's the chilling part that nobody ever mentions when they talk about the assassination. I guess it's too terrible. There were places where Kennedy was hated. Children don't cheer something like that unless their parents (or teachers) have expressed similar feelings. I turned and left the school. Never did finish the class assignment. How did all of these things influence me as a teacher? I see learning as a means of helping people understand how to make intelligent decisions. True learning gives us the freedom to think for ourselves. And we need to be careful that what children learn *is* what we really meant to teach.

But it was the tribulation of civil rights that was broached more often than all other issues and events in these interviews. This cameo by Sharon Henneborn offers a dramatic, but tragically true example of an indelibly formative experience.

> When I was around three years old in my native state of Oklahoma, there was a wonderful black family that worked and lived on my grandfather's farm. The farm was not inside the city limits, so whenever anyone came out to tell my grandfather that he was committing an unforgivable error against society, he would remind them that their jurisdiction ended at the boundary of his property, and that he would hire who he liked and live next to who he liked. I remember men coming out and telling him that the "Negroes would murder us in our beds." At that point, he would lose his patience and direct them to leave, gesturing wildly as they scurried down the drive. The mother of this black family was the first to

introduce me to the wonders of melted wax crayons. She would invite me to play and nap with her children. After our nap, she would use a razor to shave flakes from the short crayon stubs and put them into jar lids. We would set those lids filled with wax out in the hot Oklahoma sun and watch them melt into a creamy pool of color. She showed us how to dip a stick into the color and draw on the backs of cereal boxes. That was pure fun. The family was safe while they lived under my grandfather's protection. Eventually they saved enough money to buy and live above a store in town. Someone threw a flaming bottle of gasoline into the store, and most of the family perished. It seems that they were the ones who were murdered in their beds.

Living in these times, being a part of these cultural passages compelled these youths to become activists, and according to many, to "grow up fast." As Ken Wilkie said, "They just wanted to go *do* something." What became meaningful was "being a hero to somebody. Being a hero to yourself, maybe." Jeannie Siegler traveled to West Africa to teach math and art to children in Kamabai and build medical dispensary waiting sheds in The Gambia. Lloyd Sensat served in the Airforce as an illustrator in the security police squadron. All of them became teachers, many before they were 21. There was among them a consensus that the time had come to go beyond mere words. Given the Vietnam War, the Civil Rights and Women's Movements, the myriad ecological, political, and social issues raging at the forefront, in one sense or another all of them became activists. Some of them took part in marches, sit-in's, teach-in's, and demonstrations, experiencing first-hand tear gas, chaos, and the heat of ideological conflict. John Skrabalak felt the consequences of his actions for his role in designing a college yearbook protesting the Kent State shootings. Many, like Mark Phillips, whose class of 1968 shares its reunions with the solemn anniversaries of the deaths of Martin Luther King and Robert Kennedy, describe themselves as quiet participants who wore black arm bands in protest and acted more as critical observers. Lora Barrett took part in candlelight vigils, prayed for peace, and raised money for orphanages in Vietnam. It was during these times that the teachings of Paulo Freire entered into the college curricula. The ideas of achieving peace, equality, and social reform through education became dominant among the Flower Teachers.

At the same time, the majority of the teachers talked about their private lives, of family, traditions, schooling, and church as integral to forming their own character and to finding ways to build a sense of community and belonging—"to include rather than exclude." For Susie Kropa,

> My basic values were shaped by my parents. While they never
> preached to us, they modeled responsible behavior: whatever you

choose to do, do it to the best of your ability; keep your word; if you do something wrong, fess up to it, apologize, and go on with your life; be helpful; laugh a lot.

In her richly related story, Lora Barrett reveals how family and a very special teacher made her the artist and the teacher she is today:

I can still remember as a three year old, sitting in the kitchen with my mother around Christmas, cutting seasonal illustrations from the newspaper and affixing them to paper to make Christmas cards for relatives. My mother told me that I was an artist; she would introduce me to her friends as an artist. My uncle made his yearly requests for handmade Christmas cards; in my busy teens I found those requests bothersome, but reluctantly complied. I began to believe that I was an artist; I received art supplies, books, magazines as gifts. I behaved like an artist. I attended parochial elementary school where there were no art classes, so it was not until the 10th grade that I took my first art class in a school setting and was seduced by the idea that I could become an art teacher. Sr. Maurina made everything so interesting! She spoke of Dominicos Theotocopulous, of Nefratiti, of Picasso's *Girl Before a Mirror* (1932) and of Marry Cassatt. We painted and carved and looked at slides. We had student shows and art club and were called upon to be a part of every facet of school life because we could make the posters and decorations and see what needed to be done to make everything come alive. I became alive. My mother's proclamation that I was an artist was true.

But nothing hit home like the trip to my uncle's apartment at Christmas time when I came home from college for the holidays my junior year. I was just shy of my 21st birthday. The apartment was a place to wait in NYC between my bus trip from college and my father picking me up. There were many Christmas decorations in my uncle's apartment, but none more surprising to me than the 19 little handmade Christmas cards which hung on a string across his fireplace mantle. I know that children learn that they are respected and valued by the way they are treated as they are raised. I believe that I am an artist and teacher because those who I most admired and respected told me over and over again that I was an artist and that I would make a wonderful teacher.

Some of the teachers admit to having been what one called "amiable hippies," sporting the regalia—tie dye and batik, buffalo sandals, headbands, lovebeads, long hair, and driving something like Suzanne Greene's "turquoise MG with day-glow flowers." There was among them an adventurous spirit for experimentation. In Bonnie Keyser's words, "I was a 'true flower child.' When my husband returned from Vietnam, we lived in a camp on the river, with no running water and an outdoor john." Others place themselves on the periphery of the pop culture of those times, taking it all in as more passive participants. Suzanne Greene reflects,

> There were protests and rallies, and encounters with police, which I stayed away from, being the Republican that my parents had made. To me, the violence was frightening, and I didn't want any part of it. For some reason, I never questioned why we were in Vietnam. Now I wish I had.

In trying to grasp as precisely as I could the significance and impact of this formative context, I followed the direction of qualitative researchers Ryan and Bernard: If you want to understand what people are talking about, look at the words they use and how they use them (2000). In doing so, I studied the teachers' explanations of their early times, cataloguing recurring words and phrases and studying the context within which they were embedded. During this process I noticed two things. First, an apparent dichotomy emerged. On one side were descriptive expressions characterizing the outward circumstances of the social, cultural, and political realities of the times. For the most part, these descriptions were despairing, laden with disillusionment, disappointment, anger, and frustration. Abstractions like *rejection, prejudice, mistrust, disillusionment*, and *discrimination* were mentioned frequently. More concrete descriptors like *rebellion, demonstrations, turbulence, power, protests, assassination*, and *materialism* also emerged, along with events like Watergate, Vietnam, and Kent State. Taken together, they represent poignant critical assessments and denunciations of an existing climate.

On the other side of the dichotomy was something very revealing about those would-be teachers. In their retrospections of youth, they talked about things bigger than themselves. Despite their ages at the time, despite the intensity of their own lives—dealing with the complexities of maturation, working to get a college education—they clearly sought a much larger picture. There are those who look back on this generation as one of self-indulgence, hedonism—what Margaret Thatcher called "permissive claptrap," and what Alan Bloom perceived of as the dogmatic and trivial (Marwick, 1998). It is not within my means to disprove these disparagements, nor do I intend to make sweeping statements placing the participants in my study above it all. However, if there is any validity to the study of words and experiences, if we can tell something about the way people think, feel, and act by the way they choose to talk about things, then it is worthwhile to consider what these teachers recall about their formative years.

Their stories reflect a cogent social, cultural, and political awareness of their times; nearly three decades later, they speak with an historical accuracy. Along side their indictments of the existing order was a language, equally strong, of advocacy; they talked about what *could* and *should* be. They used words denoting action and transformation, like *questioning, searching, changing, affecting, helping, acting, doing, learning, listening, including, respecting,* and *sharing.* They spoke of being *accountable, informed, caring, compassionate, sensitive, unselfish,* and *fair.* In spite of their disillusionment, there were *optimism, idealism, hope, excitement, love,* and *enthusiasm.* There were *heroes* and *role models* and *possibilities for peace.* Common to all, they reflected on their early desire to act, to "fix" things that were wrong, much in the same way teachers approach their days in the classroom. From Lloyd Sensat: "These were times of great lust for life, magical, wonderful times. The intensity of the 60s created great friend-ships. Growing up in that era led us to believe that we could make the world a better place."

Whether they saw themselves as part of the vanguard or as quiet partici-pants, all of them shared a grand experience—the transitory and turbulent context of their youth. Despite the disparities in individual backgrounds, the varied places where they grew up and where they have taught, ranging from New England to the Northwest, there is among them a uniformity in their words. Within that uniformity is a common ethos: a commitment, both then and now, to something greater than their own personal circumstances. There was within these people a sense of themselves as passionate shapers of a communal good. In Ken Wilkie's summary, there is that

> sort of exotic ideal of going off and having a genuine effect, being a hero to somebody. Being a hero to yourself, maybe. And I think that kind of steers you into teaching, to be some place where you can make changes, where you can make a difference in people's lives. And it's very exciting.

Chapter 3 takes us back to their early classroom years, to the idealism and dejection, the vicissitudes of structuring, restructuring, and reform. School desegregation, its complexities and continuing progress; over-crowded classes and underdeveloped curriculum; paucity of facilities and materials; and the art teachers' struggles to gain respect for both themselves and their teaching discipline are focal points in this chapter.

Chapter 3
Pray for Absences: The Early Classroom Years

I suppose a lot of very promising art teachers have left the public schools in frustration over the conditions we have all endured. I think the survivors were those who learned to "make do" and kept their positive attitude that a better tomorrow was coming.
Carrol Morgan, King George Middle School, King George, VA

From a contemporary perspective, the intensity of the egalitarian changes in American education in the 60s and early 70s is often forgotten. No one can really say whether teaching in those years of dynamic social reformation was tougher than it is now, but certainly no one can say it was easier. There were circumstances unique to those times that held immense promise; there were also circumstances that were distressing, even dire. Those were unsettling years, the time when so many unresolved problems, questions, and seminal issues in American education were intensifying and being confronted. Reform was everywhere and situated integrally within it, as primary social institutions, were the public schools. Many promising young teachers in those days did go by the wayside, choosing careers fraught with less stress and offering more predictability and pay. Many however stayed, as Carrol Morgan said, living with the optimism that a better tomorrow would come. In reflecting on her early years in the classroom, Carolyn Skeen reveals with some humor what was then the reality for so many:
> I taught art from 1965-69 in a school that contained grades 1-8. The school was in an area that was rapidly changing from agricultural to suburban and was extremely overcrowded. I rarely had a class with under 41 students. One year I actually had 50 eighth grade boys in a room designed for a maximum of 35. It had one tiny sink, little storage, and nowhere to dry student work. My classes were back-to-back and I don't remember ever having a planning period. I taught the same 900-1000 students every week all year. Class periods were so short that students barely had time to do a little art, quickly set up for the next class and clean their hands. I was 22 years old and had lots of energy but every afternoon I would come home, stagger to the bedroom, and fall across the bed like Arnold Schwarzenegger in *Kindergarten Cop.* I made $4,300 during my first year. I was never formally observed by my principal. I understand that he stood

outside our classrooms and listened to what was going on occasionally. We were also supposed to be observed by someone from the
central office once a year until we received tenure. The first year the
personnel director walked briskly into the art room with a clipboard
in his hand. It was Friday afternoon. The last students had just left.
I was at my desk for the *only* time that day. I had closed my eyes, my
head down on the desk, my mouth open, and my arms flung wide
out. My hands dangled down off either side of the desk. I looked
like roadkill. Wet student work was scattered everywhere. There
was a week's worth of paint spills waiting to be cleaned off the
counter. His visit was a short one. I only remember his making one
comment: Maybe you should make your classes help you clean up.

Working Toward Equity

*I was the first black art teacher in a predominantly white school. So my
first job, besides teaching art, was to expose a population to a black role
model.*

Anita Winfrey, Collinsville High School, Collinsville, VA

For teachers in all disciplines during those times, the prospects for critical
change were imminent, and in the midst of the many transitions was school
desegregation. Though Brown vs. Board of Education had been legislated
some 15 years before, large-scale movement to rectify the inequities in
American education did not begin until the late 1960s and early 70s. The
reason for the acceleration in desegregation at this time was the *Civil Rights
Act* passed by Congress in 1964. Title VI of the *Civil Rights Act* provided
momentum since it mandated the withholding of federal funds from
institutions that practiced racial discrimination. In essence, Title VI states
that no person, due to race, color, or national origin could be excluded or
denied the benefits of any program receiving federal financial assistance.
To secure and maintain federal funding, then, schools moved quickly
toward integrative compliance. As it was, during their first years of
teaching, the Flower Teachers were recruited to play a starring role in
rectifying the inequities that had so long existed in our schools.

Given that neighborhoods themselves were largely segregated, in order to
equalize the opportunities in education, for the most part, school districts
chose between two desegregation plans: redistricting, that is, rearranging
attendance areas, and busing. Some districts participated in both, and in
both instances, populations of students were exchanged among schools to
achieve representative racial ratios. By 1966, faculty desegregation began.
Numerous teachers, black and white, were selected, many volunteered, to be
transferred from one school to another, shifting black teachers to predomi-

nantly white schools and white faculty to schools that had been predominantly black. Anita Winfrey, Phyllis Bosco, Ken Wilkie, Kathleen Thompson, Joan Newcomer, Carroll Morgan, Carolyn Skeen, Candy Alexander, as well as myself, were all part of these preliminary initiatives to "integrate the faculties." Kathleen Thompson's and Carolyn Skeen's first years were not unlike my own. Kathleen writes,

> That year in Clayton County Georgia, I found myself (along with the music teacher) the first white teachers at a first through twelfth grade school. It had three wings, elementary, junior high, and high school. We taught there at the elementary level one day a week. I complained to the administration that the high school did not have an art teacher, that the new "white" high school had art and a beautiful art room. So they said, "Fine, you can be their teacher." The next year I was the secondary art teacher. I had a classroom with a sink in the janitor's room for our use. I did things like papier-maché because I had no art supplies, except what the kids could pay for, so you're talking minimal… a very, very poor neighborhood called Rosetown where kids still had outhouses.

Of her first teaching job in Tennessee, Carolyn Skeen remembers,

> The school where I taught was integrated around 1967. There were only a few black students in the district. They had attended a one-room school and were the descendants of slaves and sharecroppers who had lived in a small community of African Americans that had been in the same location since the Civil War. The black children were very intimidated at first by the size of their unfamiliar, noisy, overcrowded school. There were only nine black students and someone had decided that they should be split up into different classrooms. So the students were lonely, scared, and extremely quiet at first. Eventually they adjusted well and made friends. I remember only two racial incidents. Once when my lunch group was standing in line there was some pushing and jockeying for position as someone in the back tried to squeeze in. Even the students at the front felt the domino effect of the shoving. A shy African-American girl put her hands up to ward off a six-foot-plus boy as he was shoved toward her. "Get your dirty black hands off me!" rang loud above the line. The other came when Martin Luther King, Jr. was murdered. My black students were angry and sad. The school did absolutely nothing to mark his passing. I realize that integration was a non-issue in many other parts of the country, but for us in the South it was an important step and a real milestone in our history.

My own early years of teaching were reminiscent of the experiences of several of the Flower Teachers, so in this instance, I include a memoir from my own classroom beginnings. For my first year in 1968, I volunteered to teach in a segregated African American elementary school in rural North Florida where the children lived in impoverished conditions. The elementary and secondary schools in that county were all inadequate, but those attended by the black students were far worse. The buildings and classrooms were in need of repair; there was a dearth of instructional facilities and supplies; textbooks were antiquated, often handed down from white schools, and usually shared among students; classes were crowded; and oftentimes, teachers were not certified in the subject areas in which they taught. In my particular school, supplies were nearly nonexistent in every area. A ream of ditto paper and a shoebox of broken crayons, including the much contested "flesh" color, constituted art supplies. The children's parents were sharecroppers who spent long days planting and picking cash crops, especially tobacco, for others. When the shade tobacco was in, many of my children were pulled out of class in order to help harvest the leaves. When it was cold, some couldn't come to school because the soles of their shoes gapped open. Many had no toothbrushes and lived with painful cavities. Lots of them had poor diets and pinworms living in their digestive tracts. Some of the first graders were afraid of the flush toilets in the school restrooms because they had only outhouses at home. Isolated in tiny pockets of rural communities, most of these children never had personal contact with whites. They were suspicious and reticent until they determined the goodness of the white teacher's intent. Interestingly, despite fatigue from work and family responsibility, the parents of these children participated in school affairs, bringing sweet potato pies and sugar cookies to bake sales and volunteering to run the horseshoe throw or the cakewalk at the yearly school carnivals. Teachers were not allowed to hang student artwork in the halls and there were no showcases in which to exhibit student projects, so twice a year, during PTA meetings we took the opportunity to invite parents into our rooms to see their children's work scotch-taped to the walls. Suffice it to say that the atmosphere there was stifling for both the teachers and the students. Among the images that intrude upon my memories of my first class of children is the principal chasing them down the hall, slapping at their legs with his belt to speed them to class.

Two years after that, we moved to Tampa where I accepted a position in a suburban junior high school. My school district was participating in a busing program, transporting urban black and Hispanic children to the suburbs and whites to urban schools. Our black and Hispanic students, most of whom had been raised in the city, were used to walking to neighborhood schools, frequenting neighborhood shops, having friends who lived next door or in the same apartment complex. Their playgrounds had more asphalt than grass. There were more people, more buildings than open space. Contrarily, the white children were largely from rural and suburban settings; there were farms, some clustered housing, strip malls, big open spaces, and friends whose parents occasionally brought them over to visit. For the adolescents in my newly desegregated school, there was a clash of living contexts. For the most part, they were polite and respectful to one another, but there were also forms of "re-segregation," where students separated themselves into socio-economic and racial groups. Classes were huge (some near 40); the rooms were small, and with no air-conditioning, the Florida afternoons were insufferably hot. Students, and not a few teachers, were justifiably irritable. At one point I remember my principal, usually quite sensitive, telling me, "If you can keep their arms and legs inside the windows, I'll be happy." For disorderliness, district-wide corporal punishment—paddling—was a rule, generally futile, and at times, the fomenter of things worse.

Related to the abrupt changes in their learning contexts and routines, in many schools like mine, there was a good deal of student unrest. Influenced by media coverage of political and social protests on college campuses and in other sectors of society, classes in the secondary schools were often disrupted by student walk-outs, smoke and fires, and bomb threats. Gatherings of protesting students varied as widely in their make-up as their reasons. Everything from earnest perceptions of discriminatory treatment, to dress codes, to dislike of cafeteria food could spark unrest. Sometimes there were fights in classrooms and hallways, fire alarms going off, and on several occasions, schools like mine were temporarily closed to allow time to restore calm and re-group. During the three years at this junior high school and my first year in tobacco country, I learned firsthand the necessity and the democracy of understanding my students' context, their ethnicity, economics, developmental characteristics, and more. In striving to introduce African American and Hispanic artists and authors to my students, I saw in their expressions, the recognition and connections, sometimes even the gratitude that came from studying a Jacob Lawrence or a Diego Rivera or reading Nikki Giovanni's Spin a Soft Black Song (1971).

These initial efforts in school desegregation were hard for everyone, but especially so for the students. Many had changed schools, having to find new friends, acquaint themselves with new teachers, strange surroundings, and often, differing expectations and value systems. Those who remained in their schools were surrounded with new classmates. Several Flower Teachers noted the apparent "frustration and bewilderment" of students, black and white, some of whom only vaguely understood the reasons for so much change. Though Title IV of the Civil Rights Act of 1964 offered technical assistance in providing funds for in-service training of teachers to help them deal with problems incident to desegregation, many felt that the teachers themselves were peripheral in the desegregation planning processes. Though some had been marginally consulted, many were largely on the receiving end of plans already in place. Likewise, several teachers noted that the students themselves, whose lives were most affected by education reform, had not been invited into the dialogue. Had they been, they might have better understood the why's of it all and perhaps their way would have been eased toward a more efficient, less troubling day-to-day adaptation. Though unquestionably for the good, from the perspectives of many teachers and their students "things just happened."

Integral to the egalitarian reforms within education during these times were a variety of seminal court decisions, ranging from rights of handicapped students, to granting education access to undocumented immigrants. Moreover, key pieces of legislation were passed which had significant impact on teaching and learning. There were, for example, the *Vocational Education Act* of 1963, which improved education for handicapped, low-income, and female students; the *Economic Opportunities Act* of 1964, leading to community-based education programs; the *Elementary and Secondary Education Act* of 1965, establishing broad federal support for public education; the court proceedings in Crystal City, Texas, with the ensuing *Bilingual Education Act* of 1968, providing aid for bilingual programs; and the *Higher Education Act* of 1972 which provided for sexual equality in employment in educational institutions and for sexual equality in educational programs, including preschool, elementary, and secondary schools, vocational and professional schools, and public and private undergraduate and graduate institutions.

Through the onslaught of social activism during the 60s and 70s there ensued numerous changes in the schools. From 1968 in a suburb of Atlanta, Jane Hollingsworth proudly remembers the seeds of tolerance and respect growing among her first class of high school students: "The senior class of 1970 selected *Let It Be* as their graduation song and earlier that year they had elected the first black Homecoming King." Though work toward equality in our schools was far from finished, such inchoate progress paved a path of promise and possibility that continues through today.

Today the Flower Teachers agree that school desegregation is a work in progress, a task far from finished. Nonetheless, in those first years, they savored a sense of accomplishment in the roles they were playing. At last, they were beginning to see children from all backgrounds and abilities on their way to gaining equal learning opportunities. And so it was with no small sense of irony that these teachers found themselves confronted with their first, and as it was, one of the greatest challenges to follow them throughout their careers: developing instruction for and coping with student diversity. Carroll Morgan writes of the pressing problem:

> 1968-69 was the first year of total racial desegregation in our county school, and by federal mandate, each elementary class was balanced with 40% black students and 60% white, to match the ratio of the county population. Actually, heterogeneity of life experience created the most difficulty in my teaching, as an astounding diversity of students appeared in each class.

The democratic ideal forms the heart of the teaching philosophy of every participant in the Flower Teachers' project. From their first classroom days, the Flower Teachers have worked to provide equal learning opportunity for all of their students in all of their diversity. Suzanne Greene puts it succinctly: "I guess this can sum up how I teach: Each student is seen by me as an individual, not judged by what some chart says he or she should be able to do." Marie Shack's philosophy represents the spirit:

> Students accept me for my own strengths and weaknesses I think because I accept them the way they are. I feel that it is a gift that I like all of my students; I do not judge them. I don't believe in judging adolescents, they have a long way to go. My personal teaching philosophy is to try to heighten my students' awareness of the world around them, to help them learn to really observe, not only visually but emotionally. I want students to treasure their own vision, treasure themselves, and in so doing, respect others and their visions. I know that the hundred or so students who pass my way each year are not all going to be artists, but if I can enhance their living, let them rejoice in their learning, come to love the arts and remember the time in my classroom as a period of mutual delight in each other, then I feel I am successful.

Teachers know that elementary, middle, and high school students share a ubiquitous youth culture, and, arguably, have some developmental characteristics in common. At the same time, good teachers know that if learning is to be relevant, if students are to make sense of things for themselves, and if the knowledge students discover and create is to be useful and lasting, teachers must effectively identify and work to accommodate the special needs of individuals as well as those of the group. This is precisely what the Flower Teachers realized as their student populations began to diversify. There were disparities among students' academic preparation due, in large part, to the inferior schooling imposed by racial segregation. There were ethnic differences characterized by varying day-to-day interests, linguistic

and social customs, family structure, aesthetic and entertainment prefer-
ences, and differences in values. In shifting pupil populations, economics
became another factor. Often, regardless of ethnicity, family circumstances
ranged from poverty to those who had all the advantages. There were
children from farms as well as from inner-city housing. Partly because of
previous discrepancies in school promotion and attendance policies, there
grew a wider age span within the same grade levels. According to Carrol
Morgan, "Some advanced students had skipped grades, slower students had
failed two or three grades, some disadvantaged students had been truant for
years." Indicative of the times, in most schools more than a few students
had unidentified learning disabilities and behavioral disorders. Because of
long-standing schooling deficits created by segregation, many black
students fell behind their white peers in basic reading and math skills and
ultimately in their performance on standardized tests.

As the 1960s drew to a close and the new decade began, as new college
graduates barely out of their teens, the Flower Teachers faced personal and
professional challenges that would daunt the most seasoned faculties.
Helping them cope with their momentous charge were the mindset and
character qualities developed during those years when they came of age.
With changes and advancements brought about by the Civil Rights and
Women's Movements, the emphasis on communal and global concerns,
instigated partially by the war in Vietnam, and the growing apprehension
over ecological crises, these new teachers found a natural sympathy with the
ideological convictions of the progressive educators of earlier years. Like
Dewey and the progressivists, the Flower Teachers realized a compelling
need to change the system. As part of the youth generation, they had a zest
for the hypothetical, for John Lennon's *Imagine*—if you will. They
undertook a search for new ideas and felt little compunction in rejecting
tradition that they perceived did not serve the greater good. They had had
the benefit of a forward-looking college education. Most had been inspired
by the social consciousness of professors, popular artists, musicians,
naturalists, and writers of their time. All were influenced by the political
and social activism of those days. More pressing than anything else, all of
them were confronted by the immediate needs of an increasingly heterogeneous group of students who came to them with multiple perspectives and
life experiences, and who were accustomed to understanding the world in
many different ways. Dewey's ideas of personalizing learning, nurturing
active student involvement, and educating the whole child for a whole
lifetime made sense to these young teachers. In acknowledging the life
experiences, the personal contexts, and the myriad needs of a growing and
changing body of K-12 students, and in molding curriculum around those
needs, the Flower Teachers helped prime the well for education change in
the last quarter of the century.

The stories of Candy Alexander, Phyllis Bosco, Jerry Vilenski, and Jane Hollingsworth serve as summary. Through a combination of experimental verve, sheer tenacity, and incessant optimism, their art programs achieved success. Working on the sea islands off South Carolina during these times, Candy Alexander taught three days in a segregated white school and two in a school where the children were black. Echoing the experiences of her colleagues, for her black students, "The county budget for art was zero. Supplies consisted of yellowed paper and dried tempera paint." It was Candy's ingenuity and resourcefulness that brought that art program to life. She called on fellow teachers to donate brushes, pencils, wallpaper books, and more. To subsidize a budget, students created local crafts, which were sold at yearly Christmas bizarres within that rural black community.

Phyllis Bosco's first full-time teaching job was a federally funded position in 1969. She was the first white teacher and the first art teacher at an elementary-middle school in rural Gadsen County in northern Florida.

> That year we put together an art competition with over 800 works. The reception was PTA night and the whole community showed up. I gave the student who won best of show an anatomy drawing book. He went on to receive a scholarship to Ohio State in medical illustration and then to become the art director for a CBS television affiliate. He has always been in touch.

Jane Hollingsworth remembers,

> After teaching art at Marietta High School (suburb city of Atlanta) for my first two years, I questioned whether or not I would ever be an effective teacher. Classroom management was a major problem for me—I was only 20 when I began teaching in senior high school. Students seemed to enjoy rattling my composure, and it seemed to me at the time that they didn't value my instruction. In 1970, my husband and I moved to rural North Carolina where I became the first art teacher at the county high school. The population was about 65% African-American. So many students signed up for my art class that I had to give up my planning time to teach six classes. It was one of the best years that I have ever had teaching. The students were so excited to be experiencing studio art instruction. I had no discipline problems. I encouraged students to use art to express how they felt about current issues—the War in Vietnam, civil rights, etc. Anti-war posters, calligraphed signs of protest, and other controversial pieces of art were displayed at the local bank in the small North Carolina town. I never received a single complaint from the citizens. I doubt that I could get away with that today.

Reality Struck Hard

During those years, in many school districts throughout the country, art teachers were newcomers, for it was not until the late 1960s and early 70s that interest in school art programs began to grow. At the elementary level, teachers formally certified in art were being hired to create "enrichment" programs. Before that time, most certified art teachers were hired at the secondary levels, and there were relatively few of those. Art (and music) at the elementary levels were usually taught by the regular classroom teacher. Some school districts would hire "traveling" enrichment teachers or what Yvonne Greene called a "traveling minstrel" when she did it. Generally, these were teachers who visited multiple elementary and junior high schools on a revolving basis and served as what some called "consulting" or "helping" art teachers. Suzanne Greene explains their function:

> Our district had "floating" art specialists for many years. There were three of them and they rotated to about 24 elementary schools training the classroom teachers to teach art. Sometimes they would work with a whole grade level with students and teachers then other days they would only work with the teachers. We've had full-time art teachers on every elementary campus for only the last five years. I was offered the job of floating teacher after Will [her son] was born. I chose to run CDC (campus discipline center) at a school where I had taught before rather than drive from school to school. Those teachers didn't last long since it was not an easy job and they had little praise or support.

Susie Kropa relates a similar experience:

> When I came to Iowa in 1968, there was one "art supervisor" in a nearby district. There were no elementary art teachers. Miss Chadwick trained classroom teachers in some fashion, maybe through workshops or modeling lessons. She covered all the elementary buildings. I can remember going to the spring art exhibit one year and seeing the same sorts of projects from every building. Later, after she retired, sometimes a classroom teacher who was "artsy" traded kids once a week with another teacher of the same grade level who might have been more "sciencey"; or teachers did their own thing, which could have been almost anything. That's pretty much how this school district has to this day satisfied the state art requirement; although recently they hired a first-grade teacher to teach art in all eleven K-5 buildings. It's hard to believe that a city of 30,000 can get away with that. It's amazing how many public school administrators think art should be axed, presumably to allow more time for drill in reading, math, and test-taking skills. School mission statements generally mention "life-long learning, problem-solving,

responsible citizenship" etc. but see no connection between these goals and the activities that take place in the art room.

Lloyd Sensat adds an evaluative punch line:

> I fought this concept of "helping teacher" for years. In the end, it implied that anyone could teach art. I wanted certified art teachers in the elementary schools. It is a dangerous and false assumption in our profession that anyone can teach art. Creative artist-teachers with a love for children's aesthetic capacities and an understanding of art and design concepts are essential for a quality art program.

The establishment of new art programs with certified specialists indicated a long awaited recognition of the potential role of the arts in the curriculum of the schools. Unfortunately, however, new art faculty frequently entered the schools under less desirable circumstances than teachers in other disciplines. At the elementary level, they came with the understanding that an important part of their role was providing "relief" for the classroom teacher. Seeking more instructional time, many states were expanding the school day, so to accommodate this increase school systems began scrambling to fill the time with more specialists. Relatedly, teachers' unions such as NEA and AFT, some working under collective bargaining laws, were lobbying local and state school boards for much deserved planning time for elementary teachers, similar to what high school teachers had benefited from for many years. Sharon Henneborn explains an interesting and not uncommon situation from one district in Texas in the early 70s:

> The teachers, with the help of a group of the state's urologists who bore witness to the high rate of urinary tract problems among Texas teachers, pushed for a state mandate for a half-hour duty free period during the school day. It's crazy to expect a teacher to come on duty at 8:30, eat at noon in the lunchroom with their students, and go non-stop until 4:00 before they could go to the bathroom without having to impose on someone else to cover the class.

All of this had the effect of strengthening security for the specialists' jobs because they were intrinsically linked to teacher planning time. After so many years of advocacy, teachers who believed in the efficacy of the visual arts were gaining ground for a more integral place in the curriculum. Jerry Vilenski interprets the rapidly growing interest in art specialists in a more cynical (and perhaps realistic) way: "So the net effect was that the art teachers owe their jobs to planning time much more than their administration's love of art." Anita Winfrey punctuates Jerry's statement with "Folks get mad if for some reason they miss their break due to the art teacher's absence."

Despite increasing job availability and security, many elementary art teachers were themselves excluded from the benefits of planning time and thus suffered long, strenuous days with nothing more than a half-hour for lunch. In Candy Alexander's words,

> Picture this ... the year is 1974. I am teaching in Charleston, S. C. I have one 45 minute planning period per week on Friday afternoons. The principal apologizes. He has to meet requirements to have planning time for each classroom teacher, but it is not possible for art because there is only one of me and all the classes need to fit into the schedule.

Art teachers endured more adversity when it came to instructional space and facilities. Though many academic teachers were "trailer teaching" in backyard portable classrooms, the majority of them had a permanent room of their own. The same is not true for art teachers. The reality for many was "art-on-a cart," where the teacher wheeled art into every classroom. Lora Barrett's early years offer a typical synopsis:

> Reality was that I taught art-on-a-cart in a K-7 school in the morning and in a 7-9 school in the afternoon. My supplies were limited, class size was huge, and I had no input into the schedule. I had poor classroom management skills; chaos reigned. Many students saw the weakness in me; they tortured me. The screws in my art cart were removed by the students who watched and laughed as it fell apart with all the supplies on it as I went up the three stairs in front of the principal's office. I was pathetic and had no support. I cried on a regular basis. I went home and napped several days a week. I was miserable. I stayed because I had a car loan, a college loan, and no place else to go.

After the first year, Lora moved to a new setting.

> Classroom management improved almost immediately in a new setting. I had a lovely room and an art teacher on either side of me for support. I worked for a strong no-nonsense principal... no nonsense from the kids, no nonsense from us young teachers, and there was an abundance of us. Years two through twelve, despite that brand new school with a moderate amount of materials, found me in a routine and I soon tired of the factory-type atmosphere. There were three art teachers and 1200 students. Each year I taught every seventh and eighth grader; art was an elective for ninth graders. Class size was 35; I had 35 chairs. Several classes hit 37 one year. "Play for absences" was the response I was given by the assistant principal when I complained. Each week I taught 19 different sections of students. Five sections of seventh graders came twice

each week; ten sections of eighth graders came once a week; ninth grade electives came three times a week. Every 12 weeks I had an entirely new group. Storage was a problem; we could do nothing on a grand scale. There was no sense of fulfillment. I didn't know their names or their abilities. I had no sense of connection in those days. I felt devalued, like I was filler as a means for academic teachers to have prep time. I felt no one would ever remember me; I would not remember them. I was told "No!" when I wanted to have my classes paint wall murals, "No!" when I wanted to organize an art fair. I had to get my father-in-law and our guidance counselor to help me drive my ninth graders to a cemetery to do gravestone rubbings on a day when the rotating schedule backed the art period up into the lunch/activity period. After all, we could go on an art field trip, but couldn't miss any academic time to do so.

For others it was poorly equipped makeshift conditions. Sonia Pratt describes her first year in a coal mining region in West Virginia:

I was hired directly out of college in 1972 to start a new art program for grades 1-12 in a rural area of West Virginia. Full of optimism, high energy and a dose of naivete, out to change the world. Art was never offered in this area before. I started my day in one of two isolated elementary schools where I taught on alternate weeks. One was located in an old coal camp. I rolled up my windows and locked my doors to protect myself from both the coal dust and the miners as I drove around the tipple to the top of the hill where the school was. Stray dogs were always hanging around the school and most days I would have to shout and swing my bag of supplies at the dogs to get to the front door. I had to carry all of the essentials, like scissors, from school to school. Inside were four classrooms, grades 1-4. I taught first grade on Monday, second on Tuesday, etc. I carried water in buckets from the first floor water fountain to each class. The children loved it when I came. They lived in extreme poverty and had little beauty in their lives. They loved making art and were really uninhibited. They would applaud when I came into the classroom. I haven't heard applause since then.

When I left that school, I had to race a coal train to get to the junior high school which was about seven miles away. If I didn't beat the train, I had to sit and wait for 15-20 minutes for it to pass, and I would be late for my next assignment. If I were late the principal would be at the door waiting for me and berate me for my tardiness. He said he couldn't see any reason for art in the public school anyway. In the junior high I shared a classroom with a health teacher who had never had to share his room. I was given a small student locker to store my supplies and I was never able to fill it. For all of the schools, I scrounged materials wherever I could find them. I asked for donated materials from friends, relatives, parents.

Every afternoon I taught high school art. Several years before my arrival, someone had passed away and left a house to the school to use to teach home economics wherein the students would learn to run a house. I was assigned to teach art in the living room and dining room of this house and could use the kitchen for water and clean-up. My classes were small and the kids were enthusiastic. They would sit on the living room sofa or at the dining room table while I taught them about art and art history from single copies of my college text books and demonstrated from my own sketchbook. They were an attentive group. I had no discipline problems and some of them came from some hardcore situations. Everything I taught was new to them. I was well into the groove of things when we left for Easter vacation. It was not an easy job, but I felt I was accomplishing so many things.

On Easter Sunday the junior high burned to the ground. Evidently a student teacher was trying to hatch some eggs in science class. He had left a light on some eggs nestled in hay. The hay caught fire and the school was history. We had about four days off. Our schedules were rearranged and I ended the school year teaching the junior high students in the second floor bedroom of the Home Ec. house. Chairs were arranged wall to wall and the heat was unbearable. I had only crayons, scissors, and paper with which to work. I resigned at the end of the school year.

During that first year of teaching, I learned more about surviving as a teacher than I would probably ever want to know. I did love teaching students and I still do. I moved on to a better school system that was more teacher friendly. But that early experience prepared me for many things and I look back at those students who were so excited about art with great affection. I have never been back and I often wonder what happened to some of them.

In his first teaching situation, Jerry Vilenski shared many of the same challenges and ultimate successes, yet in a context fraught with a different kind of hardship.

My first job teaching art was in the Upper Peninsula of Michigan. I taught at an Air Force Base, near Sault Ste. Marie. I was a full-time art teacher at an elementary school with a population that varied widely from around 600-800 students. Much of the school population was transient because of the military, so it was not unusual for more than 30% turnover of students during the school year. I was hired soon after graduation in 1973, a period when art teachers were in demand. I found myself literally on my own, not having a senior art teacher as a mentor and basically relying on student teaching experiences which were mostly at the secondary level. Nevertheless, I plowed ahead and built an art department from scratch. I found teaching military kids to be a mixed bag of experiences. Students' lack of ownership of anything led to a lot of vandalism and discipline problems for me and my lack of experience didn't help. Nevertheless, in four years I built a credible art department that had the support of my administration and colleagues.

The considerable political turmoil of the early 70s made educating military children a particular challenge. Some of my students' fathers didn't come back from that war. Students were transferred with their families sometimes overnight. We had students from all over the world, some with language difficulties, some with cultural differences. The experience left me with a wealth of knowledge that shaped my career and served me well in later years. After the war ended, the government closed the Air Base and 85 teachers were laid off. I returned to university to attend graduate school and do substitute teaching in local schools. A year later, I gained a position with my current district and have been there ever since.

Anita Winfrey, Mark Phillips, and John Skrabalak recall compelling reality checks in their first years. Anita recalls a short, innocently insulting question from one of her students: Did you have to go to school to be an art teacher? And in Mark's memory,

I think I was very idealistic and naive when I first started to teach, as many people were. My college preparation did not have me meet any kids until I student taught. [I had a lot of friends in college get into student teaching who realized they didn't like teaching and they wasted their four years.] We were kind of sold on the idea that the art teacher was going to be the best guy around because the kids just love art and couldn't wait to eat up the subject and they were going to love you and they were going to do wonderful things. My first week or two of school, when I began, I had a special education student, a young girl who was using a pair of scissors one day and asked me in passing, "Do you know what I'd like to do with these scissors? And I casually said "No," and she said, "I'd like to cut your f... throat." [Excuse the language.] And that made an impact on me. I was dumbfounded and I think I woke up that day and realized that not all kids are going to like art and they are not going to like me.

John Skrabalak remarks of his first "intimidating years":

The first years, the school district didn't budget for my position and thus I didn't have any supplies. I also had to share my room with two teachers who taught home arts and crafts (i. e., toll painting and ceramics). Reality struck hard. I learned right away that not everyone can be made to love art. A student was dumped into my class and refused to do anything. He threatened me with bodily harm. They didn't teach me in my undergrad training that this could happen. I plugged along though. An administrator, during an observation conference, told me that I wouldn't be a "teacher" until after five years of experience. I always wondered what exactly was I doing if it wasn't teaching.

Carol Wellein recounts hardships but remembers with fondness some goodness in those bygone days:

My first years of teaching I made $5,900. I was assigned two schools, one in what was considered a "Christian" neighborhood, the other a "Reformed Jewish" community. I was at one school for two and a half days and the other for the same. I ate my lunch in the car between the two schools. I never felt part of the faculty at either school. I had between 28 and 35 students per class and I taught grades 1-6. I averaged five to six classes per day, was responsible for bulletin boards, scenery, and an art show. But I had a good budget, a kiln in every school and an art room for the first 2 years. Yes, there was art-on-a-cart for 4 1/2 years. But I didn't care. I loved the faculty. We were all young.

And where was OSHA?

Among other circumstances encountered uniquely by art teachers in those days were hazardous conditions and potentially toxic materials. This was one of the issues not included among my original interview questions but broached instead by Sharon Henneborn, one of the teachers in the study. Not every art teacher had these difficulties, but a significant number did. The fact is, since the 1940s, The Art and Creative Materials Institute (ACMI) has been evaluating and certifying art, craft, and other creative materials to ensure that they are properly labeled for artists' use. Three certification seals have been developed over the years: CP (Certified Product) Seal; the AP (Approved Product) Seal; and the HL (Health Label) Seal. In 1998, the three seals were combined into two: the AP Seal and the CL Seal. Despite these certifications, for several reasons, potentially toxic materials found their way into elementary and secondary classrooms. In many cases, teachers had been poorly informed in their college courses about the dangers of various substances and conditions. In some instances, even commonly used materials were not labeled; in others, such as asbestos, dangers were yet unknown. Sometimes, teachers were simply cavalier about the warnings they did receive. Following are various Flower Teacher experiences and observations, which I thought it best to leave anonymous, about toxic materials and hazardous teaching conditions. Several are from teachers who, from the beginning, exercised utmost caution. Several are from those who look back now with apprehension.

1) Early on, my art room desperately needed ventilation for the firing of ceramic projects. Each year I made a budget request and each year it was denied. So I made a plan to invite some school board members' wives and administrators' wives to my room to judge an art contest. I also planned to have the ceramic kiln firing full steam at about the time they would arrive. The kiln gases were overwhelming. The next day I got two rooms in the basement with ventilation included. One for clay construction and one for glazing and firing. I discovered early how to get things done and who runs the school district.

2) I was exposed to many toxic fumes in the printmaking labs at my university when I attended college. I was aware of the lethal atmosphere in the college labs, but dismissed it as relatively unimportant because I was young and indestructible. Besides, the authorities in charge seemed to be blissfully unaware of any problem. However, I was always careful to use water-based inks and solvents when I taught printmaking in my own classroom. Fortunately in recent years, the labs at the university have also been brought up to environmental standards and the teaching staff have become acutely aware of the inherent dangers of the toxic fumes they've lived with for years.

3) I was always in trouble with the fire department since I was never given a metal storage cabinet to store paper or keep flammables. So I was usually in violation of some fire code. If they showed up at school, I would hide in the faculty room until their inspection was over.

4) When I first began teaching, my first classroom was over 50 years old. The room had one sink, lots of liquids in unmarked bottles, no kiln and numerous cans of cleaning fluids left for me "to use." I

never really trusted all the liquids and never used them—they took up storage room for a long time as no one else knew how to get rid of the stuff and I certainly didn't want to just trash it. I left these "mysterious" chemicals labeled as "unwanted" in the room when we moved to our new school years later. For the most part, I have always used watercolor markers, unleaded glazes, and white glue rather than rubber cement. If lead glazes are offered as an option, I discuss it with the students. Most students are now aware of lead poisoning and take the glaze warnings seriously.

5) Of course, when I started teaching, apart from spray varnishes and fixatives, we weren't aware of possible health hazards from art materials. I used pastels occasionally, but phased them out in favor of oil crayons. That choice had more to do with the mess of the chalk than the fixative fumes. I always sprayed after the children were out of the room, but I do recall kids and teachers complaining about the smell. Later the complaints were about the tempera paint that smelled like vomit. I called the chemist at one of the art supply retailers who told me that OSHA had banned the inclusion of preservatives in the paint.

6) The most toxic material I was exposed to and ignorantly used with glee was asbestos powder, which we mixed with wheat paste and water to produce a modeling material for puppet heads, etc. Hopefully I never breathed enough of the fibers to cause any damage...I have no symptoms. All of the dry mixing was done by me. The children used the damp modeling material. It has been a nagging worry since I first learned of its dangers.

7) In the sixties I taught grades 4-8. We had few safety guidelines. The unventilated kiln and the stove were placed next to the art room door. Between them was a wood cabinet full of fabric. I don't know where the fire marshal was. Today, I may use fixatives, etc. outside the building. Secondary students have more leeway but must be well supervised. Unofficially it is acknowledged that sometimes toxic materials have no substitutes in art at the secondary level.

8) I complained until my school system vented our kiln. The metal pieces (which hold up the ceiling tiles in the art room) above the kiln were corroded from acid gases released in firing. We were breathing that. I had developed asthma, which lasted every year as long as we were working with clay (about 2-3 weeks). I finally asked the system to build walls around the kiln. I had two students whose

father was a safety expert at a local government facility. He was the one who finally made it clear to me (and to my principal) how dangerous the situation was. I will be forever grateful to him. The vent was sort of assembled from scraps and is not especially effective, but the walls worked. I haven't had asthma since. I suspect that my students are healthier too.

9) I did order a kiln several years into my teaching—the stackable kind that leaked fumes—and it was placed on an inside wall of my room on an asbestos plate! My safety measure was to paint a red line on the floor to keep kids away. I fired it during the day and sometimes the room was full of blue smoke. I did open the windows, but we had no vent fans at the time. Because of the smell, I did more firing after school, in the evening, and on weekends. I probably had more long-term exposure to the gases than the kids, but never really thought about it. It was also during this time that lead was being removed from glazes, but as I think back, how foolish it was to have a kiln in the room! Since the early 80s, my new room has had a separate kiln room with ventilation. I don't think I poisoned anybody and I haven't had any physical problems that I know of.

10) Then, my kiln was unvented so I fired on weekends. As to the situation now, that unvented kiln is still there, still no vent, and the current teacher still fires on the weekend. Today, the board members and superintendent in my district have decided that elementary schools don't *need* kilns, so in the new schools there are no firewalls, vents, or other provisions for kilns.

11) While I was working on my B. A. degree in the early sixties, we had a visiting professor who had been poisoned through his use of plastics and the melting of plastics to create sculptural pieces. He was straightforward in telling us what had happened and how his health had been ruined. Needless to say, I was impressed with the need for caution with materials, particularly solvents and plastics.

12) Even as late as the mid-eighties my current school still had a stockpile of powdered, lead-based glazes which I mixed myself without a respirator. By that time I was fairly sure they were toxic, but I hated to see all of those wonderful packets of red and orange glaze go to waste. So I mixed them when the students were not present. I also routinely mixed wallpaper paste and breathed paraffin vapors from melted crayons and candles. This kind of thing does eventually catch up with you.

13) In the years prior to the labeling of many art materials, all of us sniffed enough rubber cement through exposure to have fried our lungs. There was dust from kilns without hoods and permanent, smelly markers.

14) Sometimes as a result of low art budgets, we had to use materials that the teachers and students bought ourselves. I had one experience in a fibers course I remember too well. One student brought in a piece of velvet when we were doing reverse-reduction dying. We were using bleach and the fumes from that cloth and Clorox mix drove us all out of the room. After that, I was more careful about fabric brought from home and about using chemicals that I can't absolutely predict.

15) Although there were never any complaints from parents, there probably should have been.

16) An art teacher friend of mine in a neighboring district taught photography for many years until she came down with leukemia. She claimed it was brought on by poor ventilation, but the district didn't want to do much about it . . . so she became a principal.

17) Now, it is often the art teachers who are best informed about potential toxics. I see it as my responsibility to keep my principal and colleagues informed—though sometimes to save money, they continue to buy what is cheap but nonetheless potentially dangerous.

18) My experience in the schools has been that people still do not realize or believe the need for caution. By raising the issue, I have been treated with suspicion or simply laughed at. One of the materials I continue to quarrel with is rubber cement, which is still widely used in unventilated elementary classrooms by both children and adults. Locally, I have discovered that the best way to tackle these issues is to work with our district purchasing agent on the pursuit of conforming to safety standards—by this means, certain items have "disappeared" from the warehouse list. Despite this, however, some toxic items persist on classroom shelves for years. For example, a highly caustic cleaning solvent intended for use by custodians in shower rooms and bathrooms was being refilled into plastic squirt bottles in classrooms, minus the warnings and directions for use, and being used as a general cleaning spray by children and adults. I became aware of this solvent because of its odor and the way in which it made me feel as if I could not breathe. It made me sick.   Working with the purchasing agent, we (the other elemen-

tary art teacher and I) were able to track this down; however, I still believe much of the solution is still in use.

19) Clay has always been a health concern. However I find stringent clean-up procedures can prevent excessive clay dust problems. We gently sweep the tables, wash the tables and pick up clay droppings from the floor after each class. That way there is not a heavy load of dried clay waiting around to be swept into the air when the custodians clean at the end of the day.

20) Kilns in two of the buildings I have served are located in the furnace room. One is in the back storage area of the kitchen. None of them are vented. The one in the kitchen is by an outside door, which is propped open when the kiln is hot; the door between the kitchen and storeroom is closed when firing. Our kilns are all about 30 years old and still going strong. A new high school opened two years ago. The kiln is fully automatic and vented.

21) I believe the issue of hazardous materials is a long, hard battle, but worth the sustained fight. As an art teacher my contact with products and materials is great, so I take the attitude of being cautious and minimizing exposure to harmful and toxic compounds. I also feel responsible to protect the children. I believe that the overall trend has been toward greater awareness of environmental hazards.

22) My first several years of teaching were influenced by a very environmentally minded teacher who opened a recycling center at our school in 1973—well ahead of the times. Our students ran the center Saturday mornings and I helped out. I share this because I think it made me very aware at an early teaching age of the importance of our environment and its care. Today we are much better informed about the products we use and we can make better selections based on our needs and safety. Our school is now visited each year by inspectors that go through my supplies and provide chemical reports that I must keep on file.

23) Teachers and administrators seem much more aware of safety now than in the sixties and seventies. There is genuine concern both for the health of students and for the possibility of litigation involving health issues. In my school district now elementary students are not allowed to use toxic products—period. If they can't eat it, they can't use it in art.

Coping, Strategizing, and Creating a New Curriculum
It was pretty hysterical and there was absolutely no support or contact from other art teachers, but I survived.
Barbara Hirokawa, Columbine High School, Littleton, CO

Given the novelty of art programs in most schools in those days, new art teachers often became the designers of new art curricula. A few of the Flower Teachers, like Joan Newcomer, were lucky enough to move into settings where a predecessor had established a strong visual arts program. In Joan's words, "There was an excellent centralized art department. We used to have workshops every Wednesday after lunch and that is where I really learned about teaching elementary art." In so many situations, however, curriculum consisted of a loosely structured program of projects at best; at worst, there was no visual arts curriculum at all. In Sonia Pratt's words, "The art curriculum was loosely constructed and the emphasis was more on everyone 'doing his own thing'." Carrol Morgan's story depicts how the new art teachers of those times coped, strategized, and charted the course for today.

I started teaching art at King George Middle School in 1968. There was no curriculum, and I was the first primary grade art teacher in the school. It was a half-time job teaching grades one through three and one 7th grade class. I signed a contract to teach 190 days half-time and work 10 in-service days full-time for a salary of $3,150. I think I taught at least four different thirty-five minute classes each day with five minutes between each. Most classes had around 30 students. I had to carry all my supplies in cardboard boxes and travel from room to room throughout the rambling two-story building. My art materials were kept in an upstairs storage room. The school had no air-conditioning and on hot days crayons melted and ran out of the wrappers.

In May of 1972, Mrs. Lavinia Potter joined me at the elementary school. Mrs. Potter, a 1940s art education graduate from R. P. I., was a friend who had resigned earlier from art teaching to raise a family. Her four children were near the ages of my three children. I begged and pleaded, and finally convinced her to return to teaching and replace me in the halftime position as I moved to fulltime teaching. Mrs. Potter was experienced, determined, and organized. She began to whip me into shape in no time. "Get a file cabinet, get organized, label the boxes, make student portfolios…." The following school year we got one big room in an old abandoned industrial shop and turned it into two art class areas. We scrounged old tables and chairs; we used an old chalkboard stand for a drying rack. And we dried clay work on an unidentifiable metal thing that was under a huge, asbestos-coated hot water tank. (Years later the tank was surrounded by a cinder block wall and the door to the enclosure was sealed with caulking.) We had no working sink because the drain in the shop sink had been irreparably stopped up years earlier with metal filings. There was an adjacent bathroom, but it was dysfunctional and eventually the maintenance department sealed the door shut. We built shelves out of benches; made plywood dividers and display boards to separate our spaces; and we taught our different classes at the same time, following the "open classroom" trend of the times. She taught me to make learning centers and independent learning packets. I learned to tolerate noise and learning centers for short periods of time. Mrs. Potter helped me to make do in less than ideal circumstances, to have high expectations, and to laugh at mistakes and messes. I'm not one for being politically correct, but I can say that I am now ashamed that between classes we smoked cigarettes in our little office and set a terrible example for our students.

In that same year, the Art Supervisor from the Virginia Department of Education came and helped Mrs. Potter and me with the long range planning and writing of our first art curriculum. He also made written recommendations to our superintendent for needed improvements. After that we managed to have the maintenance department install an old kitchen sink beside the infamous hot water tank, but we had only cold water and the sink was too high for most of our students. Our twenty-year-old kiln was unvented and we got the maintenance men to install an exhaust fan over it so we wouldn't choke on the fumes.

Also during that year, I ordered the first sets of elementary art textbooks that I had ever seen. The school board funded classroom sets of thirty art textbooks, *Art: Meaning, Methods, and Media* (Hubbard & Rouse, 1972), for each of the 1-7 grades. Mrs. Potter and I were so excited that art was considered a subject that deserved textbooks—surely art had arrived! However, the book's layout of lessons as "strands" was confusing and seemed disconnected in spite of elaborate visual keys at the top of each page; the scope and sequence overviews at the front of the teacher editions were useful. At first we tried to use the textbooks daily, but the lessons were too limiting and lacked continuity with my curriculum; however, the end-of-lesson evaluations spurred me to begin using student self-evaluations. I found that some lessons were well presented and saved me time, so I used them, but ultimately I preferred to use my own lesson plans and activities. I still have those old sixth and seventh grade texts and sometimes use them for independent assignments.

Mrs. Potter and I taught when mini-skirts, flowers, and peace symbols were in style. We let students paint pictures on the art room windows to hide the ugly view of graffiti on outside walls and to block the light so we could show slides. We had over 60 students in our two classes at the same time in the converted shop art room. The students painted flowers and peace symbols on everything, whether it related to the art lesson or not. We taught the elements of art and the principles of design before we knew that it was *formalism*. We showed slides, filmstrips, and 16mm movies that our principal thought were "over the heads" of our students, but we knew that not just our students were ignorant of the visual arts. We filled hallways and classrooms with art and had art shows. Our program got visibility and increased funding for new equipment.

Later in 1972, a new superintendent changed the art program's funding from school principal's allocations to a yearly lump sum of about $4,000 to be distributed by the Art Department Chair to each art teacher as needed. The high school art teacher was Departmental Chairman, but we all worked together to reach a consensus for allocations for each school's art program. By setting aside funds we were able to buy remote control carousel slide projectors for each art room. We began to buy art room resource books and reproductions. A lot of very good art education materials were becoming available: Reinhold Visuals Portfolios, Davis Publications' books on design, the CEMREL Aesthetic Education Program, and lots of pamphlets from NAEA. The superintendent sent all of us to an all-day workshop on the CEMREL program and bought us the teaching materials. We also became informed consumers and searched for quality art materials. We were very frugal and made a conscious effort to buy the best tools and supplies we could afford, agreeing that quality was often more important than quantity, especially in brushes and scissors.

In 1974, I was working under a dynamic young black vice principal from North Carolina, who enthusiastically supported art. I immediately liked his style and commitment to children. He was selected to become the principal of a new "upper elementary" school, which in reality became a middle school. He asked which teachers wanted to move along with him, and he selected me to be a member of his future faculty, along with others who had a special fondness for preadolescents. Choosing to move to the new middle school was the most important decision I ever made in teaching. I volunteered to serve on a committee to help plan the new school. There were many heated discussions about "open" classrooms versus "contained" classrooms. We visited model schools throughout the region. The consensus of our committee was that open classrooms had already proven to be disasters in other schools, and we settled on a modified plan of contained classrooms and large open multi-purpose resource areas—a wise choice. Using every resource I could get from NAEA, I drew floor plans for my ideal art classroom and submitted my plans to the architect in Richmond, Virginia. When King George Middle School opened in 1976, I had everything I had ever dreamed of having in an art room and extras that only an art-friendly architect could have thought of including. My previous years of experience in some of the worst possible facilities had made me aware of the essentials and the possibilities of a space designed especially for teaching art. I had asked for the sky and got it!

I smile when I think of those years and remember the organized chaos we endured together. I think we did a pretty good job of teaching art, and we were lucky to be part of the rising tide that brought art education to elementary schools in the early 1970s. In 1998, I gave the eulogy for my dear friend and co-worker, Mrs. Potter.

The accounts of fellow teachers corroborate and enhance Carrol's narrative. Susie Kropa writes,

> When I graduated from college, the prevalent thought in art educa-
> tion was a kind of laissez faire approach. It wasn't that we were "just
> letting kids create," but we were supposed to lead them to discover
> for themselves, according to Lowenfeld's *Creative and Mental
> Growth* (1957). As a first year teacher in Sidney, Ohio, I remember
> not really knowing exactly how an elementary school worked. There
> were no art rooms and I traveled between four buildings. It's all a
> blur. Curriculum guides were pretty much recipe books of projects in
> a variety of media. I do remember having lessons that weren't long
> enough, and that panicky feeling of what to do with twenty extra
> minutes and a class of noisy second-graders. I can remember being
> scared, especially of the sixth graders.

Candy Alexander had similar experiences:

> When I was hired to teach in Tennessee, I asked for a copy of the
> curriculum at my first school and there was none. They said, "Well,

you're new, and we're hiring a bunch of you at the same time. Why don't you just play with it this year? Do what you want. Consider it wide open. You can order whatever you want for materials and supplies and run it your way. And maybe in a year, we'll look at a curriculum." So I said OK, could I have a copy of the state curriculum? They didn't know whether one even existed. So I had to go through the Tennessee Art Education Association and the State Department of Education to get the state curriculum.

Yvonne Greene reflects,

In looking back I recall a relatively laissez faire atmosphere about delivering an education to the students. If it "felt right" I taught it that way. I don't think that in art I was alone in that attitude. I learned the theories of Viktor Lowenfeld. I had a firm philosophy in art education underpinning my teaching, but lacked a certain structure and concern for meaningful sequence. I was less likely to draw comparisons between art and other disciplines than I am now.

Suzanne Greene shares,

During my first six years of teaching, my district had the largest enrollment it has ever had. I was moved to four different schools during this time. My first school had five art teachers; it now has just two. The district was always changing what we were to teach from year to year, since we did not have a coordinator, nor did we have standards, textbooks, or a curriculum guide. All the art teachers at each school would get together and decide what they wanted to teach. We had our students 18 weeks and each grade level was totally separate. I also went from "contained classes" to "open concept" as our district tried out all the new ideas in designing schools.

Ken Wilkie tells of his first year of teaching when he taught first through fifth grades in two different schools in Burlington, New Jersey. On one day of the week he taught in a middle class, predominantly white school, Beverly Road Elementary. The other four days, he taught in an economically depressed area at Pinewald Elementary where the majority of the children were black and qualified for reduced or free lunches. In remembering his introduction to Pinewald, Ken explains,

Oh boy! The first year! The first district I went to, they couldn't even find a copy of their curriculum, so I was winging it from day one. I often tell new teachers, "If you can get through that first year, the second year is going to just seem like heaven." My predecessor had just retired—she was in her 60s—and she left behind coloring dittos. Like that was how she dealt with this population in this tough school—you know, give them things to color and fill in. Just the antithesis of what we were thinking of doing when we were undergraduates just the year before. You know, this was a horrible shift!

Cherie St. Pierre, Barbara Hirokawa, Mark Phillips, and Nancy Zadra echo the anxiety over the conditions they encountered in their first years. Cherie St. Pierre said,

> In the first four-to-six years of teaching, I spent 24 hours a day learning my craft. I was the only art teacher in the building. If one asked questions it was interpreted that one did not know what one was doing, so I was very quiet. I did not think I was experienced enough to take on a student teacher until my 6th year of teaching. And then I thought of it as a learning experience for me as well as the student teacher. I relied on lessons and info provided in *School Arts Magazine* and *Arts and Activities* for learning how to teach. Our department chair for our school system would not permit anyone to go to the state conferences, so educational life was very provincial. My life was hard teaching in the day and going to graduate school at night.

Barbara Hirokawa:

> I went from student teaching in high school to my first job at a huge elementary school of 1100 kids and a cart. I had six or seven classes a day and my half-hour lunch was my only break. *School Arts Magazine* saved my life, as someone had left a pile behind and I used them to dream up lessons. It was pretty hysterical, and there was absolutely no support or contact from other art teachers, but I survived. The principal was a sweetheart and let me do whatever I wanted, but he stayed out of whatever wing I was in that day so he didn't have to actually see what I was up to.

Nancy Zadra:

> I had been part of what was called the "Intern Program." Because there was a need for teachers in California, this program pushed selected college graduates immediately into jobs at regular beginning salaries. As an "Intern Teacher," I was required to attend a special summer session following graduation and return to my college campus for a seminar one night a week during the school year. The special summer session included a brief student teaching experience which was unreal since it was summer school for the kids. I remember teaching two periods of art for several weeks and it was very

pleasant. The valley weather was extremely warm and we worked at drawing and painting outdoors for much of the time. The neighborhood was graced with old Victorians under stately shade trees and that was where we worked. The seminars at night back on the college campus might have been helpful except that everyone in the group (all interns) was afraid to fess up to what was really bothering them, so the official sessions were superficial. I recall that we would spill our guts to each other during coffee breaks. We trusted each other, but not the profs. In retrospect, I believe that this Intern Program was a "sink or swim" program, but it did accomplish the goal of filling classroom positions.

When I began teaching in Roseville, California, it was 1964 and I was 21 years old. I really did not know much about the how and what of doing my job. I took my clues from teachers around me and revised as I went along. It was hard for me to deal with unmotivated and unruly high school students. I discovered art was the dumping ground for students that nobody wanted. The art department chair took pride in making art tough enough so that poorly motivated students would leave in the first week. I was not sure that this was the right thing to do.

In many school districts, particularly in the early 70s, among all disciplines, curricular innovation and reform were the norm. As Carrol Morgan discussed earlier, primary among those rapid reforms was what many considered a new humanistic era revolving around the *open classroom* and its student-centered instruction. New college courses, journal articles, and faculty meetings buzzed with the open classroom philosophy. Many schools built during the early 70s were structured around this innovative plan. Likewise older schools adapted, tearing down walls and replacing them with movable dividers to communalize the learning space. The whole idea was to activate the students, to decentralize the teacher, and following Dewey, to tailor learning to the contexts, interests, and needs of the individual learners. In a critical sense, it was a way of recognizing and accommodating the growing heterogeneity of changing student populations. Many of the liberal ideals of the *free* schools of the 1920s, like A. S. Neill's *Summerhill* (1960), resonated with the education philosophers and teachers of the 60s and 70s. The idea that freedom of development and learning nurtured students who would value peace, care, and compassion intermeshed with the open school concept.

Supervisors and faculty in every discipline, some willing, some not, joined in the push for open education. In working to place "student at the center," methods of individualized learning became a primary concern. Student learning centers took on a central role, where various areas of the classroom were dedicated to specific interests and supplied with a variety of instructional materials. Further, students were invited to plan their own course of study by constructing learning contracts and taking part in charting and evaluating their own paths of progress. There was an emphasis on group dialogue accordingly accommodated by the open learning spaces. The goal was to nurture group interaction, communal problem solving and community spirit. In those traditional schools that did not physically have the open space, teachers nonetheless worked to accommodate the open concept, creating, on a smaller scale, student learning stations, individualized learning focused on freedom of choice, and opportunities for group interaction. According to many, the open education reform movement encountered severe stumbling blocks and held substantial limitations. Several teachers like Kathleen Thompson and Joan Newcomer found themselves in schools that had embraced open education as a school-wide pedagogical approach, but for them, the day-to-day pragmatics of open schooling had little merit. In Joan Newcomer's words,

> Stewart Hill Elementary was an "open space" school, which was a disaster. The concept of an open space school for university medical students sounds great. An open space school for inner city children just leads to too many distractions to learn.

Kathleen Thompson agrees,

> There were these years in the 70s that we just really went bonkers, we went to the extreme in high school education. During that time the open classroom was everything. We had lots and lots of art students because they were into "electives," and the number of required courses you needed to graduate from high school went way down.

Despite the detrimental particulars, this group of art teachers found themselves in tune with the underlying theory. First, in placing students at center, focusing on the experiential, offering them more freedom to chose, plan, and chart their own progress, open education validated the approach already in place in the art classroom. Visual arts instruction had long recognized the essentialness of distinguishing individual styles of creativity and learning, e. g., respecting and accommodating the student's working habits and pace, expressive style, choice of technique, materials, etc. Whether they had actually worked from written contracts or not, ideally, art students were all on an individualized plan and pace. Further, relevance, that is, dissolving the dichotomy between schooling and life, was a given for this generation of art teachers. Without overt knowledge of the theory of *visual culture*, under the influence of the Pop Art Movement and its concomitant social activism, this generation of art teachers began deconstructing the boundaries between *fine art* and the aesthetics of the everyday. In describing the lessons and the projects they devised for their students, designs for Harley Davidsons, murals for Volkswagon vans, layouts for protest posters, projects for organic garden design, album covers, and peace sculptures crafted from recycled weapons emerged. The majority of the Flower Teachers in this study talked about lessons drawing naturally from "what the students already knew and liked."

Many art teachers found themselves well centered in the open education, cross-disciplinary fad of offering the popular "mini-courses" of the time, with projects derived directly from popular culture. Fibers studies were among the favorites, with tie-dye, batik, macrame, weaving, soft sculptures, and book-making. Ceramics courses were popular. Candle making, especially sand casting, was a favorite side dish. Suzanne Greene recalls,

> Bargello belts were a fashion statement along with embroidered jeans. We also taught needlepoint and stitchery. Drugs were more widely used and symbols for drugs were in their art works. I had more students coming to school stoned than now. One year my clay students decided they wanted to make pipes. I let them, but before I fired them, I plugged up the hole inside the bowl so they couldn't be used. I used to have a long list posted in my room, which told students what they could not draw. Peace signs were at the top of the list. Ironically, now I have eight balls, jokers, crossed out "o's" and other gang symbols listed.

Among the most lasting and critical developments of these times, the multicultural curriculum had its foundations in the egalitarianism of open education. By the end of the 1960s, Western canon was losing its hold, at least in the real world of the classroom. As was true in all content areas, this generation of art educators embraced diversity. Though most had experienced college programs lacking in multicultural education, through personal interest and sheer necessity they began researching on their own and introducing to their increasingly heterogeneous body of students culturally diverse artists, artworks, media, and techniques. Native American sand paintings, Asian pottery, textile designs from South and Central America, Tyi Wara headdresses, paintings by Frida Kahlo, Romare Bearden, Rhoda Williams, among a plethora of others were just beginning to find a place in the curriculum. The big problem was that examples for the classroom of diverse arts were hard to find. What the National Gallery, for example, state museums, and visual arts catalogues did not supply, art teachers had to find for themselves, making slides and mounting color images via their own devices from a multitude of found sources. Replacing the dated, red-faded filmstrips that took the joy out of learning became a symbolic act of liberation for the Flower Teachers.

Naturally intertwined with all of this is inquiry into the nature of art, its purposes, its methods, and its context. Long before they knew anything about Discipline-Based Art Education, before curriculum guides stipulated anything about teaching art history, criticism, and aesthetics, some of the Flower Teachers realized the academic obligation for inquiry in these areas. Through teachers' own admissions, art inquiry lessons were usually sporadic, non-sequenced, and informal. Nonetheless, what some called their *instinctive* and *spontaneous* classroom conversations about art are indicative of an expanding awareness in those years of what art education can and should be: full and rich and democratic. Anita Winfrey shares her awakenings:

> I was the first black art teacher in a predominantly white school. So my first job, besides teaching art, was to expose a population to a black role model. Some of the kids had little or no experience with black folks at all. This changed my basic idea of teaching art. I began to expose children to a variety of artists and artworks from different cultures. As a result, I found a great new approach, which I continue to use today to broaden children's perspectives: multicultural art history.

Carrol Morgan encapsulates the elemental nature of multicultural art education:

> Multicultural education: Was it ever a problem for an art teacher? Cultural studies form the bone and muscle of art education. How can students be asked to make a mask without being helped to understand the long cultural history and variety of mask-making—the purpose, the meaning, the media possibilities? To continue the analogy, I would say that student-created masks are the skin and adornment that create the image that symbolizes the human condition—fear, love, hate, mystery, and joy. Since 1972 when I started teaching upper elementary art I have included multicultural studies in art—it was natural and logical to include the art heritage of the non-European world. Many ideas came from readings and suggested lessons in the *Art and Man* series. In 1971, their teacher's guide covered ways to use *Art and Man* in a variety of subjects: art, music, language arts, and social studies. The suggested activities were interdisciplinary and showcased the incredibly diverse art collection of the National Gallery of Art.

Students are intrigued by the hands-on art learning about other cultures. It frees their minds to imagine from a different viewpoint. Students love to discover the secret meanings of a coded language, and that art from other cultures is like an encryption that needs to be deciphered. I get so excited when my students can read the meanings of a Japanese floor plan or a sand garden—privacy understood as a cultural belief—the idea that a sand garden can represent a philosophy of nature.

I do not claim that all or even the majority of art teachers during those years were cognizant of the omissions and committed to the need to enhance their curriculum with diversity. As for the teachers in this study, more than two-thirds addressed their forays in those early years into multicultural curriculum development. As Anita Winfrey said, school desegregation and the resulting heterogeneity of populations was a dominant impetus to adapt curriculum to the contexts of the students. As Carrol Morgan discussed, academic and social interests in cultural diversity were just beginning to impact educational resources such as school texts, magazines, slides, and visual arts reproductions. Though many art teachers weren't sure about *how* to teach multicultural concepts and content, they certainly knew *why* they were doing it.

Throughout the 60s and 70s, the Flower Teachers were fashioning a new pedagogy, designing and utilizing new materials, and constructing the components of a new visual arts curriculum. All the while, they were engendering, not only for their students but for themselves, that joy born of broadening aesthetic propensity and peaking through multicultural windows into someone else's mind.

The Measure of Those years
To this day I have not experienced such an outpouring of creativity and art. This was an era of freedom.
John Skrabalak, Altoona Area High School, Altoona, PA

Remembering those early classroom years brings a blend of incisive, sometimes biting, critical assessment tempered by pride and nostalgia. In Sonia Pratt's words, "Those early years were pretty wild. I had one administrator say to me not long ago that he didn't understand why any of us who taught in the early 70s were still teaching." They were times of progression and regression; they were uncertain, unpredictable times; most of all, they were changing times. Of all the perplexing social and pedagogical issues with which art educators, as well as those in all other disciplines, are wrestling today, most emerged and intensified during the 1960s and 70s

Educational equity; overcrowded classes; drugs and violence; the perpetual labor of constructing a relevant, democratic, and academically sound curriculum; the fight for understanding, representation and respect for the visual arts as a discipline; and obtaining adequate resources, conditions, and facilities are among the most pressing of these. Today, few of those early difficulties have been resolved. Some have been ameliorated; some have festered and grown worse; some drag on unchanged. What is important and characteristic of the Flower Teachers is that they looked upon these difficulties as opportunities and pressed for solution throughout their careers. As Ken Wilkie said, the focus was on "making change and helping others to see it." They were times to "go do something," to remediate. Inadequacy and insecurity, frustration and failure, both imagined and real, were tempered for these young teachers by a stalwart sense of determination, responsibility, and accountability. As evidenced by their professional longevity, this generation maintains an audacious desire to succeed, for their families who have believed in them, for their students and the parents who trusted them, and, as they were driven by their times, for their own satisfaction in knowing they made a difference in their world. Carrol Morgan and John Skrabalak pull it all together.

> Carrol: In 1970, all three of our county's art teachers had a lot in common: philosophies, sense of fun, the hippie era, "happenings," and a love for art in all forms. One of my closest colleagues says we were a little "bizarre." We made a good team even though we worked in different buildings. We were designated as the Countywide Art Department. We met together frequently and shared ideas and woes. Our chair was a master at writing good unit plans and was big on student contracts and self-evaluations. We borrowed ideas from each other and shared our limited A/V resources. Our program was successful and our new school superintendent supported us. He bought an overhead projector for my art room—a luxury at that time. He increased art funding in 1971, and in addition began paying for two classroom subscriptions of the new *Art and Man* (72 subscriptions cost $140.00/year, compared to $576.00 today). *Art and Man* provided excellent history articles, lesson ideas, and related filmstrips, slide sets, and recordings. We kept all the sets over the years, accumulating them as invaluable resources, which the high school art teacher and I still use. Those first six years of teaching made me the kind of teacher I am today, and the years since then have refined and embellished me, though I may not yet be a finished product.

> John: I was assigned to a basement room my second year of teaching. It was part of an old, but historically beautiful brownstone that was

scheduled for demolition, not restoration. This high school was scheduled to be "modernized" and rebuilt, instead of preserved. I got permission to paint on my classroom walls. The experience turned into a "love-in" of color for my students. I opened the cans of paint and turned my students loose. To this day I have not experienced such an outpouring of creativity and art. This was an era of freedom. Every spot on the wall was covered. When I drove by after the demolition of the brownstone, I noticed that the mounds of rubble were beautified by flecks of colored brick and spirit—flecks of memories of a bygone era—1973-74.

Chapter 4 provides an account from each teacher of the scheme of values that has sustained them day to day, year after year.

Chapter 4
When September Rolls Around

These students come to school with so many problems; some of the stories I hear from them make me wonder how they have the courage and stamina to get up every day and come to school, and I will often tell them that. And they create the most wonderful, sensitive, delightful, award-winning art; they sing with enthusiasm; they play musical instruments. They have great commitment and courage. With material like that to work with, who could possibly give up?

Lora McNeece Barrett, Holyoke Magnet Middle School for The Arts, Holyoke, MA

Sustenance and Conviction
Within the core questions of their interview, I asked the Flower Teachers to tell me about teaching philosophy, ideology, the foundation of their beliefs about art education. I wanted to know how they see themselves in their role as art educator. Directly following that, I asked them something else: *What has kept you in the classroom for so many years? What has helped sustain your commitment and enthusiasm?* Their responses to the first question were theoretically sound and clearly articulated. To be honest though, quite a few of them were a little stiff and bookish. Perhaps questions about instructional philosophy generate that kind of response; maybe teachers have answered that question too often. In another light, reactions to my second inquiry about commitment, conviction, and sustenance yielded more spontaneous explanations, more personal and philosophically telling. For the sake of both insight and interest, I have combined the teachers' responses to these two questions, pulling out statements of theory, method, and rationale from their first response and adding to that their ardent reasons to be. Following are their accounts, honest and clear.

Lora Barrett
My commitment and enthusiasm have been sustained because I genuinely delight in successes and achievements of my students. I feel like they are my family. The school is small and I know them all. I work with a wonderful team of arts instructors (as well as the health and P. E. teachers), and we meet on a daily basis to plan, share and work on solutions to problems with kids. We are not isolated from each other; we work out problems together every day. My kids for the most part are the poorest in the Commonwealth. These students come to school with so many problems; some of the stories I hear from them make me wonder how they have the courage and stamina to

get up every day and come to school, and I will often tell them that. And they create the most wonderful, sensitive, delightful, award winning art; they sing with enthusiasm; they play musical instruments. They have great commitment and courage. With material like that to work with, who could possibly give up?

What I do on a daily basis is to try to see what kids need; try to find out what their interests are and try to make connections between art and what is going on in their lives and in their heads. I talk to them in the language of studio. I talk about respect, and growth, and change. I talk about how much they can learn from each other through their weekly crits and about how much I learn from them. My goals are to get art out front everyday, to remind other teachers in a subtle way what art is all about. I try to find ways to high-profile the work of students and the school. My goal for the kids is to get them to nurture a love for art, and to understand that art is a life-long process. I share my own artwork with them, show my earlier work and current work, and I ask them for suggestions, which they *love*. It really validates their intellect to show them that I respect and trust their judgement.

I think of myself as a cheerleader and a nurturer. I believe there is beauty in every child, and sometimes they are so scared that they don't want you to find that beauty. Some of these kids have no confidence in themselves; sometimes no one besides the teachers has ever told them how special they are. And you can't just say it. These kids recognize a con job…they know when you are being sincere or insincere. So what I have to do is really be observant, and really look deep into their souls and find those good qualities in them, point them out to them, praise them, and thank them quietly for the many things they do.

Marie Shack
It is the students. From my resume you can see that I have had a variety of teaching experiences at different levels and different kinds of schools. No matter what the grade, I find that students want to learn. If they have confidence that you are going to teach them, they are receptive. They appreciate committed, bright, interesting and knowledgeable teachers. So over the 30 years, I keep learning, finding new artists that interest me, learning new techniques, perfecting others, keeping up with current curriculum trends. Because of this, not only am I growing as a person and a teacher but I can bring more to my classroom. If I'm excited, then I find the students get excited. It's a fantastic feeling…not necessarily because they might do dynamic work (sometimes that is the happy result), but if their vision is expanded. I truly feel that the art room should be a haven of joy

and delight. I take my role in the classroom as a purveyor of knowledge very seriously. I cajole, push, demand, encourage, direct, comment on the successes and on the failings. I'm very honest and don't tend to milk-coat things. One year I came back in September determined to be more mild mannered. By the end of three weeks the students were so upset with me, I was so foreign to them that I went back to my old, witty self. They know I am good hearted, but we do tease each other. If my students get more out of life, if their vision and feeling for humanity are expanded, if they become more appreciative of the arts, then that is to me more successful than any art product. I still get excited when September rolls around.

John Skrabalak
Without hesitation, the students and my involvement in the creative process have sustained me. The artistic spirit and the smiles of wonderment, discovery and success have kept me committed and enthusiastic. Also my need to grow as a teacher, as well as my desire to learn new things keep me going. My professional involvement with the Pennsylvania Art Education Association—its programming, board meetings, etc. refuel the fire in me.

I am wacky and weird, innovative and creative, a rebel, and very resource-ful. I am motivator, facilitator, problem solver, planner, observer and supporter. I give tons of praise out to my students. I believe that positive reinforcement can go a long way. I always try to find something good in every artistic expression. I believe in patience and mutual respect and consider every student's expression to be a blessing given unselfishly. I believe that anyone that takes an art course from me should have a unique and positive experience. I try to make my room environment different and unusual and I decorate accordingly. I love nature and use it as a theme frequently. The art environment should be loose yet somewhat structured. The room atmosphere should be visually stimulating. I firmly believe that all can create. I have a sign at my door that states, "Leave the *I cant's* at the door." I am there to instruct the future advocates and consumers of art. I demonstrate the skills, provide the problem or concept, prepare the materials and turn the students loose. I believe that part of art making is play and discovery, and I encourage this. I enjoy making students think in different ways. Ultimately, I am not there to make artists. I am there to teach how to see.

Sonia Pratt
Sometimes I wonder what has kept me in the classroom for so many years. There have been days that I couldn't be paid enough to do the job and days that I would teach for no pay at all. It helps to have a yearly beginning and an end to your job as a teacher. If I have a bad year at least it comes to an

end and I get a chance to start new. I've always been excited and rejuvenated when the school year begins. I am dedicated and enthusiastic, definitely student-oriented. I try to find a way to motivate every student. I try to discover their interests and ability level early in the course and work from that point. I never hold a student back who can excel nor do I push a student beyond their capabilities and create frustration for them. When I can motivate students to be enthused, and that usually comes when they find success, then I become enthused. Commitment seems to be part of my personal make-up.

Carol Wellein
My love for art and children has kept me in the classroom. I believe the teaching profession is a noble job, so I'm proud of my position. I also get to teach the subject that children love. In order to stay fresh and enthusiastic I do the following: change my curriculum, talk to other art teachers, attend all of the teacher workshops at the Baltimore Museum of Art, attend our local AIMS conferences, attend the NAEA conference when affordable, subscribe to art education magazines, go to the Internet for lesson plans, visit other schools to observe, and teach the classroom teachers some of the projects I do with the students. I am a teacher who likes children and likes to motivate them. I prepare my information carefully, I'm well organized, and I have high expectations. I include written and verbal directions as well as visuals during my motivation exercises in order to reach all learning styles. After the goals are defined, I stand back and become more of an observer. I am a facilitator during critique time, while clean-up time is very teacher centered.

Of late, my philosophy seems to be changing. I teach a combination of subject-centered, child-centered, and sometimes society-centered programs. The factor that remains constant and is most important to me is art production. I will always make that the focus of my curriculum. My goals for students are to expose them to art and artists from many cultures, to be able to develop problem-solving skills, to recognize the connection between art and other subjects, and to expose them to a variety of materials while promoting self-expression. Ultimately, I hope to lead them to an appreciation for art and to a sympathy for the values of others.

Nancy Zadra
I have continued my education and I believe this has helped keep my edge honed. Studying education is not an abstraction; it is something to be assimilated and put into practice. Teaching is attractive because it is all about human relations. Working in a school setting has always provided me with friends, social connections, and community status. Working with

students has always been basically rewarding, allowing me to learn too. I believe I should be an excellent role model and should embody the behaviors and values that I desire to build in my students. I consciously and deliberately work on this. About commitment and enthusiasm, I learned early to stay away from negative, dire-mouthed, sarcastic teachers as it is poison to the spirit. I personally work hard at being upbeat and positive. I believe it is my job to be this way.

Anita Winfrey

I am a positive, energetic "idea" person with a dedication and a desire to help kids see that art is not isolated from life. It develops life and provides balance. In my younger years, I had two excellent art teachers who both had a wealth of knowledge. They inspired me to want to teach art and they still sustain me today. I call them to consult on art ideas and problems. Also in the 70s I had a college professor who suggested we keep an art journal which I continue today. I keep a personal journal of written reflections and an idea journal for art ideas. This writing is sustenance. My belief in God and my relationships with my students have helped me to stay in the field of teaching.

Gerald Vilenski

What has kept me in the classroom so long has been largely the same motivation that got me there in the first place. There is a never-ending need for quality teachers in the arts and a never-ending need on the part of students to experience what those teachers have to offer them. My philosophy is fairly simple: to share the passion I have for the visual arts with my students by making art fun, challenging, and placing equal emphasis on process and product. I firmly believe that a well-designed art program teaches to the physical, perceptual, creative, social and intellectual development of children. I view art as the great equalizer because all students, regardless of skill or previous experience, are approaching the creative problems I set up for them for the first time. Art is creative problem solving. It is my role as an art teacher to facilitate developmentally appropriate problems for students to solve in a creative manner.

Carrol Morgan

I have been blessed with a supportive husband. He values the importance of my work as an educator and he understands that I find teaching rewarding if sometimes frustrating. His salary was adequate to support our family, so I could "afford" to teach. I love the activity of teaching art—the on-your-feet doing it. Every day is different—the excitement, the energy, the flexibility, the creative possibilities. I love watching my students grow. I get to share in their achievements—from the excitement of an art student who "gets it" for the first time, to the awards and degrees received by former students. After my initial, naïve enthusiasm for teaching, I was sustained for the next ten years by the encouragement, wise advice and direction given to me in 1972 by the Supervisor of Art of the Virginia Department of Education. In addition, my own continuing education has often sparked a renewed enthusiasm for teaching. The Getty Institute Seminars for Art Educators are highlights in my career. Being with my students keeps me feeling young and in touch with our rapidly changing culture and world.

I describe myself by what I do and how I do it. I am an art teacher—a good one. I am knowledgeable, dedicated, creative, patient, meticulous, and organized, but I am all too aware that sometimes I am ignorant, self-centered, rigid, impatient, haphazard, and unfocused. I love teaching art, but I get stressed, frustrated, and angry. I think I am very emotional, but other teachers say that I am always so calm. I will not tolerate chaos, but I love to see creative activity. I believe in art education. I believe that it imparts unique ways of seeing, knowing, doing, and feeling, which are essential to a well-balanced life. A good art education should begin as early as possible and continue through elementary, middle, and high school. It should be developmental, sequential, and comprehensive. An effective art program includes art production, art history, art criticism, and aesthetics (Discipline-Based Art Education). Twenty years ago, I used the terms "skills, attitudes, and knowledge." The basic concepts have been expanded but not changed. I believe it is my job to lead my students towards the following goals: increased visual perception, increased creativity, increased skills and knowledge, and greater art appreciation. DBAE provides the best means for reaching these goals.

I'm optimistic about art education, but I am sometimes pessimistic about current directions/trends in education. I believe that education will be improved by raising standards and expectations, and by increasing account-ability. I am worried by my students' increased use of violent or explicit subject matter and vulgar language, but I understand that they are express-ing ideas from their homes and culture—especially the popular media.

Bonnie Keyser
I am an enthusiastic and happy art teacher. How could an art teacher be anything else? I am very expressive and truthful with the students. I always try to find something good about their work before I critique it. I never coddle or lie to them. I feel my role is to stress originality and offer creative experiences that allow the student to discover and develop a personal awareness of the natural and man-made environment. I want the students to realize that art is an essential part of life. Art should be fun for

the teacher and student. I feel that I have given students a sense of achievement they may not find elsewhere in the curriculum. I strive to make everyone successful in art and to encourage them to take pride in their work.

I like the freedom that I have. We have no set art text at our school so we are on our own and have been able to develop the art curriculum. I have written three curriculum guides for our school. When I came to the high school, I was the only art teacher. Now we have two. I have worked hard to build a successful art program. I have stayed enthusiastic about teaching because of my wonderful students. It is hard to believe the talent that so many of them have—but do not know it. I realize that every student will not become an artist but will have the knowledge to appreciate art, decorate their homes, have a hobby, etc. When my students are successful with a project and take pride in their work and get excited about it, I feel satisfied and fulfilled.

Suzanne Greene
Each year I have taught students who have made a difference in my life. I have remained in the classroom primarily because of them, and, frankly, to support my family. Attending museum shows and galleries also helps keep my spirits up. It helps that my school district's art coordinator was voted the "Top Art Coordinator in the West." Through our in-services and monthly meetings, she keeps me enthusiastic about teaching. My principal has also made my life as a teacher richer. He supports my program and encourages me to display my students' work. We used to have "pro-grow" classes that we could take after school. They were taught by art teachers from other districts and artists in the greater Houston area. These kept us current and gave us a support group of fellow teachers. I keep in touch with fellow teachers. We exchange lessons and recommend what shows to go see and web sites to visit. What a godsend e-mail is! But again, it is the students who keep me going. If you take the time to see them for who they are, not what they look like or how they dress, they will give you back respect and support. Respect is not automatic. You have to earn their trust and respect by being fair, non-judgmental, and accepting.

Barbara Hirokawa
I just plain love my job! I often counsel students who are considering going into education that they will never get rich, but they will never be bored. I think what has kept me from being bored is a love of learning. I am always taking classes, attending conferences and conventions and institutes, working on curriculum writing and standards and assessment. I also love watching kids learn and discover art and often an unknown talent and career. I am a very "hard" teacher because I demand high performance

levels and behavior. But I am also very "easy" because I will go far out of
my way to help everyone meet those standards. I have been told that the
thing I do best is allow room for each student to discover their creative
potential, to solve each problem in their own way. I am enthusiastic about
what I am teaching and that carries over to the kids. I am open emotionally,
so they know who I am and they trust me. My ultimate role is to turn kids
on to art and discover the voice that art can give them.

Ken Wilkie
Teaching is rewarding emotionally. There is definitely a sense of accomplishment coming out of every day, if not every class period. It's that you
are doing something important, something that matters. It's the creativity—
that you're helping somebody come to a new point in their experience.
They reach a place where they're doing something different than what
they've done before. They've found success in something that they didn't
expect to find success in. Or maybe they hoped to find success in it and it
finally happens. And your part as the catalyst is the reward. What's helped
sustain commitment and enthusiasm is the positive feedback: parents being
appreciative, kids being appreciative, other teachers being appreciative . . .
making it clear that what I've done has made some kind of difference and
that's very rewarding. The other thing that keeps you there, keeps you from
straying is that you know you got a mortgage to meet and the stability of
knowing that it's there.

Lloyd Sensat
I enjoy teaching and getting paid. My students' accomplishments and
awards are stimulating. Teaching in a good school system and having
administrative support makes a difference. I have enjoyed a network of
good teachers and friends. I believe that it is the teacher's inspired presence
that makes the classroom a unique experience. The teacher must be a
master of subject matter, teaching all aspects of the arts. Teachers must also
know that they are a role model and mentor. Teaching is an art—intensely
personal. In my own experience as an art teacher, it has been my enthusiasm, my empathy, my role as facilitator, my commitment to my program,
and my advocacy for the arts in the schools—at the local, state, national
levels.

Joan Newcomer
My love of children and art have kept me in the classroom. My philosophy
is to present a child centered curriculum that challenges students to think
divergently and build on problem solving skills. It is important also for the
student to build self confidence in their own personal expression and to
become motivated to appreciate the artwork of master artists. I build a lot

of my curriculum around what is being studied in other subject areas and what is relevant to the student during a particular time. Relevance was the key word when I began teaching in 1970 and I still believe it is important. My role in the classroom is to explain and demonstrate the use of a vast array of art materials as well as the use of the elements and principles of design as tools for the expression of unique ideas. Once my job is over, I become a consultant and observer as I walk around the room advising.

Jeannie Siegler
My commitment and enthusiasm are sustained each semester of each year by the growth, confidence and improved visual awareness students seem to show given the opportunity. I have also moved around in school systems, which has given me a variety of experiences. My goal as a classroom art teacher is to make students aware of the possibilities of the fine arts, technology, skill development, history—and to give them some room to facilitate their own ideas. Students are eager for an avenue of expression and creativity, not always rebellious but always wanting an ear for their ideas and a place for their creativity. My philosophy is that every student has potential. Channel it constructively and watch it grow!

Sharon Henneborn
Perhaps this story will illustrate what has kept me in the classroom for so long. One year I was surprised by the level of enthusiasm my elementary school students had for Andy Warhol. It seems they couldn't get enough of him. As it was, there were two sisters who were so inspired they talked their mother into driving several hundred miles to Pittsburgh to see friends and visit the Andy Warhol Museum. They returned with a T-shirt for me and pictures and experiences to share with their classmates. The children were all impressed that there were seven floors of galleries in the Warhol Museum. One girl expressed doubt that you could visit seven floors in one day. The child presenting the discussion, a second grader, said, "Well I agree. If you were looking at Impressionist or Realist paintings you would need several days, but I think Andy Warhol is pretty much going for impact and you can see seven floors of impact in one day." All of the students agreed and she went on with her presentation. I think she summed up Andy Warhol pretty well, and I think he would agree. She also encapsulated what keeps me in education.

Susie Kropa
I wish I could say I stayed so long because I simply loved teaching. Truthfully, for many years it was just my job. I have always taken it seriously and kept up with the times and trends, but some days…months…even years, I've almost dreaded going to school. I kept teaching because we

needed the money. In my profession, I am driven! Sometimes obsessive—extremely organized—have to be! I'm pretty confident in my ability to teach, but always tinkering with lessons to make them better. My philosophy is that kids should like art and get a sense of their own worth (I am not saying self-esteem) through artistic pursuits. I believe they should understand that art requires discipline, playfulness, living with frustration, and lots of erasing! I want them to learn that working through problems to the best of their ability can give them great satisfaction and a sense of power. "Look what I did!" I believe that the art studio is a place where children can learn to respect one another's feelings and differences. They can learn to take responsibility for the care and handling of supplies and realize the importance of an organized studio space. I see myself as part artist, part role model, part coach and cheerleader, and part historian and storyteller.

Martyna Bellessis
To be perfectly honest, I have looked forward to going to school almost every day of my career. I know that is hard to believe but I have taught in some mighty fine places and I have had some great administrators and teaching colleagues who have become friends. My enthusiasm has been sustained by the quality of my students and my expectations for them. There is always so much to teach. My goals are to impart joy in learning; to teach about the vast history of art; and to use methods that result in excellent projects. Getting teaching awards has been fun. Traveling has added a new dimension to my curriculum. Having my students' artwork published is a joy and when I have an article published, it is fun to share it. I have also helped found an organization that has exhibits of international students' artwork. My school corporation and the local press have been appreciative of my efforts, sending me to NAEA conferences, international seminars, and more.

Kathleen Thompson
What has kept me going? Well, on the practical level, there's a thing that a friend of mine and I used to do. His name is Rob. We were always going to quit teaching in February. And after a while, I realized we always had this conversation in January or February. He would tell me he was going to quit teaching and go to Oklahoma to work in the oil fields. Never made it—still in teaching. He's a few years from retirement—will never leave teaching. One year, he was going to go to Alaska because the salaries were so high. And it was this fantasy that got us through the winter because those months are the time when teaching can really get to you. Sometimes at that point you want to do anything else but teach. So I think there were years when thinking I could quit or switch to college teaching or something else kind of sustained me. The point is, reality sets in after about 15 years—let's face it.

You are making a good salary, you're in the retirement system—you're not going anywhere. In the fall you love teaching...and then somehow in the middle of winter. . . . And then you've slugged through spring and then there's nothing like summer. So summer kept me in education, having the freedom to travel, do my own art, time for myself.

Ironically, the last ten years, I never want to leave teaching. It's been more satisfying. I haven't wanted to quit. I haven't needed to be sustained. And I've probably been more enthusiastic than I have ever been. I think that's unusual for teachers. I think a lot of art teachers are absolutely on their last legs those last three or four years. They're negative and just want out. But I find myself in the last ten years having the best time of all, doing the best, enjoying it the most, grateful that I could do this and spend time with kids. It's really wonderful.

In connection with all this, about eight years ago artist Miriam Shapiro spoke at the National Art Education Association convention. Her talk really affected me. It didn't change my teaching. It did allow me to put into words what I had felt for a while. It's like things coalesced and I had a level of understanding of what I was doing. And I could see why I had been frustrated for so many years by society's concept of the role of women. Shapiro talked about what she wants to acquire as "the seamless life." And I find myself in sympathy. We have compartments in our lives and they are supposed to be different. What we did at home with our children was one part and what we did in our classroom was another part of our life. What we did in our studio as artists was in another section. We had all these rooms in our house, but somehow they were separate rooms, and each of them was decorated differently and each was selected to play a different role. They don't necessarily have anything in common. You're this working woman, the artist, you're a parent, you're a spiritual person, etc. And each of these is a separate box and you have to keep them separated. Shapiro said that one of the reasons she created her feminist art was that she really rebelled at that concept—that life had to be compartmentalized. So one of the things that she did was to let her kids in her studio. Traditionally one's studio should be separate from one's children. If you were a male artist, those two things would never mix. And you know, those would be different parts of your life. In her case, she didn't do that. She didn't go to her studio. Her studio was her house and her children were part of her studio. They baked brownies, kids' toys were all around. And for her, these were not separate things. What I got from that was for me, I want a seamless life. I am a teacher. I am a nurturer. They're one in the same.

Candy Alexander
Art is creativity and teaching creativity is nourishing. I enjoy helping kids
use their own ideas and understand the pride that comes from self-creation.
I want children to see how art affects all subjects: philosophy,
multiculturalism, history, aesthetics, criticism—we try it all. I am a
facilitator, organized, creative, and take pride in having a sense of humor.

Carolyn Skeen
There is something special about art education that helps sustain commitment and enthusiasm. First most students genuinely want to be in class.
"Art day" is often a student's favorite day of the week. A parent told me
recently that the only morning that her ADHD child didn't cry and beg to
stay home from school was on art day. Art is a subject that appeals to
students with many different learning styles, a place where there are as
many solutions to a problem as there are personalities in the classroom.
What other subject comes close to involving students so thoroughly?

As a teacher I have high expectations. I expect art students (even at the
elementary level) to think and work. Art really is great fun of course, but I
believe that true creativity takes thought and time. I also believe that if
students are busy, interested, and know what is expected there won't be
many discipline problems. Good classroom management means setting
things up (rules, supplies, instructions) so that children aren't confused
about what they are supposed to do. Ideally my role in the classroom is that
of facilitator. On good days this is true. On not-so-good days I'm the drill
sergeant.

Yvonne Greene
I can sincerely say that I enjoy my career as an art teacher and do not regret
the decision I made, except for salary inadequacies. I can come home from
work every day and feel I've made a difference in one or two children's
lives. Not every career can offer that satisfaction. I view myself as a lifetime learner and in what other profession do you have the opportunity and
obligation to indulge yourself in continually exploring and learning new
things about the field you love? I love the challenge of taking youngsters
and exposing them to the hands-on learning activities and aesthetic joy that
come from the experience we call "art." My teaching philosophy is based
first on respect for children's capabilities. In addition, I feel it is essential to
provide a structured, sequential framework so children are aware of the
goals of any activity. I maintain high expectations so children feel empow-
ered to produce at the highest quality level of their capabilities. To see the
amazing growth that occurs in children after they have experienced and
internalized art concepts is immensely gratifying. I feel privileged to have

helped in the cultural enhancement of several generations of young human beings.

Cheryl Ann St. Pierre

I am single and so must make a living. I always want to do my best in all my endeavors. My own enthusiasm and commitment for eliminating boredom have sustained me throughout life. First and foremost I believe in Howard Gardner's Multiple Intelligences Theory, that art is one of the eight intelligences and that as humans we all have some capabilities in each of these. I realize that when my students enter my art room as kindergartners it is my responsibility to help nurture that intelligence and love for visual expression. It is extremely important for them to enjoy the process of making art, even more than taking a product home. The second ingredient in my philosophy is addressing the whole child, which includes Daniel Goleman's Emotional Intelligence. Not every child is fully loaded with confidence in art or experiences a happy home life. I often tell my students how smart they really are, how they need their eyes, minds, and hands to cut out a shape (no need for patterns or tracers), how we are all allowed to make mistakes, how a mistake can sometimes lead us to find a better solution, that there is no single answer in art, but many different solutions. I discuss how art includes every other subject area. Third is my emphasis on learning styles. I try to explain procedures through multiple views. The fourth ingredient is ethics. I try to treat each child with courtesy and respect. I model not only good teaching practices but also the character traits of honesty, justice, and integrity. The fifth ingredient is mystery. I like to approach each lesson with the perspective that my students and I are going on a visual adventure together. I think the ambiance of my room reflects my training by the Getty Center in Discipline-Based Art Education Theory, which requires a balanced curriculum. As I attempt to combine all of these philosophies to fulfill New York State Standards, each day flies by as we have positive, productive and contemplative experiences. In short, it's fun.

Jane Hollingsworth

The excitement and unpredictability of the classroom, especially the middle school classroom, are motivators for me. At this point in my career, classroom management and planning come naturally for me. I am no longer intimidated by the behavior of students. Consequently, I can concentrate on the most invigorating aspects of teaching art. There is always the unique or unexpected work created by the most unlikely students. The ideas generated by my adolescent and pre-adolescent students inspire awe in me. Watching students who are trying to be "cool" and detached become excited about something they have created still moves me. In middle grades, I'm able to teach students from 10 through the ages of 14. The changes and progressions within the individual students are microcosms of life itself: dependency evolves into risk-taking and sometimes rebellion but mainly into a higher level of competence and knowledge.

Lurline Lapolla

The only thing that's kept me in the classroom for 35+ years is the kids—adolescents all! I suppose I'm a perennial big sister. I enjoy the emergence of new quasi-adults. Their awareness, their difficulties, their skills are all evolving. Every minute is a new rapid in the stream. Art is an overhanging branch, something to grab onto, something steadying in the white water. I believe everyone has a talent or skill that's special. All of us have a contribution to make. My main goal is to help students be aware of and practice their special talents. I see myself as a role model. I try to practice what I preach. I am level headed. Other teachers tell me though that I am a "chanteuse," a storyteller.

Mark Phillips

What has kept me in teaching through the ups and downs of all these years boils down to the relationship among the faculty at my school. It is a close faculty. They are friends who have been there a long time. My school is a real part of the community. I teach *kids*—not exclusively *art*. Art is an experience that will brighten lives. My goal is to make art an important part of living.

Judy Williams

The joy of learning, mine and my students, has kept me in the classroom. My commitment and enthusiasm have been sustained through professional contacts and experiences outside my county. One very strong influence has been my association with the Tennessee Department of Education's Art Education Program and its director. I worked for this program a year as a consulting teacher and for over 10 years have worked with the annual Tennessee Arts Academy. The Academy is an intensive staff development experience for teachers in art, music, and drama, and for administrators K-12. I have worked with well-known and respected art educators from across the U. S. and also have met and observed sessions with music and theater educators, writers, and performers who are accomplished in their fields. The other strong influence has been my involvement with NAEA through conventions and publications and with TAEA in leadership roles. The people I have met along the way have made my life and my teaching richer. Art teachers are a sharing group.

My style is low-key. I want to give my students new information and also help them develop their thinking. I want to encourage independent ventures outside the classroom. My goal from the time I began teaching in the regular classroom in Bedford County has been to see art specialists in the elementary schools. (At that time there were no art teachers at any level.) This summer more than 25 years later, the last remaining school without one hired an art teacher.

For much of my professional life I have spent a lot of energy and time on arts advocacy. The wealth of information from NAEA has kept me up to date and given me ammunition for advocacy, formal and informal. I've talked to community clubs, on the radio, newspaper interviews, and put up many exhibits in businesses and schools that "name the learning." My role in the classroom has been to design and teach lessons that would be valuable for all students. While I want to develop visual ways of personal expression, I also want students to make aesthetic choices that will enrich their everyday lives and develop their abilities to see, understand, question and take joy in the arts and the world around them.

Phyllis Bosco
Albert Schweitzer once said, "Example is not the main thing influencing others. It is the only thing." That quote is painted on my classroom door and etched in my intellect and spirit, acknowledging that each of us has a responsibility to be an example to our students. I strive to have my classes humming with meaningful and dynamic activities. When our favorite tree was being cut down outside the classroom door, we drew the men with chain saws, read *The Giving Tree* (Silverstein, 1964) and had the log saved. The log is now becoming a totem to be installed on the grounds. Families and friends are encouraged to visit and assist in my classroom. One dad videotaped his daughter as she was having a plaster cast of her face made after our lesson on the realist sculptor Duane Hanson. I endeavor to influence my students and fellow educators to think creatively. I have a love for this profession which allows me to learn with my students, which is its own reward. I believe continued learning is the essence of vitality, no matter what the age.

But again, it is the students.
In reading these philosophies, these statements of sustenance and conviction, one begins to sense the presence of Pollyanna, Eleanor Porter's (1913) early century fictional character who was disposed to an irrepressible optimism, a tendency to find good in everything—even when it was not there. For all of these teachers, sometimes Pollyanna does enter the scene, especially as they reflect over a long, intense, and fulfilling career. In the acts of remembering and retelling, we unconsciously edit and refine. We see reflections as more radiant and complete. And after all, it is a given that

the 30 teachers in this study are a biased sample. They are the ones who stayed, for better and for worse. They are the survivors who learned to make do and who kept their positive attitude that a better tomorrow would come. The point is, with so many of today's teachers dropping out after only a few years in the classroom, these veteran teachers might help us understand what it is that can keep a teacher on the job, dedicated to a lifetime in instruction.

Throughout their lives as teachers there have been myriad experiences and scores of individuals who have provided sustenance. To revisit Carrol Morgan's words, "I have come a long way but it has not been a lonely journey."

From all that these teachers have said about teaching and philosophy and years spent in the classroom, there are two concepts that unite their thinking and overarch everything else. They are inexorably convinced, in Anita Winfrey's words, that "art develops life and provides balance." They are staunch, opportunistic, and self admittedly, shameless advocates for art education. They are convinced of the interdisciplinary ties, the cognitive, perceptual, emotional, and social skills that study in art can promote. At the same time, their sights are set beyond the subject they teach. For their students, they see the life-long picture. They conceive of themselves as catalysts. Once students are motivated, so much is possible. For their students, they want personal fulfillment, the pursuance of perpetual learning, and the propensity to see a little further, to envision something more.

These teachers take pleasure in people, especially when they are in the state of being kids. They are generous and without jealousy, finding their peak of fulfillment when their students succeed. They are cautious and healthy in skepticism, yet they strive to avoid the dead-end that comes from cynicism. They are honest, sometimes to their own detriment. Time and experience have made them pragmatic and self-critical. Most of all, they are not complacent. They are perpetual learners with a love for creative adventure, always inquiring, always looking for a better way. All of these defining qualities are apparent in the way they talk about their teaching philosophy and in the way they speak about the longevity of their careers. Suzanne Greene and John Skrabalak encapsulate:

> Suzanne: But again, it is the students who keep me going. If you take the time to see them for who they are, not what they look like or how they dress, they will give you back respect and support.

> John: It all comes down to the children. That is why we are here. Close

the door and open their minds and hearts to a new world called *art*. They deserve everything we do for them. They are our future advocates. I am honored to be an art teacher. My path has gone in the right direction. I have gotten so much from teaching and it's unconditional. There aren't many jobs out there where I see people leaving from work smiling. I can honestly say that I leave most of my days with a smile on my face—a smile that shows contentment and love for my craft.

In Chapter 5, teachers describe and critique the changes they have seen and experienced over the past four and five decades.

Chapter 5
"For the times they are a-changin'."

The Times They Are A-Changin', Bob Dylan, 1963
*I really get fed up with people moaning about the good old days and why
can't education be like it was when they were in school. Thank God it's not!*
Barbara Hirokawa, Columbine High School, Littleton, CO

If we are to discover better places in the world of education, it is essential
that we know where we've been, what we've done, when we have flourished or faltered, and most important, why. One of the most productive
lines of education research is inquiry into change and in the case of the
Flower Teachers this is something they know a lot about. The kinds of
changes that take place over decades, these are the shifts and movements in
teaching and learning that I wanted them to talk about. In asking teachers to
contemplate education in the broader context of time and to talk about
change, or the lack of it, I was requiring of them a complex of thinking, for
the study of change is a comparative process, a look across time at the
whole as well as the parts. Inherent in comparisons are contrasts, so I was
asking teachers to search for similarities and highlight differences. I wanted
to know, for example, about more pervasive differences in the profession,
pedagogical approaches and curricular trends and issues. I also wanted their
opinions about changes in the people with whom they work, in particular,
the students and their parents.   More specifically, I asked them to focus on
art education, hallmarks they have seen, reforms that have rooted and taken
hold, reforms that failed.

Corresponding with all of this, I wanted something fundamentally linked
with the ethos of this generation. So, I asked them about changes within
their own teaching, about the progress and contributions they have made
along the way. What I was really trying to get at was how close they were
coming to the white knight dreams they envisioned when they were wearing
bellbottoms, attending pop art exhibits, and thriving on the music of Joan
Baez and the Beatles. In the midst of their deliberations over the coming
and going of their school years, I asked them to sum up, to take the measure
of their successes and failures. In the grand scheme, I wanted them to talk
about the fluidity and the discontinuity—all the things that have deterred
them or moved them forward in their mission over the years.

Let no one mistake these teachers for uncritical optimists. Because they like what they do, through habit, they look for the good. But they see, every working day, the faults, the inadequate, the deficiencies — and they call it when they see it. They are master teachers but they have also attained the credentials of education critics. They know what works and they know the impediments that snag and encumber the work they need to do. In this light, they are qualified to judge and evaluate. In talking about the transformations they have seen and experienced in the world of teaching, the Flower Teachers move back and forth between generalizations and particulars. In doing so, they offer their own analysis and interpretation and, sometimes, inconvenient truths of the way classrooms have or have not changed and the reasons they believe to be behind it all.

Following are their responses to a sequence of four interview questions designed to elicit reflection and disclosure about their perceptions of the variations, the transitions, twists and turns they have seen over time. Differing from the other chapters, every teacher in the project is represented through direct quotation here; paraphrase violated accuracy, specificity, and bypassed voice. From my position, it is essential that each teacher's perspectives be presented as they were offered. It is then, a long chapter. As is true throughout the interview, teachers' responses varied in length from individual to individual and from question to question. Some are sparing, "just the facts." In a few instances, teachers did not respond to specific items, so those categories are omitted for them. Others offered extended descriptions interspersed with examples and anecdotes; many of these had to be abbreviated. Typical too of responses to open-ended questions, teachers tended to intermix their ideas on various aspects of change, blending categories and spilling thoughts from one interview item to another. This intermixing, of course, made it difficult to organize responses for the reader. For the sake of organization, and to be as clear and accurate as possible, I have created seven broad categories into which I have grouped each teacher's thoughts: *Teaching* (changes in teaching and education); *Students/Parents* (changes in students and their parents); *Hindrance* (obstacles to teaching effectiveness); *Help* (facilitators to teaching effectiveness); *Personal* (contributions and individual change); and *Stories of Failure* and *Stories of Success*.

In their own words . . .
Carrol Morgan: *As a profession, teaching has primarily changed from an instructionally focused task to more complex therapeutic and social engineering tasks.*

Teaching: Since I started working in public schools, new philosophies, management styles, socio-cultural influences, and new technology have changed teaching. The changes have included expanding administrative management, restructuring schools, team teaching, block scheduling, evolving modes of instruction, increased guidance and counseling staff, increased focus on special needs education, and the incorporation of computer technology, all of which have profoundly affected teaching.

Block scheduling and team teaching have rotated in and out of favor. I'm convinced that block scheduling is implemented to maximize classroom use and teaching positions. (For every five teachers on a block schedule teaching three classes each day, either alternating days or by semester, an additional position is gained without hiring a teacher, because teachers who were teaching five classes are teaching six during a school year.) Team teaching has two connotations. During the 1970s it meant two or more teachers cooperating to teach one class/subject. Now, it means a group of three to five teachers teaching different subjects to one group/team of students. It is now part of the middle school concept.

I believe that the "open classroom" concept came into vogue during the 1970s due to budget constraints. It was cheaper to build schools with fewer walls. Now, most of those buildings have been renovated into closed classroom spaces—the noise and confusion of open classrooms was unbearable. The open "resource areas" of the 1970s and 80s were very practical spaces for large group activities, but sadly, most of those spaces have been divided into classrooms for growing enrollments and additional special education classes. The trend in elementary and middle school buildings of the 1990s is a pod or separate wing for each grade level or team. In this era of concern for safety, the separation of students by age seems to be a "divide and conquer" approach, in spite of the claim that it makes students feel more secure belonging to a smaller group. Students and teachers are isolated by grade level or team; and the mini-schools or schools-within-a-school have destroyed the old concept of school spirit— the students' school community shrinks into mini-groups, and students are separated from neighborhood friends and often alienated from the members of other teams or grade levels.

I started teaching under an earlier form of management hierarchy when decision-making was from top down, especially from principal to teacher. Administration meant a superintendent, director of instruction, principal, and vice-principal, and it included one secretary for each position. I personally knew each person. Today I can't even name all of the adminis-trative positions in my school system, and communication between teachers and upper level administrators is practically nonexistent. I have always been the only art teacher in my middle school (and County-wide Art Department Chairperson since 1973), so I have been able to make my own curriculum and instructional decisions. However, most teachers are no longer that fortunate. School administration and instructional management have developed into layers and clusters of decision-makers, including supervisory personnel, guidance counselors, department chairpersons, grade level chairpersons, team leaders, committees, ad hoc groups, and the PTA. Thanks to the Demming quality control philosophy of the 1990s!

National and international changes in industrial and commercial management styles have carried over into education—the quality control and focus team approaches. The original intent of the new philosophies was to increase productivity in organizations where output can be precisely measured and controlled. I question the application and effectiveness of the newer philosophies in education where precise outputs and control groups are debatable. The intent is admirable, but the means are questionable. Please! Save me from another "School Renewal" committee with its endless problem solving sessions that lead to decisions that no teachers have been given the authority to implement.

As a profession, teaching has primarily changed from an instructionally focused task to more complex therapeutic and social engineering tasks. An increasing concern for meeting the educational needs of a more diverse student population has changed the direction and philosophy of teaching practices. Equal opportunity and civil rights court decisions have had a tremendous influence on education. In the 1970s, achieving racial integration became a primary goal and teachers had to focus more attention on social issues: conflict and classroom management, changing standards and increasing retention, increasing awareness of Black History and various cultural differences. Those issues continue to be addressed and have been joined by an increasing amount of attention devoted to other areas: multicultural education, alternative life-style choices, sex education, drug use awareness and prevention, child abuse and violence, and community involvement in education. The middle school trend to implement the "teacher-advisor" concept is a part of the move towards putting teachers in the role of parents. In my role as an educator, I am expected to be all things to all students, but I must walk an increasingly fine line between the roles of parent and teacher in order to avoid policy conflicts and infringing on the rights of my students.

In art education itself, I have seen the following changes, which I have listed, from my perspective, in their order of importance: the nationwide movement in the 1970s towards art education specialists in public schools; Lowenfeld's theories of creativity and expression in child art; availability of art education textbooks and resource materials; the strong advocacy by the NAEA for public school art education; emphasis placed on the humanities during the 1980s, after the earlier post-Sputnik focus on science and math; *Virginia State Standards of Learning in Art* published in 1988; school integration and the movement in art education towards multicultural curricula; introduction and diffusion of DBAE theory and practice as a cohesive approach to art education; increased funding and facilities (sporadic and disparate) for art education.

The rapid advance of computer technology into education has changed *how* teachers do their everyday tasks. Most paperwork has been transferred to computer generated documents. Teachers have to meet minimal levels of computer literacy and learn to incorporate computer technology into all subject areas. In order to be competent teachers, we must be able to select and use an ever-expanding array of devices: computers, printers, scanners, digital cameras, and whatever comes next. Teachers must be able to select appropriate software programs for personal use and for student instruction. E-mail communications and Internet access are now being introduced into every classroom and we need to know how to use them effectively, efficiently, and safely. Teachers must keep up or they will be left behind in the race to prove themselves technologically qualified to teach in today's classrooms. I see a continuous need for additional pre-service and in-service training for teachers.

In looking back, I have learned how good and how bad a school or system can be. In retrospect, I think something went seriously wrong in about 1989, when it became a trend for administrators to establish a Mission Statement in education. I think that was the beginning of the meaningless, politically/socially correct statements that generalized platitudes until they became warm, fuzzy drivel—a mission statement became a vision with no focus. Statements promised educational nirvana, while administrators went rushing out with their warm fuzzies to make their students and teachers feel good—pseudo social events to improve morale, food-candy-trinket awards to even the poorest achievers, and trumped up claims of success. Being a generally cooperative person, I went along with each new trend, but I think I have been misled.

This year a former art teacher became a new principal at a prestigious new high school in an adjoining county. I hope that he starts a trend, because I truly believe that art teachers have a better global understanding of students and schools. (Do I suffer from delusions of grandeur that may come from staying in teaching too long? Am I delusional to believe that art teachers could make better decisions, spend money more wisely, plan better buildings, and have more concern for meeting students' needs?) Those experienced art teachers who choose to enter administration will bring a new and better perspective to educational problem solving, and that is one new trend in school administration that I can advocate.

Students/Parents: Increasingly, only high tech, intensely stimulating or inter-active media engages students. Today, many students know more about current technology than ever before and many are more computer literate than their teachers. Most students want to keep a music device plugged into their ears, and more students are willing to break rules in order to satisfy their wants. More students demand and expect individual attention, immediately and for longer periods of time. More students are likely to have expensive material possessions and clothes that are fads, which appeal to a need for acceptance and popularity. More students are obese, refuse to engage in physical activity, and have poor eating habits—canned sodas and sweet cakes for lunch! Fewer students model the qualities of civility, democratic principles, and tolerance. More students know and use anti-social manipulation skills on a regular basis to deliberately establish an atmosphere of anarchy and gang mentality in the classroom; this, I believe, reflects changes in entertainment, families, schools, communities, and the nation's culture in general. For 30 years, I have taught some disruptive and uncooperative students, and they were individuals with problems, but the growing gang mentality in my community threatens to take control of classrooms, halls, and schools.

As far back as I can remember (1950s), some students have cut initials in their arms and written into their skin with pens, but the frequency, extent and intensity among today's students has increased to alarming rates. I think it represents students' increased emotional, rather than rational response to their feelings of isolation and stress. They decorate or mutilate their bodies with symbols to represent who they are and what they feel. I think that the growing social acceptability of tattooing and body piercing has contributed to the trend. An increasing number of my students are being diagnosed as clinically depressed and/or emotionally disturbed. Their bizarre behaviors are extremely upsetting and have frightening effects on my other students and me. I recently had a "depressed" seventh grade student who deliberately cut his arm with an exacto-knife and told a classmate to "Watch me bleed." (He was sent to the student assistant counselor.) A seventh grade girl pierced her tongue at home, collected her blood in a jar, and brought it to school to drink at lunch. (She was given three days on out-of-school suspension.)

When I first started teaching, the majority of my students came from two-parent homes, and many of their mothers were stay-at-home moms. Now the majority of my students have experienced at least one divorce in their

families and most of them are "latch-key" kids. They wear house keys
around their necks and many live in different houses on the week-end.
They are often dealing with neglect, abuse, alcohol, or drugs. When or if
these problems existed 30 years ago, students were more likely to hide them
from teachers and the few available guidance counselors.

How do I compare students? Are they getting worse? I hear those questions all the time. I am not really sure about the answer, in spite of the
preceding paragraphs. Since I started teaching, the sad fact is that over the
years I have taught many students who have become criminals and destroyed lives figuratively and literally. Some of them have managed to
straighten out their lives and become successful adults. I read the criminal
indictments in the newspaper and recognize the names all too frequently.
Twenty-eight years ago I taught a seventh grader who killed his twelve-year
old cousin with a shotgun. He was back in school three weeks later. Last
year, a former sixth grader whom I taught seven years ago, shot and killed a
man in a drug-deal-gone-bad. He will be tried as an adult for first degree
murder. In my heart, I knew that those students were potentially dangerous
when I taught them—they had no sense of right or wrong. In contrast,
twenty-five years ago, I taught two girls who ransacked a new home and did
thousands of dollars of damage. Their parents were better off and made
restitution. This year I taught two boys who ransacked a home and did
thousands in damage. They were sent to a detention center. One boy was
detained and the other was sent back to school, and my class. Two decades
ago, I never suspected those girls were capable of criminal behavior because
their personal problems were so well hidden; but this year, I strongly
suspected that those boys were headed for trouble—their art spoke volumes.

Art teachers have a special window into the minds of students; their artwork
and behavior in the open atmosphere of an art room can show us more than
we want to know about their lives and emotions. During my earliest years
of teaching elementary art, I concentrated on art that was decorative or
illustrative, and based on formal design principles. My students' art was
what I would call benign, but that has changed. Twenty-five years ago, I
began to include lessons that elicited more personal expression and symbol-
ism. Students' art began to reflect their parents' and the country's concerns
about Vietnam, racial equality, and the environment. Flowers and the
circular peace symbols emerged and then flooded students' artwork. That
era was followed in the 80s by artwork that sometimes displayed graphic
depictions of violence, war, crime, and sexuality. Only the most disturbed
students had created such images in the 1970s. During the 1990s, the
artwork of students has become more violent, more emotional, and more
sexually explicit. Now I frequently see images of gun violence, robbing,

stabbing, decapitation, blood, feces, huge partially exposed breasts, male genitalia, and symbols of hate groups. Almost exclusively, these images appear in the art of males. Media exposure and violent or abusive lives have produced a new generation of youth whose artwork is reflecting the world as they see it. Flowers and peace symbols, along with more positive images, continue to appear in the artwork. Young girls still draw pictures of horses, friendship and love. But frequently those traditional symbols of love and peace are not singular or decorative images. I am more likely to see such symbols juxtaposed to vivid depictions of war, hate, crime, lust, and violence. I can't fix their broken or unhappy lives, but I do the best I can to help them through art.

I am dealing with a whole new generation of parents today. Many of them don't seem connected to their children at all, while some are so involved in managing their child's every moment that it is difficult to determine the line between the parent's ego and the child's life. I'm sure that both kinds of parents have always existed, but I seem to notice the extremes more frequently today.

I started out this discussion with the deliberate intent of listing positive changes in students over the past 30 years, but by exempting individually outstanding students not covered by these generalities, I have developed a list of negative changes. So, as I reflect on the above writings, I am forced to ask myself, "Why do I stay in teaching if this is the way I view my students?" Well, hope springs eternal, and next year will be better.

Hindrance: In 1973, I taught the one elementary self-contained class for the special needs students, and I had only one seventh grade student who was identified as hyperactive. He was allowed to drink coffee during class and walk about the room at will. In 1998, I taught 70 inclusion students from special education classes, and 26 students identified as ADDHD. On average my art classes are 24% special education inclusion students. I have to read, sign, and follow each student's Individual Education Plan (IEP). At 7:30 A. M., the school nurse begins administering hyperactivity medications to a line of students and continues throughout the day—dispensing Ritalin is one of her main functions.

The fear of litigation is overwhelming the administrators and the teachers. In the upcoming year of 1999-2000 I will have to sign *every* student's agenda everyday in every class to insure that each student has copied the lesson objective, and homework assignments, and any upcoming tests within three days. I don't believe educators have been successfully dealing with these special education problems, and the additional amount of required paperwork is staggering: IEP's and countless forms to document behaviors; parent and teacher communications; interim progress reports and individualized copies of lesson plans, etc. An increasing amount of my time is spent on required in-service training for inclusion of special needs students. In addition, there are required in-service classes to address multicultural education.

I believe that teachers are being stretched to their limits, more than ever, to the detriment of their instructional focus on subject content, planning, and research. Increased teacher accountability looms on the horizon as higher expectations and raised standards of learning are being implemented. Since 1995, I have seen greater emphasis on curriculum planning, alignment of curriculum with state and national standards, learning objectives, and standardized testing. [Teachers are being forced to teach to the test.]

The causes of our educational dilemmas are multifaceted and often beyond our control as teachers. I can think of parenting, cultural values, poverty, and the justice system. Commentators from every niche of society—the media, psychologists, educators, and politicians—provide their own opinions of the causes or cures for the problems in education. Peddlers of new educational fads and theories get the political establishment on their bandwagon, and before long, a new trend is rolling along and additional funds are needed. The cycle repeats itself. The cures for our dilemmas, if possible at all, are somewhere in the future.

Frustrated teachers hop from school to school looking for better conditions and they leave the profession at alarming rates. There is an increasing shortage of teachers and a dwindling number of qualified young people entering the profession. At the current rate of increasing pre-service and in-service requirements, an educator in the year 2010 will need two Masters Degrees and a Doctorate in order to be qualified to teach—not to mention millions of dollars worth of liability insurance. I love my profession, but if I had to start over in today's world, I don't believe I would deliberately choose education.

Help: It takes a bit of reflection to identify the greatest facilitators, because the less evident underlying ones may be the most important. When I try to strip away all the non-essentials, what is left? What have I done without, and what could I have done without? I think my teaching was effective long before now, in very poor facilities and with a lot less of everything. But I also know that I have become more effective as I got more of everything. I am going to try to list the facilitators in order of priority.

1) I have come to the conclusion that I am responsible for effective teaching, and a positive attitude is the greatest facilitator. I can do, I will do, and I will make do. Risks are worth taking. Every student has some good qualities and the potential to succeed in some area.

2) A great facilitator is my belief that my subject is important and will benefit my students.

3) My commitment to planning (curriculum, unit plans, daily lesson plans, long-range and short-range plans) has made my teaching more effective.

4) I am a better teacher because some administrators, co-workers, students, and parents have supported my program and me, and they have thanked me for my efforts. My positive attitude is supported by the knowledge of their appreciation for what I do.

5) My breadth and depth of experience, knowledge, skills, and methods help me to motivate my students to learn about art, enjoy their art experiences, and develop positive attributes.

6) I am supported by my expectations of success, willingness to improvise and try innovative ideas, my ability to adjust to new circumstances, and my expectation that tomorrow will be better.

7) I have been lucky and have worked hard to deserve the support of administrators who control the purse strings for my art program.

8) My middle school room has been a great facilitator to effective teaching. It has all the necessities and many luxuries.

9) My teaching has been improved by NAEA publications and conferences; two Getty Institutes; the sharing of ideas with other teachers; and the use of materials produced by the Virginia Department of Education under the Art Supervisor of the 1970s.

Personal: Oh yes! I see myself differently now. I am the "old guard." I was "the new kid." I am the "keeper of archives." I was "without a clue" and didn't have a file cabinet to keep one in. I used to say, "What are we going to do?" Too often now I hear myself say, "We used to ..." or "We already tried . . . ." It is so difficult not to say, "We are reinventing the wheel here." Then there are those days when somebody says, " Go see Mrs. Morgan. She will remember how we did that." Somewhere along the way I became the accepted guru of curriculum, policy, and school history. I don't know if that is a compliment or an invisible hand pointing toward the retirement sign. I never thought I would stay in teaching until I was one of the last teachers who remembered working for our first middle school principal. There are only five of us left. I do remember looking at some gray-haired teachers with bad attitudes and thinking that it was time for them to retire. Now I realize that a bad attitude can develop at any age, and some "mature" teachers have excellent attitudes and make their best contributions to education in their later years.

Over the past 30 years, my approach to teaching has changed, been revised, returned to tried and true methods, and remained open to new strategies. In other words, I use any method that works. Among others, I have used the following approaches: "winging it," letting students make choices in their own directions, using learning centers and individualized learning packets, lecturing, debating, modeling procedures, and using the Madeline Hunter method. I have used student self-evaluation, student contracts, portfolio assessment, independent study, guided discovery, computer assisted learning, and teacher-directed instruction. I have learned to individualize instruction, to adapt and adjust for diverse abilities, and to use student agenda books for recording assignments, stating objectives and communicating with parents. I anticipate success, but I can change directions when an approach isn't working. I have learned that some approaches work most of the time, some work some of the time, but none work all of the time. Individual students and even whole classes can be so vastly different that I have to be ready to change what I am doing and how I am doing it at any time. Experience has provided me with so many choices to use that it is surprising when a workshop or seminar presents a novel method of teaching. As for the latest trend in cooperative learning—three days of required in-service training and many failed attempts to successfully apply it in the classroom have convinced me that it is not a magic formula. The traditional art education methods that use multi-sensory experiences and hands-on activities are almost guaranteed to work and I have relied on them for over thirty years to teach art concepts and skills.

Some areas of my general educational philosophy have swung like a pendulum or come full circle. My basic art teaching philosophy has not changed very much, but it has broadened and matured. Is homogeneous grouping better than heterogeneous grouping? I'm still not sure—both have merit depending on the circumstances. Mainstreaming and inclusion of special education students—I have come full circle here and believe again that it is detrimental to the education of the general student population when inclusion infringes on *their* right to learn. I now believe that the "least restrictive environment" has to include equal concern for all students. Should students be failed or retained? I can remember sitting in end-of-the-year retention meetings and voting to retain failing students. I now believe that students fail to learn, but they should not "be failed." I believe in the new concept of alternative education, but there has to be a better alternative than the limited program I see in my school system. I actually had a seventh grade "alternative education" student assigned to my advanced eighth grade art class because that was the only choice that fit her sched-ule—a seventh grader who couldn't do sixth grade work was in an advanced eighth grade art class!

I believe that I have built a middle school art program that I can be proud of. It has gained the respect of administrators, students, parents, and the community. It is a legacy that I hope will continue with the art teachers who follow me. Art class is viewed as more than a frill at King George Elementary School.

I believe that my Art Mentorship Program has been a significant contribu-tion to the idea that mentors *do* make a difference in the lives of children. In 1987, it was a novel idea that has now become routine in many school systems. The students benefited and the adult artists benefited from their experiences together, and there have been long lasting rewards for both. To see a twelve-year old discussing the fine points of art production and evaluation with an adult artist, in an atmosphere of mutual respect and interest, is an incredibly satisfying experience for this teacher. I am afraid that the program will not continue into the future because it requires commitment and a great amount of after-school time, which I don't see coming with many new teachers.

I believe my students are the most important contribution that I have made. Each one who has passed through my classroom and achieved even a small success is better for their art education experiences. Some of my students are or will become artists who will make a difference with their creativity and commitment to the visual arts. I have taught my students that art is more than pretty pictures. They can interpret art meanings, discuss aesthet-ics knowledgeably, create and evaluate art forms, and apply many art skills to creatively solve problems. They know that art is all around them and that it does make a difference in the quality of their lives. I believe that I have given them what I so desperately lacked in my own early education in the visual arts.

Stories of Failure: I've become a pragmatist—I won't be able to reach every child. As early as my first years of teaching, I had students who just seemed headed in the wrong direction—their lack of respect, their perverse behavior. Well, some of them are in jail, some are now deceased. I try and try again to make connections with dysfunctional children, but with some, I eventually accept that they will make bad choices, and I am not the solution to their problems.

I have seen the art of severely abused children—it's frightening. I have referred students to guidance counselors and school psychologists. A few good school counselors have made a difference. Why is it that the art teacher is often the only one who sees that a child is severely troubled or learning impaired? I believe that art can produce a self-portrait that is often beyond the conscious effort to conceal reality.

Finally, I always feel like a failure when I see art students throw their portfolios, artwork, or note folders in the trash or just leave them behind on a table at the end of the term. It saddens me that they have no attachment to their work.

Stories of Success: My success stories are the stories of my personal success and survival as an art teacher and the stories of my students who became better people because of their art experiences. They became more percep- tive, more creative, skilled, and more able to communicate visually and to appreciate art in its many, varied forms. I have taught thousands of students and many of them could be the subjects of success stories. Their art education has and will make a difference in their world. Two groups of students stand out, and they are the gifted/talented in art and the highly interested who are self-motivated. Since my second year as a middle school art teacher, I have fought for and established different methods of reaching these special students.

Carolyn Skeen: *School security is a big issue now. My little elementary school has locked outer entrances, lockdown drills, security cameras, and a gate in the office that can only be activated from a specific point. We have a school emergency plan that has the art room listed as the morgue (because I have large tables). Have we gone too far? Are we approaching paranoia?*

Teaching: The word "restricted" comes to mind when I think about how teaching has changed. At every turn there are more laws, more forms, more regulations, more restraints. The positive side of these restrictions is that teachers are expected to follow standards and show results. We are now held accountable for student learning. When I began teaching (in another system), my art program was whatever I wanted it to be. I'm not sure that that district had an art curriculum until after 1968. If we did, I never saw it. The only standards that art teachers in my old district had to live up to were our own. If I skipped an important aspect of art, nobody knew or cared. The teacher that I replaced had taught all of the seventh graders to knit. She had been a home economics major. The students loved knitting and had spent a good bit of the previous school year on their projects. They couldn't understand why I wasn't interested in letting them continue to knit in the eighth grade too. I lost the opportunity to invite my grandmother to come to school as a Visiting Artist. Seriously, I think fibers are an important part of an art program, but I just could not justify more knitting (and I only had to justify it to myself).

In the 60s teachers had no M-Teams, IEP's, inclusion notebooks, or due process hearings to deal with. Sadly there were few modifications for students with disabilities either. Now we are buried in a mountain of paperwork for these children. However, special students are finally being helped. That's the thing about most of these restrictions and regulations, they were at least created to solve problems.

School security is a big issue now. My little elementary school has locked outer entrances, lockdown drills, security cameras, and a gate in the office that can only be activated from a specific point within the school. We have a school emergency plan that has the art room listed as the morgue (because I have large tables). I have taught students who were so in danger of being kidnapped by a non-custodial parent, that we were requested to lock our room doors whenever those children were with us. Have we gone too far? Are we approaching paranoia? I would have said yes, but I confess that after recent school shootings and terrorist attacks, I no longer know. When school began in August this year one principal handed out the agenda for the first staff meeting. Teachers laughed at some of the items on the list. Those who had been teaching for years noted that the times had certainly changed.

> Samples:
> Your inclusion notebook must be current and in plain sight.
> Harassment—child must fear for safety—remember we have a form.
> E-mail is not private.
> Parent volunteers who work with children should be in your sight.
> To charge a student for possession of an illegal item we must show that the student had knowledge of possession.
> Document all death threats.

Teachers are expected to include drug awareness, ethics, values, good manners, personal safety, conflict resolution, gender equity, etc. in with the regular curriculum. Teacher certification and evaluation have become more rigorous and we now have National Boards. Teachers now have a much greater role in deciding how schools are run. Parents have too. Parents expect more of schools, but at the same time there is a curious abrogation of parent responsibility. Raising the child also becomes the job of the school, coaches, scout leaders, after-school programs, and the television set. The South Park kids become role models by default.

We now have National Standards for the arts and increasingly these standards drive a formal curriculum. Professional organizations are strong and teacher pay is better. In general, there is more (but not nearly enough) money for student instruction, much in the form of grants. Public schools now have growing competition from religious schools, charter schools, and home schooling.

Factors? I think a lot of the positive changes in teaching have been brought about because we have strong professional organizations. In some circles it is popular to bash the NEA (National Education Association), but I started teaching when NEA was relatively weak and I know that many changes benefiting public schools would never have occurred without lobbying efforts by a stronger NEA. Another factor that has lead to positive changes is that colleges have better teacher preparation programs. New teachers are more aware of issues, possible pitfalls, and resources now. Further, I believe that the Women's Movement has had an impact in making female teachers able to stand up for themselves and in promoting gender equity in the classroom.

There are also some negative factors working here. Some changes have taken place because self-serving politicians and other public figures have made education into a "whipping boy." It's so much easier to blame the schools for failing to solve many of the country's problems than to actually do something to eliminate the problems at their roots. It's such a frequently used old political strategy. Fix blame and then you don't have to deal with the problem. Making public education into a scapegoat for social ills has left many Americans with negative and suspicious attitudes towards schools.

Specific to art education, the following have impacted my own classroom: the *Americans with Disabilities Act*, and therefore inclusion; site-based management; cooperative learning; multiple intelligence theory and other research into how the brain works; multiculturalism; National Standards and Boards; early intervention strategies; integrated learning; and technology in the art room.

DBAE has to have had the most significant impact on art education. It really has revolutionized the way we teach art and the way college programs prepare their students to teach. DBAE has forced teachers to re-evaluate their programs in terms of content and emphasis. DBAE has also probably had the most impact on my students, even though they may not realize how much it influences what they are learning.

Students/Parents: I don't think today's children place much trust in the world. Two weeks after the events of September 11 my students are still tense and jumpy. A garbage truck backed up to the school Thursday. It beeped as it backed and there was a loud crash as it emptied the dumpster. Several of my second grade students looked panic stricken. They were utterly still. One actually turned pale. "What's that?" he whispered more to himself than to classmates. You could hear his whisper across the room. There was a self-conscious chuckling and a feeling of relief in the room when I explained the noise. It will take a while for all of us to get over the tragedy of New York City. There are still scars, even for children far away from the sites of the terrorist attacks.

Students are less afraid to speak up now. Some would say that they are less respectful. I know that they are not as polite. I really miss good manners. I think students today are not as afraid of expressing their thoughts though, and that's good. Students are much more cynical, even at the elementary level. They are pessimistic, more suspicious of adults, and more sophisticated. Students today are more stressed and more street-smart. They know more, have more information. They have more material goods.

Children may be more afraid of change. This is a surprise. Children seem to adapt so well to technology. While they are not in the least intimidated (in fact, they are thrilled) by buttons and switches, in general, the world is a scary place for them. Students have little trust in the world and not much faith in anything. The illusion of safety that students had in the early years is gone now. Children do adapt to a frightening, fast-paced, rather regimented environment, but the cost is the loss of freedom and childhood.

Parents love their children every bit as much. They are busier and more stressed. They work longer hours and spend less time at home. They spend much more time hauling the children to endless rounds of after-school activities. Parents are, in general, more vocal about what schools should be doing for students. Parent conferences are more frequent. In spite of killer schedules, some parents are still volunteering to help at school. I see more parents on drugs.

Hindrance: With the exception of one school year, the need for money to support the art program has always been a major obstacle. You can't have a great art program without money for supplies. I've had six principals in my career. Three of them did not understand that art is vital for young children.

Art teachers talk about money a lot. We exchange information about budgets, fund raising, how to get free or inexpensive instructional supplies at every conference and workshop. "How much money do you have per student?" is a frequently asked question. So many art teachers do not have enough. As state budgets across the U.S. get tighter and funds for education dry up, art teachers (especially at the elementary level) lose their jobs. Teachers who remain are often asked to spread themselves too thin. The thinking is that a diluted art program is better than none at all. At a recent NAEA conference, I talked with a teacher whose entire program for the year exists on 25 cents per pupil. Legislators and administrators are tempted to agree on funding cuts for the arts because in many cases they simply have little exposure to the arts themselves. We do not miss what we have never experienced.

Help: The greatest help came from three principals who *did* understand that the visual arts are vital for children. And there have been the activities of the TAEA (Tennessee Art Education Association) and the NAEA (National Art Education Association) conventions, which have been like "revivals" for art teachers. NAEA publications have been lifelines. Likewise I have been helped by the Oak Ridge art teachers (real friends—we whine, swap ideas, gripe, try new products, and cheer each other on). Arrowmont School of the Arts and Crafts has provided renewal. The Tennessee Arts Academy has been there for teachers until its funding was cut this year. Elliot W. Eisner's thoughtful and thought-provoking writings have facilitated me in my profession. The Getty website has offered a great deal too.

Personal: I see myself as a professional now, as an expert in what I do, a specialist. This expertise was hard won and has taken many years to accumulate. I don't think I had much of a teaching philosophy, etc. when I started. The fact that I was so unprepared for teaching art after college was not the fault of my art and art education professors. The state simply did not have many requirements for certification in art. At the beginning of my career, I just muddled through and learned by making mistakes. Art ed. interns are much better prepared now. They have to be. New teachers today have to be good right from the first day that they stand in front of a class. They are not given the luxury of time to make many errors.

My major contribution is enriching the lives of my students through art. I have taught several students who later became art teachers themselves. I know that's a contribution to teaching.

Stories of Failure: Thirty years ago I had a child in an 8th grade class who I tried very hard to reach but just couldn't. The failure still stings. He was highly intelligent but was an average art student. I never thought that he was particularly motivated. He just seemed to endure art class, never a spark of enthusiasm. I would like to be able to confirm my suspicion that his parents told him that art was a waste of his valuable time. But I don't know this as fact. I was told not to cross the parents under any circumstances and not to call them. Apparently, they had a history of giving teachers and administrators a hard time. The real trouble started with a stitchery (done on burlap stretched over a wood frame). The assignment was to use the entire burlap surface for the design and to use at least three kinds of stitches. Students could (and did) take the stitcheries home to work on them. Steven did a very small (about 3-4 inches long) flying bird and nothing else on the large piece. I complimented him on the neatness of the one stitch he had used, his choice of colors, and gave him a "C." The next day I received a note from his parents saying that in the future, Steven was to use my class as a study period because that would be more valuable to him in his career as an engineer or scientist. After a week of watching him struggle to keep his math homework out of the paint in an overcrowded art room, I sent him out into the hall to work at a regular student desk. This enraged Steven's parents. I got another note saying that I was treating him unfairly. I wrote them a long letter (against the advice of my principal) explaining my decision to put him in the hall and asking them to consider letting their son resume art class. As I type this, I see how the situation should have been handled and how similar this incident was to incidents that frequently happen now to other teachers at the middle school level. This was about poor communication between parents and teacher, about the administrator who put expediency over the welfare of a child, and probably about the need for assessment techniques that can clearly show students and their parents what class assignment expectations are and how the student is dealing with those expectations.

I have experienced failure in another way too. Many of my elementary students go on to take art at the secondary level. However, with only a few shining exceptions, my *best* students never make it to high school art. My brightest, most skilled, most wonderfully original children never take art again beyond the minimum required in middle school (two nine-week sessions). They get lost in the requirements for "success" at the middle school level. If they take band, chorus, strings, advanced math, foreign language, etc., they can never have elective art. The middle school art teacher tells me that her best students don't generally take much art in high school beyond the state-mandated single course. We are losing our best students at every level beyond elementary. Each year the art teachers in my system meet and whine about this problem, but we never actually come up with a plan. It's time we did.

Stories of Success: Recently, I've had some wonderful teaching experiences using an integrated approach with the music and physical education teachers

at my elementary school. We did a project called "People in Motion."
Students created paintings which showed several of the various movements
in a favorite sport or physical activity. Individually, they composed short
pieces of music which reminded them of their painting. Using a "layering'
technique, they then made longer class musical compositions. Music was
performed and recorded. Each child then choreographed two dance
sequences ("shapes and actions") based on their own painting. The movement sequences were created and performed to the class musical composition. It was easy to spot the children's paintings in their dance routines. We
all got raves from school administrators. But most important, the students
loved the whole project and each segment gave them opportunities to create.

One of the teachers where I once taught, was about as "left-brained" as
people get. He was very analytical and detail-oriented. He had no clue
about what art is or why anyone would want to do it, or even look at it for
more than a few seconds. I get the impression that art genuinely puzzled
him. He once asked his class to write about the thing they like most about
school. He told me that more than half of the class wrote that they liked art
best. He was amazed. He showed me the papers. I suspect that there is
now a slim file labeled "art" in the perfect filing cabinet that is his mind.

Lloyd Sensat: *I've never worked harder than I am working now because of
the excessive demands and expectations put on the school system.*

Teaching: Things were better when we were Flower Teachers. I've never
worked harder than I am working now because of the excessive demands
and expectations put on the school system. When I first started teaching
they actually "let" you teach. Now there are so many demands on teachers'
time. Society expects teachers to succeed with *everyone*. There is a great
deal of talk about accountability, including testing and its implications.
There is a great deal that is not about teaching. My planning period is not
used for preparing for my art classes; instead it is taken up with administrative paperwork and often, workshops. Now schools are run more like a
business. Schools are like a factory: Teachers are workers and the learning
outcomes of their students are products. This industrial conception denies
the complexity of what real education is about. We need to help those in
"management" understand this fundamental flaw.

In my last years of teaching, I did not expect to be teaching with hired
policemen in the school nor with new accounts of students murdering one
another in the schools of America. Columbine High School could have
been a description of the high school in which I have been teaching.

Students/Parents: I have noticed tremendous changes in the students I have taught over the past three decades. Motivation, work ethics, task commitment have all declined. There is a worrisome need for instant gratification. We are almost afraid to teach, in that, we are scared to tell the students to sit down, listen, think, and learn. We are afraid to ask them to master the basics. "Works" of art take *work*. Creativity is not painless. Many students today fail to see—don't want to see—what really goes into a finished project. There is a lack of commitment. Students don't want to work at home; if they can't finish it in class, they won't bring it home. For many, there is no sense of passion. In art, you must have passion! They wander in and out without a sense of direction. It's ultimately kind of sad.

Hindrance: What I would call "basic" art education is still nonexistent. Art is still considered as a "nicety" versus a necessity. Moreover, administrators who react to life like robots are among the major stumbling blocks to education today. So often there seems to be no leadership and those in control seem oblivious to the pain.

Help: Help has come from a team of teachers that became friends, a support system. When I first started teaching, I joined the Louisiana Art Education Association, serving intermittently as district chair, executive council member and president of the organization. I created the group's first newsletter and led the movement to consolidate with the National Art Education Association. Belonging to and more important, being active in both groups have been facilitators to my teaching. Collaboration with colleagues statewide and nationally certainly helped me grow and develop as a teacher. There have also been some supportive administrators. Working in a rich, talented art program and in the St. Charles Parish has been enriching.

Personal: I have worked on every level in the public schools, elementary through high school and have enjoyed many honors for my teaching and service. As the report *Toward Civilization* asserts, I believe that art is at the very core of what we are and what we should know about life. I have always considered myself both an artist and a teacher and I believe in Kennedy's words: "I look forward to an America that admires beauty." I believe that art is a fundamental catalyst in the critical thinking process. Throughout my career, these are the concepts and values that I worked to promote in my teaching.

Stories of Failure: The failure...this is the hardest and most painful of all the questions. The failure has come in trying to deal with administrators

whose goal it is to turn a wonderful school into a technological concentra-
tion camp and the faculty and staff into machines. I mourned the loss of
humanity, creativity, and originality for both teachers and students in a
setting like this.

Stories of Success: My most important awards and success stories have been
my students. It never occurred to me that I had a student who could not
achieve or succeed. I have always had great expectations for them and they
never let me down. In fact, many of my former students have gone on to
advanced studies in the various fields of art. Toward the end of my teaching
career, I am teaching students whose parents had been in my class and they
all remember the "Sensat influence."

Barbara Hirokawa: *The biggest thing by far that has happened to art
education is DBAE. Essentially, this curriculum approach validated a lot of
things I had already begun to realize.*

Teaching: I really get fed up with people moaning about the good old days
and why can't education be like it was when they were in school. Thank
God it's not! I agree with those who say we do not need to memorize
everything like we did when I was in school. There's just too much
information out there for anyone to know it all, and what is important is that
they care to find it and know where to look. I see our role as visual arts
educators as one of teaching visual literacy so that the kids have the
knowledge and awareness to interpret their very visual world. We are of
course educating the artists of the future, but mostly we are educating those
who will be consumers of art. My school is very lucky that we have the
foresight and the ability to become very up to date in technology resources
and our kids use that technology in all of their classes.

The biggest thing by far that has happened to art education is DBAE.
Essentially, this curriculum approach validated a lot of things I had already
begun to realize. It revolutionized our discipline beyond all imagination
and eventually led logically to the standards based movement as it pertains
to art education. We suddenly (or eventually) were recognized as "real"
teachers of a "real" subject, something which we knew all along!

The paradigm shift to the philosophy of standards based education, the idea
that all students will have the opportunity to learn, has consequently made a
significant difference. I agree with this concept in that it replaces the "I
taught it, too bad they didn't learn it" attitude we used to work under. When
our state was looking at legislating standards in six core subjects, and I was
involved in extending that legislation to include art, that lead the way to art

being treated equally in our state, on paper at least! Our department has been the example in standards and assessment since before our district standards were even written.

Students/Parents: Most of the changes I see in the schools are societal. Kids are different in so many ways from what they were like in 1969. The changes have been good and bad, but for the most part I really like the kids I've had the past few years. They are more knowledgeable about the world thanks to the prevalence of technology.

I have been lucky in that most of the parents at Columbine are supportive of education. They attend conferences, try to encourage their kids, have and are willing to send money for fees and extra expenses, and most have the expectation that their child will graduate and go on to some kind of higher education. When I started at Columbine, it was a new school in a new community. The changes I have seen come from the community being more established and settled. There is a tradition of excellence, and a lot of our parents are former graduates. The only down side I see is that with increased affluence comes a lack of appreciation for all they have.

Personal: I am not the same person that started in this career. Most of the changes can be accounted for by the changes in education and art education during that time. I worked for 20 years with a man who, when he retired, was still teaching the same as he always had, and I was determined to never be like him. Then I would have been bored and boring. My philosophy has not really changed, but it has evolved and strengthened with time and constant learning. I have become more of a leader in my school, district and state, from a desire to share what I have learned and pay back what I have received from my many mentors. One of the biggest changes came with the end of our year-round school calendar. That gave me a whole semester with kids instead of eight weeks. My instructional approach has changed the most since the advent of standards based education, and my work on the state and district standards writing teams. I think that has made me a much more effective teacher and allowed my students to learn more and better.

My biggest contributions have come through my role as leader in my district and in the state association. I think when I retire my role will be historian for the Colorado Art Education Association because I have to do something with all those years of files. Above all else are the effects I hope I have had on the lives of my students.

Stories of Failure: It's the students who never graduate or never go on to fulfill their dreams. Marcy, who chose colleges and majors dependent upon her latest boyfriend, not her wants and dreams. Teddy who is making a fortune in New York, but still hasn't, may never, grow up and be human. Linda who is talented but never able to function in this world. Tim who thinks he has more talent than he does and is constantly disappointed. It's hard to accept these situations and let go. Luckily you never find out about a lot of them, or it would be depressing.

Stories of Success: They are my students and there are so many to try to remember. I suppose the easiest ones are those I have maintained friendships with since their graduations. Barry goes the furthest back, graduating in 1979. He had a rotten family life and art was his savior. He babysat my boys, lived in our house when we were gone for a year, and loved our cats and our ghosts. He eventually became a designer and worked on some important projects locally. He died of AIDS four years ago and I still miss him. Sherry works at a foundry in San Francisco and is competing for the Columbine Memorial job. Meryl was brilliant but a high school drop-out. Her mother persuaded her to try school again. She had me for photo first hour, got hooked, and graduated with awards in art, yearbook, newspaper, and academic grades. She graduated from Brooks Institute and is now a successful freelance nature and travel photographer. Larry got a scholarship to Pratt, has been an artist in various places around the world and now designs web pages and makes a fortune. Kelly was an installer for the Art of the Motorcycle show at the Guggenheim last summer and now works for the Museum of Contemporary Art in Chicago. Sharon and Heather were not much into art in high school, but missed it in college and eventually became art teachers. I ran into Sharon at the Colorado State Art conference, and Heather at Nationals in Houston. What great surprises! I have two favorite young friends at the College of Santa Fe, both on scholarships, and one at UC Santa Cruz who went there for creative writing but switched to an art major. And four of my best ever students from the class of '99 are going to major in Art Education. Many successes you usually never know about, but I have been lucky to find out about some because of renewed communications concerning the tragedy here at Columbine. Some good comes out of everything.

Lora Barrett: *And when I can't think of how to respond because the story they tell me about their lives is just so horrific and foreign to me, that's failure on my part because I can't help them if I don't know what to say.*

Teaching: Collective bargaining has changed things in my school district. We increased the elementary art faculty from two full timers to eight full time teachers (one per building). One of the results of a teacher strike was an increase in elementary classroom teacher prep. time, and in order for that to happen, more art, PE, and music teachers had to be hired. Locally, that has had the greatest impact. I see the kids coming to middle school much better prepared in art because of this faculty increase.

Inclusion students with special needs, without a teaching aide to accompany them to the art room has been another focal change. This causes obvious stress on the art teacher, the other students, and the special education students.

Among the other changes impacting our academic programs, education finance has improved, increasing the school budget and therefore the art budget. Multicultural education has brought about change, though it still has a long way to go. Other curriculum changes have not impacted art in our district as we were already well ahead of the trends in the discipline.

Students/Parents: The community where I have always worked has become poorer over the past several decades, and with poverty comes a whole spectrum of issues which are very removed from the life I was raised in and the life in which I live. Some people say that kids are tougher now than they were 20 years ago. That might be, but I'm better equipped to work with them than I was back then because I bring an encyclopedia of practical experience to bear on my teaching style. The issue of liability has become one to worry about; you can't ever be alone with a kid, and you're not supposed to touch them, but kids hang on me all the time and they never would have done that 20 years ago. We have a police officer in every secondary school in the district, not because of what has happened in our schools, but because of what happened in Columbine High School. I find the kids have a narrower frame of reference, and that sports are king. But a lot of that has to do with the fact that the families my students come from don't have the resources or educational backgrounds themselves to partici-pate in enrichment activities. I find children warmer than when I first started teaching. I find them needier, poorer, nicer, more open, less pre-pared. I find the parents more defensive, more narrow in their focus, more likely to judge before having all the facts, more likely to take the side of the children even when they have incriminating facts, less likely to support the school, less likely to come to school even when their child is in a perfor-mance.

I hear more kids say, "I hate to read" than ever before and find that many more are passive receptors of information and have difficulty formulating a critique or argument. Some of these changes are brought about by poverty; some of it is that it's easy to be passive and sit in front of the TV or video game; some of it is that the family adults are out working long hours and the kids park in front of the TV for security. Society has changed, and I'm not sure we have changed the way schools operate in order to address these changes.

Hindrance: Some of the greatest obstacles to my teaching effectiveness have been in this order: class size, lack of facilities and technology, loud-speaker interruptions, schedule changes without ample notice, and disruptive students.

Help: Some of the greatest facilitators in my teaching effectiveness have been mentoring new teachers and student teachers. Likewise, teaching part time in the Art Education Department at the University of Massachusetts at Amherst has helped. Other teachers who have served as role models, my own drive and innate stamina, and my will to plunge ahead despite diversity have all served me well.

Personal: I have changed. I'm not the naïve, young teacher I once was. I'm far more patient, find much more humor in situations and don't take myself so seriously. Life is too short. I'm no longer searching for that ultra talented student who will become famous some day, and because I'm no longer hung up on that, I'm sure I'm closer to finding that quality in so many more students.

My most significant contributions have been mentoring younger teachers, deliberately seeking out newer teachers and giving them tips. I have established a strong arts component in the school that is supported by the principal. I have consistently set high standards for students as well as adults, including myself. I have a sense of humor, the ability to laugh at myself. I treat others, both students and adults, as I would expect to be treated. I put art out front at all times.

Stories of Failure: When kids have been troubled and I haven't been able to reach them; when we've been unable to get them into a counseling program, that's failure. And when I can't think of how to respond because the story they tell me about their lives is just so horrific and foreign to me, that's failure on my part because I can't help them if I don't know what to say.

Stories of Success: I've had my share of students who are Gold and Silver Key winners in the Scholastic Art Contest. My kids have won Grand Prize for every float they've ever entered in Holyoke St. Patrick's Day Parade. They've received accolades for operas they've written and have won countless local and state contests. But I think the biggest success stories are those that are intangible. Many of the kids I work with are so very poor.

When they come to the school, many of them have such low expectations of themselves. When I can get a kid to come out of his or her shell, and to take a leadership role among their peers, that's success.

I consider it a success when a kid sits in my office and pours their heart out to me, whether it's about an abusive relationship that I can report, or a kid who is thinking about suicide and we can get him or her counseling, or when a kid agrees to be good in another class because I'm going to check on them and they think they will be letting me down if they don't pull through. Successes are measured in having kids who show up every day and who, at the end of the semester, ask if I will keep one of their pieces of artwork in a frame in the classroom for other kids to see. That's pride. That's self-confidence. That's generosity. That's success.

Sharon Henneborn: *I eagerly attend as many courses and conferences as time and money will allow. I read as much as time allows and visit museums and gallery shows. We must come out of our classrooms and learn from each other.*

Teaching: Thirty years ago I spent a good percentage of my time working to gain the respect for the arts that they deserve. Today the arts have a more respected position. Though art curriculum has changed for others, my instructional approach hasn't changed all that much. Interestingly, many years ago colleagues would say that I "talked too much." It was because I would include art history and cultural context. I spent a lot of class time with group critiques. I used a cross-curricular approach to my teaching. Now DBAE is recommended by the district and state art organizations, as well as many state departments of education.

In reference to discipline, when I first came to my current school district, the conditions were often hazardous and if a teacher was assaulted, it was considered an embarrassment and not to be mentioned. Fortunately for me, I was strong enough to fight defensively and was never badly hurt, but others were. As an example, in 1969, I was on recess duty and went to break up a fight. No teacher would ever approach the huge fifth grade bully involved, so I must have taken him by surprise when I pulled him off the two boys he was pummeling. Once I had him of course I couldn't let him go! While he was still off balance, I lifted him up with my long arms and pushed him up against the wall, his feet dangling and kicking. He was flailing with his short arms. Every kid he had ever bullied was circling and taunting him. I spent an eternity pressing his chest against that wall. I can still remember his plaid flannel shirt—funny what you remember. Finally I convinced one of his tormentors to go and get some very large men to help.

In the big picture, our district has come a long way since those early years. The schools are safer, the teachers union is strong, yet there are still challenges to meet.

Hindrance: To name a few, I am my state's Elementary Arts Division Chair and I am concerned that our elementary art teachers are teaching from carts, have no space allotted to them and have schedules that would drain the life out of any human. I am concerned that our state teachers are required to teach special needs students mainstreamed in large numbers without the training they need.

Help: Staff development has been a great help. I eagerly attend as many courses and conferences as time and money will allow. I read as much as time allows and visit museum and gallery shows. We must come out of our classrooms and learn from each other.

The proliferation of commercial visuals and publications for children's art in the last 15 years is a godsend! So are color copiers, scanners, digital cameras, and the Web. All of these things help me get information to the children. I used to have to make my own visuals and transport library books, and write my own text.

Stories of Success: When I asked to move to middle school it was a very exciting time. The district had made a decision to embrace the new middle school philosophy and test the methods in our largest middle school. The staff was sent for intensive training in the summer. For me, this was a new grade level and a new philosophy. Fortunately for me, I had taught many of the students in the lower grades. The challenge came from students who were not used to my methods. One sixth grader let me know from the first day that he did not like art and that he would be doing minimal work. He was definitely a leader and I could see him rallying the troops to produce the minimum and spend the rest of the class time tormenting me and entertaining his peers. That was his plan and it had worked for him in the past. He liked to do defiant, irreverent, provocative little cartoon ink drawings instead of the assignments. These were meant to distract other students and irritate the teacher. I knew that I must find the latch hook to open this rebel to the possibilities of art for himself or we would have a rough time together for three years. It has been my belief that if a child has ideas, I can teach him or her to express those ideas in an art form. His little doodles were bursting with ideas, so he was really easy to hook. I challenged him to find a way to meet all the assigned objectives with those cartoon drawings. He became so occupied with his drawings that he forgot to lead the rebels and I could get them to focus on learning. He signed up to work with me on the school newspaper and produced many interesting illustrations. He was a constant challenge and kept me on my toes for three years, but we were producing and learning together. He went on to a school of visual arts, studied and taught art at various locations around the country, and when there was an opening in our district, returned to teach in the school where it all began for him. He is an excellent teacher. It is very exciting to have him as a colleague and a dear friend. He wrote, illustrated, published and distributed a book of his provocative cartoons. A delightful young law student read that book and declared that she must meet the author; later, she became his wife. As I finished typing this interview, he celebrated his thirtieth birthday and the arrival of their first child.

Suzie Kropa: *By the mid-90s, I became aware of postmodernism. It took me a while to figure out what it meant and how it applied to teaching art. I now realize that art teachers have been postmodernists for a long time.*

Teaching: The biggest change in public education between then and now is the range of abilities we see all thrown into the same classroom. If we saw special needs children at all in the 70s, they were in separate classes. Behavior disordered students weren't even around. In Mt. Pleasant they attended school at a special institute or in a special classroom in another district.

The other big change I perceive is curricular. In the early years we had "curriculum guides," recipe books of art projects in a variety of media. In the early 70s, crafts like stitchery and macrame were prime. DBAE (Discipline-based Art Education) hit in the 80s and had a significant impact on my teaching. It helped me develop a logical sequence of skills that build over time. At the same time that DBAE was introduced, our district adopted the *Discover Art* series (1985) by Laura Chapman. We never used it as written, but it did help us with "scope and sequence," to use popular 80s jargon. By the mid-90s, I became aware of postmodernism. It took me a while to figure out what it meant and how it applied to teaching art. I now realize that art teachers have been postmodernists for a long time. In the last five years, I've noticed an increase in the availability of teaching materials on the arts of diverse cultures and of women. I have also been focusing more on living, working artists than I used to.

The most recent trends of standards development, benchmarks, curriculum cadres, and assessment loom large and worry me. I am concerned about the way assessment is being touted—at what price? Kids need a coach, somebody to be right there helping and guiding, not a scorekeeper with a clipboard. Laura Chapman said, at the NAEA convention in Chicago in 1998, that we would do well just to have our students enjoy art.

Students/Parents: In many ways students are brighter than ever. Many have home computers, are active in lessons such as dance, music, and sports at an early age, and have parents who want the best for them. On the other hand, I see a loss of some of the simple joys of childhood that I remember, when parents weren't organizing every moment. At the other extreme are the kids who are left entirely to themselves. The gap is wider than it was thirty years ago, the extremes greater. I think day-care has changed the way children are socialized. Warehoused children are a different breed from the ones who have stay-at-home moms.

Another change we've all observed is cultural diversity. Because of where I teach, my students in the early years were largely white. Now we have a sizable Laotian population and are beginning to see more Hispanic children.

Hindrance: The problem of poor faculties has been perpetually trying, but I have not let it become a major obstacle or dictate the curriculum. Scheduling has been and continues to be a problem—not enough time between classes, changing buildings every day at noon, having three different grade levels in a row. Now we are inundated with printed materials, and since Iowa has no state-wide mandated curriculum, we teachers are putting in many hours, discussing and writing our own. Ironically, all of this extra work begins to get in the way of what we were hired for in the first place, to teach.

It's hard juggling work and family, traveling between schools with no art rooms anywhere, feeling somewhat like an outsider, and just lately, being overwhelmed with curriculum development—too many meetings, too much jargon as the educational pendulum continues to swing.

Help: We've always had a budget to support whatever supplies and materials we need. Our principals are helpful in contacting maintenance for needed repairs to equipment like kilns. Most classroom teachers are supportive of the art program and follow through when students misbehave in art class or when they need extra time for work.

Personal: Is there a difference between a 22 year old and a 56 year old? Of course I see myself differently now. I'm wiser, more relaxed, more in charge, much more confident, and not as silly. I relate to children better now, having reared two of my own. I can let the kid in me come out more now that my hair is streaked with gray and my face more grandmotherly than motherly. My philosophy hasn't changed all that much—instructional approach, yes. I use more variety—slides, films, overheads, story-telling, songs, and humor. I am conscious of trying to attend to every student, if only for a moment. In my youth, I wasn't empathic. It was "me" and "them." Now it's "us." We're all in it together.

I've been a role model in and out of school. I've made it a point to paint on location in places where my students are likely to see me at work. I support the arts in the community—the symphony, community theater, and concert association. I was one of the initiators of our Youth Art Month exhibit, which is in its twenty-fourth year. I think I've given hundreds of children good memories of their elementary art experience.

Stories of Failure: I have had many projects that flopped. But the failures that get to me the most are those with individual students—a situation that gets out of control or my failure to listen carefully or keep my temper. These are the things that keep me awake at night trying to figure out what I could have done or what I might do differently.

Stories of Success: Several years ago, I introduced a castle drawing lesson to my third grade classes. The drawings were done with black sharpie markers over pencil. I was surprised when kids started asking how to draw rocks, bricks, shingles, and other textures to make their drawings interesting. So we looked at David Macaulay's *Castle* (1977) and *Cathedral* (1973), and I supplied a bigger variety of markers, from sharpie to razor-sharpie; and the student drawings progressed way beyond my expectations. Since there is a video of *Castle* (1977), I asked the third grade teachers if they might have time to show it to their classes. And *they* began to get interested. The students were obviously highly motivated and their finished drawings showed it. In the years that followed, teachers built whole units around the castle drawing project. One teacher staged a medieval feast in the lunchroom, complete with high school musicians and mothers dressed as servants. Another invited a college professor from Ireland to come and tell castle stories. The elementary music teacher got into the act too, teaching medieval dances and explaining the origin of "Ring Around the Rosie." Students have come to look forward to the castle project and have memories of it well beyond third grade. Castles are so captivating because they represent every aspect of life during the Middle Ages; everything happened in and around castle walls. How intriguing to try to imagine what it must have been like to live then and to think about how that life compares with ours.

Teaching children how to draw castles revealed to me that a quality educational experience is all encompassing. World Wide Web advocates like to talk about how easy it is to jump from site to site, accumulating information that leads to understanding. The castle project taught me that when children are motivated, they learn like that, seeking knowledge from whatever sources are available to them until they are satisfied. While some lessons are not as enthralling as others, I think the wise teacher tries to make connections that arouse curiosity and cause students to ask for more.

In sum, I think my best years are happening now. I don't know if it's the students I have at the moment or that I finally have my own room to teach in. It's probably both of these things and one more—I feel like I finally know what I'm doing. I've seen trends come and go, and after thirty years of experimenting, I know what works, and I know what is important.

Judy Williams: *T-cap is our Tennessee skills test starting at third grade. The Sanders "value added model," using these scores, looks at how an individual teacher's students improve during the time she has them. It's not popular here.*

Teaching: Early in my career I remember parents scrubbing the floor of an unused storeroom so we could do art and other activities there. I remember a mother bringing a snake to school that she found in her garden and we looked it up and identified it. I remember parents dropping in to talk often. Teaching a child the consequences of his behavior was a joint effort and discipline at school was supported. Books and supplies were handled carefully. Now, parents have to plan carefully to come to school for special activities or when a problem arises. It's very difficult to find volunteers to help with special projects. Many times parents take the child's side in incidents of misbehavior. Some children do not take care of classroom equipment and materials and parents are irate if asked to pay for damage. The most disturbing change is the increasing number of emotional and behavior problems that I see, the lack of good care at home—nutrition, rest, cleanliness, self-control. It would be simplistic to say that this is because more mothers work because I see problems in the children of stay-at-home mothers.

I worked for 25 years in my county to see full-time elementary art teachers finally hired. Now, after 29 years, these teachers are losing their rooms and the teachers who have left for better salaries are not being replaced or are being replaced with classroom certified teachers. (In all fairness, there is a shortage of certified art teachers in our area.)

In my county, and in the workshops I conduct in the area, art teachers are trying to educate peers about how art reinforces T-cap tested skills. T-cap is our Tennessee skills test starting at third grade. The Sanders "value added model," using these scores, looks at how an individual teacher's students improve during the time she has them. It's not popular here. We live with it and wonder when it will become the basis for employment, tenure, etc.

Students/Parents: The most visible change I have observed in my students is the increasing lack of effort. At the high school level, more and more students do just enough to get by and the apathy is so pronounced in some that they don't even do that much; they are just there so they can keep their driver's license (by Tennessee law). I hear the same complaint from the AP English teacher. At the elementary level I notice lack of respect for the teacher, even to the point of rudeness, and also unwillingness to put forth much effort. On the plus side, I notice that more students have seen great art (through travel, on TV, the Internet) and that more have art materials at home.

Parents are actually at school less. More of them disagree with and do not support teachers' decisions regarding grades and discipline. Most recently, however, I have been teaching children of my former students and those parents have been supportive and value art in the school.

Hindrance: Scheduling and inadequate facilities have been on-going problems. At the high school level, the basic course, Art I is comprised of students from the entire population of the school—14-18 year olds. To say the least, it's difficult to engage every leaner effectively in a group with that kind of diversity. At both the high school and elementary levels, I have used a lot of time and energy finding free supplies; this is time that I could have spent on planning and preparation. Inadequate facilities and equipment have always plagued my program. Teaching art in a room with no sink is no fun.

Help: Help has come from administrators who valued what I was doing and told me so and who backed that up with consideration in scheduling and at least some money and support for the program. I would also add here the printed material from NAEA (National Art Education Association) and TAEA (Tennessee Art Education Association) workshops. Another help nowadays is the abundance of wonderful visuals.

Personal: My instructional approach has changed in that I encourage a lot more "talking about art" due both to my increasing knowledge and the availability of reproductions and other visuals. I am also more careful and structured about directions for production and do more explaining and discussion before beginning a production activity.

I know now that I cannot save the world nor even give every student all that they need. What I have tried to do over all these years is to help both teachers and students realize that the ability to create and enjoy art is for everyone. The ability to draw or paint is not visited magically upon a selected few, but is developed by interest, study, and practice. One community member actually told me he thought art was for the elite—he had a nice collection and considered himself one of the elite. There is a place for art in everyone's life and it is a place filled with joy.

Stories of Failure: Failure came with the talented student to whom I paid particular attention early in my career and lost touch with after high school. He was in prison for several years. When he got out, his sister brought me some of his drawings hoping I could suggest job opportunities. His work had not progressed much. Now I look back and wonder if it would have helped if I had kept in touch and corresponded during those years. When I think of failure in a more general sense, I think of the talented and interested students I could have helped more had I not (of necessity) spent so much time and energy in scrounging for supplies and dealing with students who were disruptive or apathetic.

Stories of Success: My success stories are general—the former student, now the young parent, who tells me in the grocery store that he/she's painted a mural on a Sunday school room wall or applied a faux finish to her living room wall or visited a museum "off" somewhere, or drawn a portrait of her child, or bought some original painting for her home. Yesterday, when I went to a museum, the visitor's brochure was illustrated by a former student. Several former students have successful graphic design careers; some are actors whom I see occasionally on national TV. [My students designed sets, lighting, and costumes, and also acted]. A few are art teachers; some are factory workers and business owners. When I see them they often tell me what they are doing art-wise or they call to ask where to find certain supplies. These are my success stories—men and women going about their daily business of working, rearing families, and serving their community and enjoying the art in their lives.

Lurline Lapolla: *We've sent work throughout the world and all of it is selected from regular class assignments. It makes me feel like my students are ambassadors for peace.*

Teaching: For me, the emphasis in art education has changed from formal to expressive interests—the emphasis is on the experience of the work and on the solving of problems.

Today, as always, I work to help my students understand that they are individuals and they each have their own special talents.

Students/Parents: Today's students are waiting to be entertained. Perhaps the Internet and video games have given them instant gratification. The work today is sloppier with less attention to craftsmanship and less willingness to alter it or to make adjustments and refinements. Today's kids are louder too. Today's parents don't expect the kids to produce. They expect us to be "nice" to the children—the arts after all are likened to recess.

Hindrance: Art has always been a second class subject. The perception has been that it's good experience, but only counts for the talented or those who have no success elsewhere. It's structured recess, not a discipline. Many administrators, parents, and students seem to share this attitude.

Help: The greatest facilitators to my teaching are three younger brothers whom I helped raise and who have been very supportive. Also a fantastic former department chair who shows me unthought of ways to accomplish what I want to do.

Personal: I know I've influenced hundreds of children (and some of their children). Standing out in my mind are the various international exhibits into which I have brought my students. Their personal satisfaction in sharing their work has been greatly rewarding for me. Throughout my years in teaching, I have been known as a "glass-half-full" person to be counted on.

Stories of Failure: There have been many teen suicides in our town—one every year or two. Sometimes I feel the arts have failed because they gave these kids no anchor in the storm of real life. Art, music, and books have always been there for me in times of personal trial. Somehow, I feel I should have better instilled these sources of hope in my students. Realistically, it can't always happen.

Stories of Success: My most memorable successes have been with my students and their participation in various international exhibits. We've sent work to Japan for over 18 years. In 1998, a whole class worked together for an exhibition in the Slovak Republic. We were the only U. S. school represented. In Latvia, there were only two U. S. schools represented. We've exchanged videotapes and artwork with Hungary. We've sent work throughout the world. All of this artwork is selected from regular class assignments. We've done local exhibits too, but the international ones make me feel like the students are ambassadors for peace.

Yvonne Greene: *I've grown beyond my early teaching days when I basically taught unrelated lessons conceived in a panic the night before, to a philosophy that believes in structure, sequence, and building one art experience upon another.*

Teaching: The teachers and administrators in the public schools have become much more self-aware and accountable than we were in the '60s when I began teaching. In looking back, I recall a relatively laissez-faire atmosphere. With the emphasis on testing and with more students remaining in school until high school graduation, we are more specifically goal-oriented.

Mandated teacher preparation periods for elementary classroom teachers in Texas gave me the foot in the door to develop an art program where I currently teach. As the academic disciplines have had to measure up and more time is spent preparing for the mandated achievement tests, art classes have had to justify their existence even more definitively. The Discipline-Based Art Education (DBAE) philosophy has added more depth and purpose to our curriculum planning and delivery of lessons. It has enlarged the instructional scope to reinforce studio activities with exposure to diverse works from art history, aesthetic questions, and art criticism.

Enhanced global awareness, as well as a long overdue recognition of the ethnic diversity within our own culture has given rise to a multicultural investigation of art from many perspectives. Recognition of women's contributions to the arts has added yet another dimension to teaching art as an inherent expression of all humankind. Fortunately a wide range of quality art reproductions is finally readily available to art teachers for use in their classrooms. I shudder to remember building my personal library of art examples by cutting out woefully small art images from magazines whenever I happened upon them or awkwardly holding up art books for my classes to see reproductions of artworks to illustrate a concept I was teaching.

Interesting to note, the time-honored teaching practices by art educators have now made their way into mainstream instructional practices. I admit to a little resentment when generic staff development sessions bandy about terms like *creative problem-solving, discovery learning, hands-on activities, open-ended questioning, giving students opportunities to arrive at innovative rather than prescribed solutions to problems*—all without giving credit to the art education philosophies that have taught these concepts for decades.

Students/Parents: I began teaching in a rural, homogeneous white working class community. Then I taught in an urban setting with children from middle and upper middle class families. Finally, I teach now in a small town with a large poverty level. The children are from Anglo, Hispanic, and African-American populations. So, my view of students has changed with the nature of the communities in which I've taught, as well as with time. What I perceive in today's children is that underneath all the current undisciplined behavior and the thin veneer of street-wise social sophistication, they are still as fragile and vulnerable inside as children ever were. And I must remind myself that it is necessary to search for and reach the soft interior of them, rather than react to the tough outer coating manifested in their abrasive social behavior. I am happy to report that the quality of art production is as high as it has ever been, at least among the youngster set (K-3) which I teach.

Assumptions that we may hold about the stability of the home environment from which our students come may reflect memories of our own childhood more than the contemporary reality. Many parents are very young and I find we deal with them *and* custodial grandparents jointly. Often there is only one parent in the household and she (it's most often *she*) has very little time, inclination, or comprehension of the value of providing enriching experiences for children at home. Parents are often hostile when the school attempts to discipline youngsters in ways deemed acceptable to previous generations. Parents are still very proud of their children's accomplishments and really appreciate positive messages from school. Art can provide much positive communication.

Hindrance: Sadly we are undergoing one of the most difficult times in West Texas right now. We survived a tumultuous spring (2001), with fears of my program being cut due to draconian budget cuts. Unlike the rest of the country, West Texas is losing student population so there is no teacher shortage here. And with the decline in enrollment, belt tightening happened. Anyway, unfortunately music was cut from our school (I hope temporarily), but art remains, in great part due to the three art teachers in Slaton hustling for the past few years to bring our students' art before the community with exhibits, calendars, billboards, etc. In fact they added fourth grade from the other elementary school to my schedule. In sum, they added six more art classes, cut my three pre-K classes, so art takes up the slack where music filled in. I am enjoying teaching the fourth graders and I don't really miss the four-year olds. However, I am teaching eight classes on Mondays and seven the rest of the week...too many classes and not conducive to adequate planning nor materials preparation...but I remind myself that I still have a job. I plan to teach four more years to be able to receive a modest retirement from the Texas system.

Throughout the years there has been the lack of "wholehearted" support from administrators: "We are really fortunate to have you. You do such a good job—of course, be aware that if there were any positions cut, yours would be one of the first to go. Your job exists basically to provide a conference period for classroom teachers . . . we could always arrange the day so that all teachers' conference times were at the end of the day and still be within the law."

Help: When my supervisor recognizes the value of my program; when the art budget is maintained at a level so that I don't have to scrounge materials or rely solely on recycled junk materials; when I attend staff development sessions that apply to me as an art teacher, like the Texas Art Education convention, these are the kinds of things that help.

Personal: Age and experience have increased my confidence as a teacher and as an advocate for art education. I've grown beyond my early teaching days when I basically taught unrelated lessons conceived in a panic the night before, to a philosophy that believes in structure, sequence, and building one art experience upon another. I am more likely to articulate goals to the children for what I teach them now and I spend more time and energy on relating how historical master art works illustrate the concepts we are currently exploring.

Several thousand students have spent four years coming to my art room. I feel I have had a positive impact on their lives in ways they could never explain. Their art experience has become an internalized part of them that will be with them all their lives. They may not remember my name years hence, but they will make "artful" decisions about their lives because of what they learned from me.

Stories of Failure: Failure is the inability to "do it all . . .," to be a human being, wife, mother, housekeeper, teacher, artist. It's having to choose what to spend less time on and having to chose to sacrifice being an artist, except during summers and someday, retirement. There are those days when I have inadvertently made a hurtful or exasperated comment to a student…they will remember my insensitivity all their lives.

Stories of Success: Receiving an unexpected national award for efforts in teaching art via radio felt like a great success years ago. Being able to convince administrators of the viability of an art program at the elementary school where I now teach exemplifies success. Creating a high visibility art program through local, regional, state, and national exhibits, billboards, calendars, and more is a sign of success. Likewise, I have felt reward through recognition at the local and state Youth Art Month celebrations and through being nominated for Texas Elementary Art Educator of the year.

Mark Phillips: *More and more, time and scheduling are working against us. We try to wedge so much into our curriculum—character education, guidance groups, kids are pulled out of classes a lot and all of this upsets the continuity of learning.*

Teaching: There have been major changes over the past 30 years. Accountability for one. The various governmental agencies and the public demand it. We must do a better job. Since teachers are being better paid, we must be more accountable and I think we are better for that.

Today art is much more of an academic discipline; it's not considered "fluff." We now have a formal curriculum and learning assessments. At one time we had the "open classroom" with "workstations" and independent studies. Things were far more informal. Now we have gone in a different direction; we talk about portfolios and assessment rubrics—it may not be the right direction but we are moving. Today we have "special needs" students. At first these students were not intermixed into a class—now they are. It's better for the students but harder to deal with all the different levels and needs. We have everyone from non-readers to gifted learners.

Students/Parents: Twenty-seven years ago, kids were kids. Now they are more world-wise given the Internet, MTV, etc. Kids are more alike now all over the U. S.; witness the clothes, hair, fads, and interests. Even the rural kids are more world-wise. There has been an increase in school violence. Today's kids are better off, having the resources to become more educated sooner, but they have lost their childhood innocence at an earlier age—this is especially evident at the middle school level—6th graders are now like 8th graders used to be. I miss the innocence along the way.

Hindrance: More and more, time and scheduling are working against us. We try to wedge so much into our curriculum—character education, guidance groups, kids are pulled out of classes a lot and all of this upsets the continuity of learning. Paperwork—and the computer has added to this— has proliferated. Teaching is almost secondary to filling out forms. Class loads—I have taught 500 students a year. My classes are big with 32-34 kids—I have always had these big numbers. My room is packed. Impacting our visual arts discipline have been DBAE, learning outcomes, and standards. Politics and government have their hand in all of it. More and more, I've got to teach the way they have it spelled out. Some days I think it is almost impossible to teach anymore.

Help: It has helped that my district has supported art, even in the lean years. We've had a good staff; we are friends and work well together.

Personal: I am different now. I am a better teacher. In fact, I sometimes tell my former students that I wish I could bring them back. I would do so much more for them. I must be more of an entertainer now. I have to catch their attention and sell my program. My most significant contribution to teaching over the years is that I have given 110%. I have worked to be a good friend and teacher. I will leave knowing that I have done all that I could, that I have done my very best.

Stories of Failure: It's the reality checks when we remember that not all kids like art. It's finding very angry kids who hate art and everyone and everything around them. It's so hard to get them interested. I have, for some reason, had more failures this past year than I have ever had. I fret about it. It bothers me that I can't seem to turn the switch on to get them to learn.

Stories of Success: I remember Robert, a student in my art club. He wanted to do oil or acrylic painting at the middle school level. He wanted to do a big canvas, so I stretched a canvas for him and set him to work. He was phenomenal! He was in the art classroom every possible hour of the day and night. He knocked me over with his abilities! He graduated in art from college and is now a commercial artist.

Jane Hollingsworth: *Authentic assessment is another area that impacts art education. Public schools are asked to find other ways of evaluating student achievement: portfolios, individualized rubrics, performance criteria, etc. Yet colleges and universities still base admissions on GPA's and SAT scores.*

Teaching: In 1968, it was assumed by both the employer and the public that if you were certified by the State Board of Education to teach, you were qualified. That translated to much more confidence and support from administration and from the students' homes than exists today. Now, additional documentation and accountability seem to be the two watch-words which pervade the educational environment. While parents usually will support the teacher in a dispute with the student, they expect teachers to be able to support what they say with concrete evidence. Teachers are much more likely to be questioned about their motives and actions. In terms of parental support, I believe that began to erode with my generation when we began questioning authority. The courts and the media have also under-mined the public's faith in its institutions and their employees.

In terms of educational trends, proposals have been made for national testing of both teachers and students. National Standards have been established in almost all subjects, including art. As with most educational trends it is a mixed blessing. National Standards and testing "legitimize" to lawmakers and the public the subject areas being tested. This could be especially important in art since it is not considered a "core" academic subject. The best minds in specific disciplines are usually pooled to write standards and test questions, so a wealth of information in the content area is therefore synthesized and disseminated to the pubic. On the other hand, National Standards are a culmination of objectives that are created on the national level. Individualization and regionalism are basically ignored. In art, that omits the flavor and essence of artistic expression. Standardized evaluations of art programs therefore may not reflect the quality of individual programs. Authentic assessment is another area that impacts art education. Public schools are asked to find other ways of evaluating student achievement: portfolios, individualized rubrics, performance criteria, etc. Yet colleges and universities still base admissions on GPA's and SAT scores.

On a positive note, public schools in 1999 have more funds and smaller class size than when I first began to teach. My art program is supported with a larger budget, and I can apply for local grants to obtain equipment and materials that I need for my program. I consider 24 to be a large class now; when I began my career around 30 would be a normal size.

Students/Parents: Since my career began during the turbulent 60s in a newly integrated metropolitan high school, my perspectives on student behavior are different from many of my current colleagues. Most teachers will say that the demeanor of the students we presently teach is much worse than it was 30 years ago. I don't see it that way. I remember that a class at Marietta High School made me cry by uniting in their misbehavior. I remember clay fights. I remember students being jailed. I remember bomb threats. Not much has changed. The media portrays incidents in public schools with much more zeal than it did in 1968. The public is more aware of infractions at school, and more tax dollars are spent to deal with disruptive students. Sometimes I think it boils down to sheer numbers. With the increased population come increased problems. By and large, most students in the classroom today are "good kids." They have the same values their parents had—they may express them differently, but they're the same. The parents of today's youth are much better educated than their counterparts 30 years ago. That may explain why they feel more at ease in questioning a teacher. More mothers work and the lives of parents are more hectic. It can no longer be assumed that you can reach a parent at home by telephone. Mothers and fathers want their children to do well in school, but many don't know how to encourage them. A disturbing trend that I've noticed recently is competitiveness among parents for their children to excel academically, socially, and athletically. Parent involvement in this effort is extremely overt. It's important to parents to *see* measurable results from their children's efforts—they want to publish honor rolls, athletic recognition, contests and competitions. Sometimes I worry that they're taking childhood away from their own children. The trend is especially apparent and disturbing for an art teacher. Art involves free expression, search, reflection—activities that cannot and should not be subject to measurement and comparison.

Hindrance: The mentality of administrators and colleagues about "non-academic" classes is probably the biggest obstacle any art teacher will face, especially in the middle grades. Art is still not seen as important as math, social studies, language arts, or science. At some point I began to believe that if I was good enough—if I obtained an advanced education and built up an award-winning art program, I would be recognized by getting a better schedule. For me a better schedule would include longer art classes and possibly advanced art classes. In the end, it doesn't matter how effective the teacher is or how rich the art program; art is still what they call an "exploratory" subject and art classes will continue to be secondary and adapted to the academic class schedule.

To illustrate, this year has been the lowest point in my career. Since 1978, I've taught art at the same middle school and I've had an extremely successful experience. The administration has fostered a supportive environment for the arts. However, last year, for reasons unrelated to the arts programs, my school was restructuring; teachers were involved in the process and we met once a week for an hour after school. At the end of the year, most of us were looking forward to returning to jobs that were going to be even better than they were before. At the beginning of this year, I returned to work to find that my teaching time in art class had been reduced to 35-40 minutes per class and that I was on full-time, permanent lunch duty for the whole year. This schedule was developed on the spur of the moment to accommodate 70-minute academic classes and to provide academic teachers with 30 minutes of duty-free lunch. After earning my Ed.S. and certification in gifted education, I was looking forward to implementing some of the ideas I had developed in graduate school. This was out of the question with the teaching schedule I had been given. I've spent the whole year trying to make the best of a bad situation at a point in my career when I'd thought I could be reaching new plateaus of instruction.

Help: Great facilitators to teaching art are the Georgia Art Education Association and the National Art Education Association. Each year I attend the state conference and interact with colleagues from all over Georgia. Contact with other art educators energizes me. I feed off the ideas and motivation of my colleagues. Returning to graduate school was also a boost to my teaching effectiveness. I now know what postmodernism is and I've incorporated the instruction in aesthetics more formally into my curriculum. Supportive parents facilitate my teaching: each year, parents come by my room to tell me how glad they are that their children were able to take my class. Many relate things their sons or daughters told them that they learned or tell me how they've displayed their work at home. Our school and community are very good about recognizing our art programs. We have system-wide exhibits and an on-going art exchange between Gainesville and two cities in Japan and Hungary. Student work is displayed in frames at the district's Central Office. At the risk of sounding corny, watching the involvement of the students in studio work or in aesthetic discussions is probably the biggest facilitator of my effectiveness. I still get a rush when I watch students get excited about their work.

Personal: Today I view myself as a master teacher who can motivate and facilitate students to greater levels of knowledge about art. At the beginning of my career, I was idealistic enough to believe I could open up the world of art to my students and they would change the world through artistic expression. I believed that with proper instruction all students could create great art. Today my goals are different. I no longer believe that producing great art is possible for all students. But I do believe that all students will benefit from knowing more about the nature of artistic expression. Topics such as art criticism and aesthetics occupy much of my curriculum today, whereas in the beginning years, I moved from one studio project to another.

My greatest contribution to teaching art has probably been establishing myself as an effective role model within the public school system. Art purists might rail against the constraints that public education puts on the creativity involved in teaching art. Many artists are non-conformists; therefore they would not be able to tolerate the institutional atmosphere of public schools. I've made it work. My peers, I believe, see me as a disciplined yet creative member of the staff. They view my classes as controlled and involved in their work. I've often been told by academic teachers that I'm "one of the few *normal* art teachers" they've ever seen. I take that as a compliment, even allowing for the obvious narrow-mindedness reflected in the statement.

Stories of Failure: I have experienced inadequacies as a classroom teacher, but "failure" would be too strong of a word to describe them. For example, I have never been able to develop a foolproof solution for students who rush through their work, bring it to me, and tell me they're through. I have strategies that I use, but they don't always work. Another on-going problem in teaching painting is to motivate students to devise their own, original ideas. Most students want to paint "pretty pictures" of mountains and sunsets. Sometimes I force them to use prescribed subject matter such as still lifes or drawings from the garden, but I would like to be more success-ful in motivating creative, artistic thinking processes. A specific situation has arisen in recent years that has forced me to change my approach to free choice: I have always allowed students to decorate ceramics work with designs that they devise themselves. However, our community has recently reacted strongly to visual evidence of gangs. As one point, students were forced to destroy their designs because it was determined that they were gang symbols. I wonder whether censorship is an aesthetic issue.

Stories of Success: Several years ago, I offered an independent study to one of my talented students. Her assignment was to design and cast over 200 ceramic tiles to form a tessellation to cover an outdoor wall. She made the plaster mold and cast all the tiles. They were fired and glazed, and a professional tile setter volunteered to put them up for us. They are now a permanent part of the school building and the student's name is fired onto one of the tiles. She can bring her grandchildren to see her work.

This year on the spur of the moment I decided to take a sixth grade class outside to draw pictures of the garden we'd established many years ago. Students made sketches of specific plants and labeled them with their biological names. I had a large picture frame in storage. At a building supply store, I bought a piece of plywood and had it cut to fit the frame. Each day I let some of my sixth graders bring their sketches to the plywood board and draw their plants. I assigned all students painting duties and soon a lovely picture of a garden emerged in acrylics. Students presented this picture to the school on honors day; it's hanging conspicuously in the sixth grade hall—it's absolutely gorgeous!

John Skrabalak: *Now portfolios are big. We art teachers have been doing portfolios since the invention of fire. Give credit where it is deserved.*

Teaching: I have written and re-written my curriculum more times in the past ten years than I did my first 20 years. There was more flexibility and less accountability in the past than today. Everything we've been doing all along now has a name for it. Each new state administration has their perspective of how things should be done, which usually means re-writing the curriculum. In my teaching situation, there are more people, who are not in the field of art, telling me how to teach than ever before. There are more restrictions resulting in less freedom. In addition, the current perspective on school violence has created a highly restrictive, somewhat paranoid environment in my particular situation.

In the past decade, there have been rapid changes. In art education, there has been a DBAE Renaissance, which has had a great impact; it has validated what many of us have done all along. In order for it to work, it needs to be sequentially placed in a K-12 curriculum, then it won't come as a shock when the student gets to senior high. Unfortunately, my school district has no sequential art curriculum and I don't always know what is being taught in the lower grades. Many teachers now purposefully teach art history, criticism, aesthetics, and production. Having state standards that include the four areas is a big help. For me personally, aesthetics is the area where I have been neglectful, but even that is changing. It is a comprehensive teaching modality that requires more planning; it is a real challenge. The value that DBAE has for the divergent thinker is incredible. Along with these changes, arts assessment is being instituted; this brings accountability—which is good for our profession. Now portfolios are big. We art teachers have been doing portfolios since the invention of fire. Give credit where it is deserved.

More broadly, there has been a swift transition from outcome-based education to standards. Block scheduling, site-based management (if it does what it's supposed to do and if the administration will relinquish control), and the existence of magnet and charter schools have also made an impact.

Students/Parents: I feel the students were more responsible and free when I first started teaching. Now kids are more needy. In earlier years, a student would never ask me if he or she was getting extra credit for completing a minimal task. Students today seem to expect something in return for any small action, etc. They are very grade conscious. Peer pressure and cliques are more evident than before. Students are more afraid to take risks as learners. Students get bored faster. They are the TV remote generation. They can turn a teacher on or off as they choose. The students seem to lose their innocence earlier than before. They are openly sexual and more promiscuous. They are more fatalistic. They see the future and career options as limited. More kids are working and own cars today. Drugs are a real issue of concern. At times, I feel I am a surrogate parent to many of my students. There are more parents working and many children go home to empty houses. The parents want the teachers to be everything to their children. Parents today are more critical of both teacher and school and are more apt to take the side of their son or daughter in learning and disciplinary issues. Parents want to be friends with children rather than parents. Roles are fused. Parents are more apathetic when it comes to participation in such things as conferences.

Positively, the quality of my students' artwork has improved and I attribute this to my own advancement in instructional expertise as well as my development as an artist.

Hindrance: My school district and its school board take pride in the fact that they have not raised property taxes for 16 years. I have not had a budget increase in art for 14 years, yet they found money to resurface the already astro-turfed football field another time. I have had to spend exorbitant amounts of my own money to buy art supplies for my program. As far as scheduling goes, I wish some of my art courses were year-long courses. I have so much to share with these kids. Complaining falls on hostile, deaf ears. I was dealt this card and I kept it. I can honestly say that I have been blessed that my program hasn't been cut, however, the future looks shaky.

There is also a lack of administrative support. Some administrators were inadequate as teachers and yet they observe and evaluate your performance. Many administrators are threatened by the arts and have major control issues. I am convinced that many had a bad art experience when they were young. I feel at times that I am working in a vacuum. With the exception of one art colleague, there is little interest in my district to improve the quality of the art program. Incompetence among a few teachers here doesn't help our cause. They are set in their ways. Progress scares them.

Help: My drive and motivation to keep current with art education methodology and trends have facilitated my teaching effectiveness. I love to go to museums of all kinds as well as attend arts festivals. I attend all state conferences and a few national ones, if approval is granted. I love to buy and read books in my field. A day at a bookstore is common for me. I like to apply for grants to learn new concepts and skills. Recently, I received a grant to research, purchase materials, and to introduce aesthetics into my Art I curriculum.

Personal: I haven't changed internally and philosophically. I am still loose, but with caution. In the past, I could make a lot of decisions on my own. I could get away with a lot more. It was more free. The school was more accessible. Today, everything requires approval, and it is usually denied.

Being an advocate is tiring but necessary for survival in this job. I never had to be as accountable as I am today. My art room door is closed more than in the past.

Art is very visible in my school. None of the ten course offerings in my program have been cut because of my active role in advocacy—my activity in the state art education association and my willingness to learn and share new ideas and trends with my students and colleagues.

Stories of Failure: I have a list of failures to offer. We still don't have a sequential K-12 curriculum in my district. We lost one art teacher and an art room in the senior high where I teach. We have only two art teachers for 10, yes 10, elementary schools. No matter how hard I advocate, communicate, exhibit, etc., my efforts mean nothing to the majority of administrators who make these decisions. I haven't been able to teach a "re-written" curriculum for one year in the past 15 years before it had to be "re-written" again. The arts are still second class in this district. And finally, there are the students that I did not reach, or at least I thought I didn't reach.

Stories of Success: There has been a great deal of success with my courses: All of the art courses that I wrote and introduced during the 1973-74 school year are still in existence. Success stories are those students who went on in an art field of study and are now practicing art. Success stories are those average students you had 20+ years ago—names forgotten—who come up to you and tell you how much they enjoyed your class. Success is all the discoveries, all the happenings, all the creations, all the fun, all the joys, and finally all the awards I have been fortunate and blessed to have received. Success stories are all about having the children of former students in your art classes, and the parents reminiscing during conferences about the good old days in art class . . . and having these same parents commenting that I haven't changed a bit!

Phyllis Bosco: *The examples children receive now are through a barrage of media vying for the brief attention spans of younger and younger children. These examples are often not positive role models.*

Teaching: Our educational system has a broader range of responsibility than it did even a decade ago. Like it or not school has become one of the most stable factors in the early formative years of a child's life. Today, not only toddlers, but also more and more infants are attending nursery schools. After-school programs keep children busy and safe, making the school day even longer. Previously, religious and cultural traditions and/or common work environments helped establish strong roots from which children grew and developed into productive citizens. If job opportunity wasn't there, at least the work ethic was. If a household was in need, the extended family, the religious establishment or community took on the responsibility of helping out. There was more of a sense of security. That type of caring environment is not as prevalent these days. Children are uprooted regularly. Many have a fragmented and inconsistent existence. The examples children receive now are through a barrage of media vying for the brief attention spans of younger and younger children. These examples are often not positive role models.

Conscientious parents who strive to instill a moral consciousness, love of the pursuance of knowledge, and respect for the environment must concentrate their efforts into fragmented periods of time. Today parents cannot model behavior under a variety of life experiences if they aren't available to take advantage of those situations as they naturally occur. Because they must work hard to be financially stable for the physical child, at times the nurturing of the intellectual and spiritual child is being neglected.

Personal: The role of education today must include not only the teaching of skills, but also the teaching of *vision*. We need to teach children to value the power of knowledge. This can be taught through all disciplines. Children need to be given challenges that will help build their confidence. They also need to be given encouragement in their efforts to express themselves creatively. When our children begin to understand that they alone are responsible for realizing their dreams, no matter what obstacle in life they may face, we will have succeeded in establishing the foundation for productive children. All of this is what I have striven for in my teaching.

Stories of Success: Success is having at least one good chuckle a day at school. Some days I literally get goose bumps when I realize a student has "got it." An example occurred when one of my first graders asked a question that stumped me. As students are entering my classroom, I play classical music. They mime an instrument while going to their seats. When the music stops, they are quiet and listening. I had been playing Tchaikovsky's *Nutcracker Suite*. In the fall we had been studying the works of Kandinsky. Falicia raised her hand to ask, "Ms. Bosco, since Tchaikovsky and Kandinsky were both from Russia and lived a long, long time ago, were they friends?" A connection had been made: the knowledge had been applied and formulated into an insightful inquiry.

Cherie St. Pierre: *The teaching philosophy in art education today is the opposite from that of the 60s and 70s . . . . I think I was ready for these philosophies early in the 70s since I never really "bought into" the Lowenfeld approach.*

Teaching: Over the years, my school system has tried to maintain an art room with a kiln for each elementary school, which says a lot for the quality of my district. However, I have traveled on a cart, up and down stairs from classroom to classroom with cardboard boxes filled with supplies at various times throughout my career. The quality of my school system increased dramatically in the 80s and 90s due to a superintendent with a vision. Upon his retirement we have swung to the opposite on the pendulum due to the conservative right wing. We have hate groups competing to be on our Board of Education, and one newspaper that is against the schools, constantly publishing "yellow journalism." In spite of all of this, I think our teachers are better prepared when they come out of college, we have better hiring systems consisting of team interviews, and on-site management. Our teachers' union is extremely strong, taking the lead in the implementation of the latest techniques and methods in education, forcing administration to follow its lead. Our Staff Development Center is one of the best in the state. I think the requirement of the state to have administrators study and intern for an administrative certificate has improved the quality of administrators and eliminated the "good old boys" network, at least in my system. I am basically proud of the growth in education in the 1990s. I think we owe this growth to philosophers like Bernice McCarthy with her *4-Mat System*, and to Howard Gardner's research in cognitive psychology, and also to Jerome Bruner.

The teaching philosophy in art education today is the opposite from that of the 60s and 70s. I was trained in the early 90s in Discipline-Based Art Education, a paradigm shift that differs from the creative self-expression approach to art education which dominated the field for 40 years. The self-expression approach (the Lowenfeld approach) placed great emphasis on art making through a variety of art materials and methods that were non-related and non-sequential. The supposition was that the learner was innately creative and expressive, needed nurture rather than instruction; exposure to adult art images inhibited learners' natural creative development. In contrast, DBAE requires a sequential, balanced curriculum emphasizing content from the four art disciplines of aesthetics, art criticism, art production, and art history from world cultures. The focus is on art as a discipline of study, interrelated with language and other subjects. The learner needs instruction and exposure to adult works of art, both Western and non-Western. The teacher still provides motivation and support, but also helps the child understand valid art concepts at the child's level. Creativity is treated as unconventional behavior that can occur as conventional art understandings are attained. I like this philosophy coupled with Howard Gardner's design on performance-based assessment, education for understanding, and the use of multiple intelligences to achieve a more personalized curriculum, instruction, and assessment. I think I was ready for these philosophies early in the 70s since I never really "bought into" the Lowenfeld approach. I have always encouraged multicultural learning with my slides and artifacts from my world travels and I have long enjoyed teaching visual concepts.

Students/Parents: I think students continue to appreciate any teacher who is enthusiastic and motivating, and who does not belittle or insult them. Children are good judges of character. If you are not honest or just, you lose their respect and your credibility immediately. As for parents, they usually appreciate good teachers.

Hindrance: The greatest obstacles have been the lack of an art room. So much time and energy are wasted because of this. It is impossible to ensure great quality in the lesson. You are invading someone else's teaching space when you enter their milieu. Another obstacle is having a principal who does not see art as a valid subject area and who constantly limits funds for supplies.

Help: Actually, having two masters' degrees and a doctorate has gained respect for me. At least no one challenges me unless they have adequate references for their arguments. I am also a leader by example. I mean that I am not aggressive in leadership qualities, but instead it is my performance that gains respect for me.

Personal: I think I gained more respect for myself and for art when I became a faculty mentor. It is a difficult position to attain in my school system. There are rigorous references, paperwork, and a 15 member interview team with whom to interview. The training and position gave me confidence to contribute to staff development in teaching many courses to my peers. Maybe when you become older, you are more brave.

Stories of Failure: I am not a Pollyanna, but I do not blame myself for any failures. Maybe I see them as educational challenges to overcome and from which to grow.

Stories of Success: I have had many former students seek art careers due to my teaching and motivation. I taught the kindergarten teacher's children. When her daughter saw my slides of Italy in sixth grade, she said to herself that she was going to study in the same program when she got older, and she did. Today she is married to a Frenchman, works for an international insurance company, has worked for them in England, France, Switzerland, and Italy. Her mother blames me for having to go abroad to visit her grandchildren. The same thing happened to the school secretary's children. I motivated them to study art and foreign languages and her son works for a Japanese bank in Hong Kong. And there is my elementary student who said I was the reason she wanted to become an art teacher.

Sonia Pratt: *I am not opposed to accountability. And I am very much in favor of a structured curriculum, but we still need to allow for chance, open ended assignments and exploration of materials and ideas.*

Teaching: I see a lot more pressure on the teacher. More pressure to be accountable for results and more pressure from the threat of violence. When I started teaching, I never dreamed that we could have lock down drills, fear of violence, physical restraint teams and rampant use of behavior medication. For art teachers, I feel apprehension over the standardized testing in the arts. I am open to it. Time will tell. But the pressure to produce could be detrimental to the creative process. I heard a well-known poet speak at a local university recently. A question rose from the audience. "How do you teach poetry?" He said, " You don't. You set students' souls on fire. The poetry comes from that." I am not opposed to accountability. And I am very much in favor of a structured curriculum, but we still need to allow for chance, open ended assignments and exploration of materials and ideas.

Art curricula now seem more in line with other disciplines, moving from unstructured to structured. In the early years, the focus was on "doing your own thing." Now, we emphasize the structure of art, the elements and principles, and at the same time, we teach the role of art in society, the historical and social influences. DBAE offers a good approach, though I haven't totally embraced it. I visit the Getty Center website for ideas and have found it to be useful. A mandatory fine arts requirement has made a positive impact on our own program. Art is now seen as a legitimate discipline, not recreation.

Students/Parents: Students today are much better behaved and have a more positive attitude towards art. A fine arts requirement to graduate has been in effect for some time in the state of Maryland. I see a definite change of attitude because of that requirement. I see a less sexist attitude also. When I first started teaching, I couldn't get a boy to sew anything and I couldn't get a girl to saw a board. Today it isn't a problem.

The parents today are much more involved. I have more of them coming to conferences, attending art shows, and going on field trips. Usually when I call home over a discipline problem, the parent is supportive.

Hindrance: Keeping up with technology has become one of the most difficult aspects of teaching. So much has been thrust upon us so quickly. Bureaucracy is an ever-present hindrance.

Help: It has always been the enthusiastic students who have been my greatest help.

Personal: I definitely see myself differently now than when I first started teaching. I am much more structured and goal oriented than when I first began. I had one college instructor relay the *joys* of the "Summer Hill" approach to education. I gave it a try and it nearly blew me out of the classroom. I am in charge of the class and we all follow basic rules and there is plenty of latitude for creativity. After all of these years, I know I have made a difference in a lot of people's lives.

Stories of Failure: Failure is having a student fail the AP art exam.

Stories of Success: The Baltimore Museum of Art had a statewide competition in conjunction with the Victoria and Albert Exhibit that was being held there. We organized a team of students and two teachers to create a project for the competition. We worked several months on the project. I had no idea how our team would do coming from a rural environment and competing with predominantly magnet schools. We were in the top five finalists. Our students were overjoyed. So was I.

Suzanne Greene: *Abused and neglected kids are more and more common, and they are not just the poor children. My school serves kids who live in one of the richest areas in the US, but we also serve some of the poorest in Houston. All of these kids can and do have problems that are far more serious than the problems in the 70s.*

Teaching: When I first began teaching, teachers were still respected persons. Today you have to earn that respect; it is no longer a given. I believe that society as a whole does not respect what teachers do. Just look at the money we make. In Houston, a garbage collector makes more money than I do. A single teacher with more than one child and who has no other support qualifies for reduced lunches for their children.

Parents have more power now than in the 70s. Many do not believe a teacher when their child has a problem or misbehaves. I've had parents tell me that I am lying when I call them to report their child for cheating or hitting another student, while others tell me that they have never had a teacher complain about their child. Today's parents will try to solve their child's problem for them or try to force the school to solve it for them, rather than letting the child learn from what they have done wrong. I had a student with a knife at school, which automatically means that the child must be sent to an alternative school. The mom works for an attorney, and she argued that the blade on his knife was less than 4" long, and he should not be punished for it. She won. But that knife could have done just as much damage as one that was longer.

The computer has changed the way I teach. Now I use the TV hooked up to my computer and the Internet to visit museums and research artists. I can quickly download something from the Louvre or print out an art piece that was created last week. These kids know computers and create as many drawings on a computer as they do on paper. I take as many computer classes as I can just to keep up with them, but I am falling behind. Computer use is a part of every student's education. It is so common in most homes that one of our eighth graders set up his own web page which contained the answers to each week's English vocabulary test. His classmates would visit his web page, print out the answers, then pass the test that week. We didn't know about this site until one of his classmates forgot to hide the sheet containing the answers.

In the state of Texas, students are now required to take at least a year of fine arts in both middle and high school in order to graduate. There is a great importance being placed on these classes and our state has set many standards which must be followed. This has all come about within the last 10 years.

There are various other changes too. For example, contained classrooms have replaced open classrooms in my district. The open concept junior high where I once taught reopened as a contained classroom school. Other schools within my district that were once open have built walls for containment. Lengths of semester classes have varied from 18 weeks to 12 weeks and then back to 18. Block scheduling versus traditional scheduling varies from school to school. Each school has "site-based management," which means that each school decides its own curriculum, class times and size, etc. based on what that campus needs or wants. Length of the school year and starting and ending dates have also changed from year to year.

Of all of these changes, it is the computer that has impacted my own teaching the most: using the Internet rather than posters, slides, or going to the library; holding classes in a computer lab, where each of my students creates an art work using a draw or paint program; scanning art work or photos into the computer; altering what has been scanned, then either burning it to a CD Rom or printing it out on a color printer. I must keep up with this technology, so I am taking nine hours of computer training this summer. My goal this year was to have every one of my students create an original artwork using the computer. Next year I want each class to create their own web page. I see all the money my school receives going into buying better and faster computers. It is eerie to go to the library and see one room that we call the "computer graveyard," those that are too slow or limited to do a good job. In reference to the effects of the computer on curricular changes, I have seen the addition of a course in computer generated art now being taught in many of our schools. However, the major art shows have been slow in accepting this form of art into their contests.

Students/Parents: When I first started teaching, I caught kids with chewing tobacco and joints. Now I still find the same things, plus guns, knives, and brass knuckles too. Kids still fight, but now they get a ticket and a trip to court. If they cuss you out, that too is a ticket and a court trip. I have more kids on probation every year, and they are very open about it. They know that if they do not follow the rules, they will be in trouble with the school and the probation officer, and this has made many students change their behavior. We give an award every year called the "Comeback Kid." It is given to a student who has really changed his or her lifestyle and is staying in school.

The biggest change is the presence of gang members and stronger drugs in our schools. We have a zero tolerance for gangs. They are identified, photographed, and fingerprinted by our school district police. We have our own police department with over 30 officers and a drug dog. We were the first district in the nation to have these in place. The dog has greatly reduced the amount of drugs coming into our school. But the drug problem is still here. It used to be marijuana and sometimes LSD; now it's stronger versions of those drugs, plus crack, heroin, and others. Alcohol is the number one drug of choice even among the sixth graders.

Abused and neglected kids are more and more common, and they are not just the poor children. My school serves kids who live in one of the richest areas in the US, but we also serve some of the poorest in Houston. All of these kids can and do have problems that are far more serious than the problems in the 70s. I see more attempted suicides and runaways now.

To share an anecdote from 1987, I remember a parent who posed an ironic question on a written evaluation of an open house: "Why do teachers talk down to us when we are better educated than they are?" Today, the majority of the parents want the best for their child and they want to work with teachers to reach this goal.

Hindrance: The hardest part of being a teacher is the constant demands placed on you. I work with over 150 kids a day. Each needs my help and direction, which can become overwhelming. If you have never been in a classroom, then you cannot understand how much these kids take from you day after day. You really have to want to be with them and laugh at yourself or you will burn out. Sometimes I'll just take my 6th graders outside and make them run for a while, and I'll run with them; then we all feel better. Some days I go home just totally drained, but then I have dinner to cook, homework to help with, and a house to keep up. I am no longer a good housekeeper. I just can't do it anymore. Some nights I wish I had a "wife" at home who would have dinner ready when I come home, especially those nights when I stay late at school. I get so depressed when I open my door and a messy, cluttered home greets me—that isn't how I was raised. Take last night: We didn't eat until 8:00 and all I had to do was reheat and cook in the microwave.

Help: What helps me most in my teaching is my drama background. Rather than just lecturing, I role-play, change my walk, my voice, and present a lesson in a more effective manner. I know how to use my voice to keep my kids tuned in, and I know when to stop. I really like kids and I really like interacting with them, so I spend a lot of class time just talking with them. They know they can come to me with anything and I will listen to them without judging them. If they give me information that needs to be given to a principal, I will protect their identity. Also the support I receive from our art coordinator and my colleagues makes me a stronger teacher.

Personal: The event that affected my teaching style (more than anything else) was my son. He was born 2 1/2 months early, and he fought so hard to live that we changed his name to Will. When he started school, he began showing signs of learning problems, although his IQ was very high and he was way beyond his classmates in verbal communication. His teacher said he was just a behavior problem and didn't change her attitude until we had him tested for special education. After that, we made many changes in how we worked with Will. We started giving him Ritalin and hired a tutor. Within two years he was a different student—one who could stay on task and learn. As a result, I am much more aware of students with any kind of disability. Too many teachers have no understanding at all of how students struggle to learn. I'm glad my district is training teachers in whole brain learning styles. Teachers need to consider all parts of the brain in planning lessons. This is why an art teacher creates interest and success in their classroom. When I present a lesson, I do it orally, write the steps as an outline, and demonstrate each step before the students start. I also do not set deadlines for work, except at the end of the semester. Kids are allowed to work in my room before and after school and/or at lunch. They may also check out materials and work at home. I have left a love of art and a joy for producing it in many people, and I will leave a school that is filled with student art work, not "bought" art.

Stories of Failure: I had a pair of twins who were probably two of the most gifted students I have ever taught. They could draw anything perfectly and created beautiful sculptures. But they were mean—and not just bully mean. They were sadistic and evil. One tried to rape a girl during a science movie. His brother tried to slash another boy's throat with a knife in the boy's bathroom. If a teacher hadn't heard the boy cry out and gone in there, he would have succeeded. (This was before we put in a "no knife" policy.) I tried to reach these boys through art: "You can be a professional. You have talent that I will never possess and you can be somebody." My words were met with cold, icy stares. One of them once tried to attack me, and I asked to have him removed from my classroom, but my principal said "No." They both failed my class along with their regular classes. They just didn't care about art or school. As a result, they were in our school for five years instead of three, and we finally sent them to high school because they were now 16. The next year they murdered a man and his son, dragged their bodies into a car and set it on fire. They are both in prison.

Another girl who had such promise just wanted to run with her gang and be with her man (at age 13). She too was an outstanding artist, but she refused to draw anything that didn't have gang signs in it. She even applied gang signs to her clay cylinder. I bought her some *Low Rider* magazines and showed her that her own work was far better than what was being published there. I told her I would submit her work to the magazine if she would stay in school. She has now been missing for weeks. I fear for her. Her friends think she is "tight." I try to talk to them about the dangers of street life, but they say she can take care of herself.

The saddest was a beautiful girl whose work reflected an amazing talent, but she drew pictures of bleeding wrists again and again. I shared her work with a school counselor, who brushed me off. People don't realize how much a student's art can tell you about that child. Several weeks later she slit her wrists, and then did it again three more times during that school year. She is now in an institution.

In my first year as a teacher, I had a young boy who would never look at me or talk to anyone. He said art was "boring." I tried to think of projects that might interest him, but finally I just gave up and let him sit there and fail. Over the winter break, he went into a closet and shot himself. Could I have helped him? I don't know, but I should have kept trying.

Stories of Success: Kids that I taught years ago still stop in to see me and talk. They tell me that what they learned in my class has stayed with them and helped them in their careers. One boy from my photography class told me that every time he looks through his camera lens for his TV station, he remembers me telling him to "Frame your shot." Parents have written me letters thanking me for enriching their child's life and telling me how much their children now know about art. One mother was amazed at how many styles of art her son knew when they went to MOMA. Then there are the many students whom I have helped cope with the problems in their daily lives. One former student called me from the University of Texas to ask me if I thought she should still be an art teacher. She came to spend the next day with me in her old classroom just observing. She now has her BFA in Art Ed. Last Saturday I received the following note from a student about to graduate from high school.

> Mrs. Greene, I wanted to include you in this moment, for you have known me for so long. I will be attending the University of Houston in the fall. They have a good art program and I'm looking at the possibility of majoring in interior design and minoring in photography. I just finished the 40 piece portfolio which you advised me on. Thank you for all your help, advice, and inspiration!

I also worked for over 20 years to convince my school board that a "real" art teacher was needed in every elementary school. In 1978, we were allowed four art teachers who would rotate through the 22 elementary schools to teach the classroom teachers how to teach art. To me, that was not acceptable, and it wasn't until our current art coordinator was hired that things started to change. We started with a few PTA's and convinced them to support the hiring of art teachers. This became a wake-up call and now we have district elementary teachers in EVERY school as of 1996.

Sudee Sanders: *I am committed to breaking the chain of condemnation caused by limited thinking.*

Teaching: In Cherry Hill, New Jersey, the definition of "good teaching" has changed. It now means helping students to meet national and state standards made more personal through developing local standards. In reference to the National Visual Arts Standards (and thus the state and local), they provide a framework to help students learn about art by using various means to express themselves and to evaluate the merits of their efforts. The Standards promote fluency in new ways of thinking, working, and communicating. They also develop habits of applying art knowledge to the world outside the classroom. They are structured to recognize a broad range of visual arts that can be used to accomplish specific educational objectives. Creation is at the heart of this instruction as students learn to coordinate their hands and minds and gain experience in making choices that help them to communicate their ideas. The arts education standards have the potential to make a difference because they address the fundamental issues of quality and accountability.

Students/Parents: For most of my thirty-four year teaching career, I have been process rather than product oriented and I have often been misunderstood. It used to be that honoring the creative process almost automatically yielded exciting products. Now, many students rush the process and refuse to value effort; instead, they want fast fixes of instant success without sustained work time. Their sloppiness satisfies them and the products they produce barely meet the minimum expected. They are engaged in the process but the results are not "pretty" because they are not produced with care; they are not produced with honest effort; they lack integrity due to the attitudes of the many young artists who are often in a hurry to move on to the next event. I know that it's OK to fail, but I'm not sure that they know when they have failed, and what's worse is that many of them don't seem to care.

Personal: My world is multicultural and I want my influence in it to reach beyond my own grass roots. I am committed to breaking the chain of condemnation caused by limited thinking. Biologically, I have no children, but professionally, I have thousands. As an art teacher for thirty four years, I have assembled a very large family filled with students of all colors. It is my best intention to show them that I have no prejudice as I praise their work or call on them for answers. As recent studies have shown, like other forms of prejudice, gender bias can be subtle and destructive. With understanding, respect rises above ritual, and prejudice becomes less prevalent.

Anita Winfrey: *People give lip service that art is important but many art teachers still teach from a cart or travel from school to school to meet students.*

Teaching: Who would have thought twenty years ago that teachers might have to wear bulletproof vests to school? That is a big change. Many organizations like the NAEA and the Getty Foundation have launched a big push to promote the cause of the visual arts, but at the grassroots level, folks get mad if for some reason they miss their break due to the art teacher's absence. On the national level, there is a push to require art for all students. On the local level, some schools barely issue grades in art. People give lip service that art is important but many art teachers still teach from a cart or travel from school to school to meet students. There is still little or no funding for art budgets and little respect from other teachers. I even had one student ask me if I went to school to be an art teacher. Thankfully, we now have multicultural education. We have moved from isolated celebrations of religious festivals around the world to more broad based multicultural studies.

Students/Parents: Parents now seem to see the importance of being directly involved in their child's education. I get more calls, more visits, and see more folks for conferences.

Hindrance: Sometimes race has been an obstacle. Sometimes being female has been too. Sometimes the way art education itself is perceived presents an obstacle. Most students enjoy art but when they don't get grades that count, their attitude is one of "art is play time." In the same vein, many students are "mainstreamed" into art because it is perceived as an easy subject to pass.

Help: Fellowshipping with other art teachers and seeing that everyone has similar problems and experiences helps a great deal.

Personal: Throughout it all, I have always kept a positive attitude. I have a constant willingness to change and grow, an openness to try something new. I have been in teaching long enough to have had some of my students' children. Those parents remember me and their children behave in my classroom, so I must have had some positive effect on them.

Stories of Failure: Kids that feel turned off about art are always a challenge; I have to realize that everyone is not going to love art.

Stories of Success: When I enter kids' work in art contests, they win! They feel special. Equally rewarding, I have a regular "Student Artist of the Month" whom I chose from different grade levels, and at the end of the year, I recognize them with a treat, such as a gift certificate for pizza and a more formal award.

Gerald Vilenski: *Distilling a child's education down to the results of a standardized test and restructuring entire curricula in order to teach to that test does a major disservice to both educators and students.*

Teaching: The teaching profession has definitely changed since I started my career, and in many ways not for the better. Political pressures to improve public education have done little to help education, but rather were put into place by misguided legislators as punitive measures, not to help educators do their jobs better. The issue of accountability has probably been the most profound change I have observed in education. Most educators have felt the pressure of trying to conform to uniform standards imposed by legislators and embraced by school boards. Distilling a child's education down to the results of a standardized test and restructuring entire curricula in order to teach to that test does a major disservice to both educators and students. The end result is that schools have changed literally for the sake of change. Apparently, those who are driving this movement believe that if students are tested enough, they will be better learners. I believe that a child's school experience is far more complex than any test can indicate. Children learn in such varied styles that testing alone cannot possibly reflect the entire learning process. Teachers, on the other hand, have been expected to deliver more and more, with less and less. Less time, less money, larger class sizes, fractured schedules, and poor leadership all have contributed to rising concern among educators. Academic reform is, in many cases, less good education than it is opportunistic politics.

Accountability reform is taking place at the expense of a varied and rich set of educational experiences, and because of the emphasis on core academics, once again, the arts have been placed on the back burner, relegating them to "enrichment activities" or in most cases, planning time for academic teachers.

Although accountability reforms may have effected some improvement in the hard sciences and mathematics, the accompanying standards and measurements are very often in direct conflict with the elements that make art education special. The free expression of ideas, individuality, and creative problem solving do not fall within the perimeters of standardized criteria. I firmly believe that teaching, no matter what the subject, is far more an "art" than it is a science, despite attempts by non educators and educators alike to make it so.

DBAE was an early attempt to rationalize art education by applying academic standards to the arts. While there is much to admire in the DBAE model, the practical considerations of personnel, budgets, facilities and scheduling that real life arts teachers face have made the implementation of the principles difficult at best. It is highly unlikely, for instance, that an elementary art teacher who teaches 600 students per week, pushes a cart from room to room, and has a budget of $500.00 per year will have an awful lot of time or energy to employ the elements of DBAE.

Students/Parents: I am observing many more students coming to school unprepared for the rigors of school life. Many students come from extremely dysfunctional family lives, and in many cases it makes the schools the only "normal" place they can go. I do not recall in my early days as a teacher encountering so many children from broken homes, abusive situations, being raised by grandparents or moving from school to school several times because of domestic situations. Many of these kids come to school not understanding basic social skills, frequently getting into trouble, having poor academic performance, bad nutrition, and lack of rest. All of this contributes to the feeling on the part of many teachers that they have, in effect, become the first line of defense for these students, and have added "social worker" to their job description. This adds yet another layer of complexity to the job of educating our children. It takes time and energy away from the many kids we teach who *do* come to us ready and eager to learn, with supportive parents and stable lives. It makes me wonder out loud why the perception among the public is that educators are not performing up to standard. How can we, when we have among our other duties, the job of curing societal problems within the restricted time we have with our students?

Parents of my students have gone through some significant changes over the years since I began teaching. Most noticeable, as I have already mentioned, is the increasing lack of responsibility for the actions of their children while they are in school. Parents are more reluctant to back up the schools when their children present discipline problems, and as a result, problems that once were more prominent in the secondary schools are showing up regularly in the elementary classrooms. Still, however, there are a good many parents who do participate in their child's education by volunteering in the schools, helping out at school events, raising money, and tutoring. The presence and support of these parents has become an essential factor in the success of both their own children and the school in general. This is something that did not exist in any common way when I first began teaching.

Hindrance: The greatest obstacles to my effectiveness as a teacher are lack of administrative support, poor facilities and schedules that are developmentally inappropriate for students. It is extremely difficult to convince others of the value of art education when decision- makers are not sensitive to the contribution art makes to the children we serve. The facilities I teach in are converted classrooms, without adequate storage, safety equipment or room for the students to work. Block scheduling simply serves classroom teachers and their planning time and presents an inherently inflexible system that does not serve the needs of children in the arts.

Pressure from the state to improve curriculum has resulted in hastily put together programs that look great on paper, but fail to address the realities faced in the classroom. Compounding all of this, the overall value of school districts is being distilled down to a single set of test results.

Help: Strangely enough, one of the greatest facilitators to my teaching effectiveness has been the availability of an art room. Inadequate as they may be, having an academic home is extremely liberating for the teaching of art. I find it incredible that as we turn the century, we still have hordes of art professionals pushing carts down hallways in order to provide their students with art experiences. There are many, many art activities that I would not be able to teach if it were not for the existence of an art room. I have turned down better paying teaching jobs with large budgets because they did not provide art rooms—it is that important to me.

Personal: I am a very different teacher now than I was at the beginning. Experience and expertise in the field are among the obvious reasons why, but there is more to it than that. I have made a concerted effort to grow professionally during the years I have taught. I believe that I have continually evolved as a teacher in relation to changes in society and education. An important element in my teaching style is modeling behaviors that illustrate my passion for art: I am a practicing professional artist. I show my work in galleries, belong to various arts associations, judge exhibits, present workshops for adult artists and serve on art-related boards. I believe that while these are strictly extra-curricular activities, it serves to represent art education and my school system in the region and has become an integral part of who I am as an art educator. I have never considered myself to be an "arts" and "crafts" teacher. Even though I teach at the primary level, I have always approached art as a serious, separate subject to study in its own right, not a frill, not planning time for others. I place far more emphasis on content in my lessons than before and maintain a higher standard of excellence for both my students and for me.

As I near retirement, among my most significant contributions is the legacy I will leave to future generations of art teachers. I have provided a stable department that is no longer subject to being cut during financial crises, a solid curriculum that is developmentally correct for students, a community that is beginning to recognize the value of the arts for cultural and financial contributions to citizens, and widespread parental and student support. Even though I have irritated decision-makers and administrators with my advocacy, I believe they begrudgingly accept that little would have changed without my leadership. Hopefully, I will have inspired others to lead when I have gone.

Stories of Failure: I have to count among my failures the inability to significantly change the attitude of many of my fellow teachers and administrators towards the arts. On a regular basis, I still find myself in the position of having to justify my program to decision-makers. It seems that every change of leadership brings a need to re-educate those leaders in the value of arts education.

Stories of Success: I believe that I have enjoyed significant successes as an art educator and advocate. Among them are the building of a first-class elementary visual arts program; attaining a complete K-12 visual art faculty; helping found a community arts council; instituting a county-wide summer arts school for middle-school students; producing two award-winning student animated films; and helping educate several student teachers.

Joan Newcomer: *Administration seems to be encouraging all teachers to challenge themselves to take an interdisciplinary approach to their teaching. This is an approach that art teachers like myself have taken since day one.*

Teaching: I have seen the philosophy of art education becoming more important in classrooms throughout the curriculum. DBAE has had an important impact. Studies and workshops by the Getty Institute have had a definite effect. Classroom teachers at the elementary level are including more art in their projects and developing imaginative thinking processes. Administration seems to be encouraging all teachers to challenge themselves to take an interdisciplinary approach to their teaching. This is an approach that art teachers like myself have taken since day one. I am seeing this happening more and more all the time. In addition, multicultural education has definitely had a big impact on teaching and learning.

Students/Parents: I would say there is more harmony among my students today than there was when I first began teaching. I remember having playground duty and having one student after another come up to me to complain about one another. This was the normal mode. Now it is more of a rare occurrence. Children are playing group games or sitting on swings together. They rarely need me. There also has been a major increase in the use of Ritalin.

I myself have more of a desire to get to know the parents. This is probably because I am a parent now. When I first began teaching, I don't think that I was as friendly towards the parents. Parents actually were more supportive of teachers back them. Today's parents are quicker to criticize teachers in the public schools. It doesn't take as much for them to speak their mind.

Hindrance: My last few years of teaching 5th grade met with particular obstacles to my teaching effectiveness. The students came to me once a week for 45 minutes. They were always late because they were coming from the other side of campus. I had to constantly re-teach lessons because a week was a long time to carry things over and there was never enough time. I had previously taught them for double periods (90 minutes), so I knew what the class could have been, which made it particularly frustrating. Administration is responsible for providing their faculty with enough time to teach their students effectively. I would have long talks with the administrators about this, but it was like talking to a wall.

Help: The workshops on Wednesday afternoons when I first began teaching art in the Baltimore City Public Schools were definitely one of the greatest facilitators which got me off on a strong footing. We had workshops on many different art activities, such as picture-making, stitchery and applique, papier-mâché, painting, puppets, discipline, and lots more. I learned so much about my field from these workshops, things that I never got in college.

I also need to give credit to a certain angel in my life who was and still is a facilitator to my teaching effectiveness. I met her when she was a fourth grade teacher; later she became a math specialist before she retired. She had a love for art and was always very supportive of my program. I had lots of fun building rain forests with her class and making tessellations. When she retired, she came back to school every Friday to be my assistant during my three newly acquired kindergarten classes. I was as nervous as a new mother having to take on five year olds. She was wonderful with them. She did this as a volunteer out of the kindness of her heart and to make a point that an assistant should be hired to help me in the art room. Our student body was growing and she could see more clearly than I did the demands of my job. With her help and that of our art department chair, we now have a paid part time assistant who helps me in the art room. There have also been parents who served as angels. One mother would come to my art room with her earphones, water bottle and apple and spend time getting all my artwork framed and labeled for exhibit.

Personal: I hope that I have instilled a love for art to the thousands of young faces who have been in the process of blooming as they passed back and forth through the art room door during their stay at my school. I hope that I have helped these students to develop a sense of self-confidence in their own abilities as creative thinkers and problem solvers. The joy of art adds meaning and passion to our lives. I hope that I have inspired my students to try their best, and not to forget to take on the responsibilities of clean up time. Life presents us with lots of clean up times too!

Stories of Failure: Teachers are always learning from their students too. I've had students that weren't happy working in the art room. One child in particular just did not have much aptitude in fine motor skills and I had lots of problems with him. He evidently felt he was trying and he also told me that he thought that I didn't like his work. I learned from him to be more careful about indicating that I think students are not putting forth their best effort. On the other hand, he was a great soccer goalie and he ended up on the same soccer team as my son. When I told him what a great job I thought he did out on the field, he thanked me and knew that the compliment was sincere.

Stories of Success: I know that some of my grown students have become artists or have gone into careers that involve art. I see the paintings of one of my former students in my doctor's office. He went off to New York to work on his art. I've run into mothers who tell me that they still have the artwork that their child did in elementary school. There is a sense of pride and accomplishment that a young child feels when they are able to hand make their own artwork. Somehow it is a way of preserving that short-lived part of their life known as childhood. I have adults come through our art exhibits who tell me that they like this artwork better than the work of adults. There is an energy, a beauty, a certain magic that can only be created by the hands of a child.

Martyna Bellessis: *It is a sad commentary on life in the United States when a six year old is dropped off at a before school program at 6:30 am, fed breakfast, then lunch, and finally picked up at an after school program at 6:30 PM.*

Teaching: My role in the classroom has most definitely changed. In the 1960s, I was into the Lowenfeldian theory where I was handing out supplies and constantly telling everyone how good their artwork was looking. As time passed and students kept begging for knowledge, asking questions about how to draw this or how to finish that, I knew they needed to be taught methods and while encouragement should be given, there has to be more substance in the teaching. When you say that every project is good, kids just don't believe you and your opinion is devalued.

Over the years, the greatest change and impact on me and my students is multicultural education. There are now 42 native languages in our local population. We have a wonderful time with this aspect of education. But

I'm afraid that in many schools this topic is covered by the making of Kachina dolls, which according to my Native American students is very insulting.

DBAE has been another effective cause for change. Educators respect money and when the Getty began its support for art education, many people took notice. If it's good enough for the Getty, it must be good for us. Yes, I have embraced DBAE in some aspects of my curriculum in grades 5 and 6. I think DBAE's curriculum reform is positive to a point, but we don't want to intellectualize ad nauseam. Kids like projects and products.

Students/Parents: Students today need someone to listen to them. When I sit down with them at the art tables, I really share in their lives. I want them to be active listeners too and I want them to be enjoying their art experience. Early in my career I never thought about the enjoyment factor.

Hindrance: Children do not see their parents enough. Time is of essence. Sometimes parents don't know how to say "no," and they think everything their child does is "cute." Teaching has changed because we are the ones who must teach listening skills, sharing, and respect for others. It is a sad commentary on life in the United States when a six year old is dropped off at a before school program at 6:30 am, fed breakfast, then lunch, and finally picked up at an after school program at 6:30 PM. Dinner is at a fast food restaurant and then on to some type of practice: soccer, ballet, baseball— depending on the season. This is the lifestyle of a high percentage of children. Parenting used to be a priority. Sadly, today it is not a very important factor. I wonder how other cultures are coping with these problems.

Also of significance, in my state, funding problems continue to be an issue vital to art education. Our state formula is outdated. Our art budgets are constantly being decreased. We have to depend on our Pots for extra funding.

The inclusion of special needs students into the regular classroom is the topic of a whole paper by itself. I'm sure the high school art teachers can tell you many stories of complex difficulties.

Help: Having school board members, whom I helped to elect, value art instruction and change conditions to facilitate education in the arts, has been a big help. The respect that my administrators and teachers have for my program helps a great deal too.

Personal: In October 2001, my faculty had a retirement dinner for me. Their show of admiration and their comments helped me to write a response concerning my contributions to the world of art teaching. My most significant contributions to teaching were having an enthusiasm for teaching elementary art that was "catching," for school board members (for whom I had campaigned), administrators, faculty, and staff. In seminars locally, statewide and nationally, I have worked to help others understand and share in the idea that elementary art is not comprised only of creative projects. It is at the same time an intellectual activity where knowledge should be constructed. Art is vital in the education of the whole child. My role in my profession has been to provide a positive, far-reaching force for elementary art education.

Stories of Failure: I can share two examples. Once I suggested to a third grader that her bird needed some texture such as feathers. Her mother, an assistant instructor at Indiana University, called and told me never to criticize her daughter's artwork again or I would lose my job. In another instance, an early childhood studies instructor at the same university told me that my elementary students needed to play more in art class. Her son was in the fourth grade at the time! Somewhere here, there was failure.

Stories of Success: This past year a sixth grade girl told a group of mothers that she wanted to be just like Dr. Bellessis, an elementary art teacher who gives people presents (sometimes I have raffles in my room). At our sixth grade graduation ceremony, two of the three speakers (one per sixth grade classroom) publicly thanked me for being their teacher and friend. They really meant a "mentor," but they are unaccustomed to using that word. Finally, there is the Korean mother who called and told me in her halting English that her fourth grade daughter's winning of a local art contest would go into the writing of their family history.

Nancy Zadra: *I have held my present job for ten years, and for nine of the ten my position has been threatened and "on the chopping block." Now I am in the habit of attending every school board meeting and sitting near the front because I want to provide a conscience to the board and their actions.*

Teaching: I see teachers as commanding less respect. Elementary teachers must work especially hard in this area. Most unfortunately, an overlying theme has been the increasing scarcity of funds and the threat to the arts. I have held my present job for ten years, and for nine of the ten my position has been threatened and "on the chopping block." Now I am in the habit of attending every school board meeting and sitting near the front because I want to provide a conscience to the board and their actions. When appropriate, I take the podium and speak. I select my words with care, stating it in terms of the children and their needs. I talk about the role of art in the life of a child.

In the past decade particularly, teaching has changed from a solitary activity to one in partnership with other adults. The classroom is more open and accessible. Mainstreaming marked a change: students and their assistants coming in and out of the classroom. In my district, the flow of adult helpers is constant. There are teaching assistants from the university, paid aides, volunteers, foster grandparents, and parent helpers, as well as the special ed. teachers and assistants. I personally have cultivated the use of parent helpers and make sure I always give the parents meaningful jobs in the art lesson. My use of parents is motivated by the need for adult help as well as by the opportunity to acquaint adults with the art program and thus build support. With all of the people coming and going, teaching becomes a public activity, and I find that I am constantly aware of the need to be sharp and professional in every aspect.

In art education in particular, there has been a change from a loose, disorganized study (exemplified by some of the high school art classes I took in the late fifties) to the development of a highly organized approach as seen in DBAE. Although I have not taken it as a "total package," I have incorporated DBAE into my existing curriculum. In my own experience as a teacher I believe that the more solid and substantial art study becomes, the better. This is a positive trend, helping to assure the continuance of art in the curriculum.

Students/Parents: At the elementary level I see kids coming in with fewer skills and less social sense. Kids have a tough time learning to monitor and guide their own behavior. It's as if not much has been expected at home, and not much attention paid to guiding the child. It seems to be that most parents work and have less time to spend with their children.

Hindrance: When class groups are oversized and physical space is tight, the program becomes altered in unfavorable ways. You cannot do the same lessons or use the same materials. Students remind me of those experiments with laboratory rats under crowded conditions, because their behavior changes as space becomes more crowded. Behavior deteriorates.

It has sometimes shocked me to discover the strange ways that art teachers are sometimes perceived. By some, art teachers may be viewed as less intelligent. At the same time, it is believed that they are able to accomplish more with less, thus being capable of miracles. There is always some magic about art, thus some distrust.

Help: Good friends, good role models, collegiality, and professional studies all have helped greatly. In my present job, I teach art to half the elementary school children in six buildings, and my colleague Janet teaches the other half in another six buildings. We started our current employment at the same time, both entering with prior teaching experience in a variety of places. Our partnership approach has been highly productive and personally rewarding. We share resources and originate and develop ideas together.

Personal: I now see myself as competent and masterful. I am organized, focused on my goals. Today I am truly in tune with the developmental level and interest of each particular group. In short, I know what I am doing and how to go about it. I continue to seek input and to learn, but I realize at the same time that others seek out my expertise.

Stories of Failure: Especially as I began my career, I really did not realize how much personal choice I had in selecting and organizing what I did. A teacher's awareness of these freedoms is important. In another light, there are always those students you simply did not reach. That brings a sense of regret.

Stories of Success: Along the way, I have had students who did not excel at other subjects but who found their niche and their place of excellence in the art classroom. It has come to my attention many times that often it is best not to know what your students *aren't* supposed to be able to do. I have extracted remarkable results when I did not know about their limitations.

Bonnie Keyser: *Many of the parents tell me they can't do anything with their kids. So what in the world are* we *supposed to do?*

Teaching: I personally feel that teaching in the public schools has not changed that much. Sadly, we still don't have enough funding or the proper equipment. We are still one of the few school systems in Virginia that does not have an elementary art program. In addition, students are having to meet more requirements, which does not give them much chance to take art as an elective. We were recently informed that students who do not pass the Virginia Standards of Learning must take remediation courses. There is no money in the school budget for teaching these new courses which will be classified as "electives." The students who require remediation will not be able to take art electives, so the art, music, and drafting teachers will be responsible for those courses.

Right now, we are on the block schedule where classes are 90 minutes. It is hard to believe that when I first started teaching, classes were only 45 minutes. We taught eight classes a day compared to the four we now teach. I definitely love the block, but most teachers are against it and constantly complain so I am not sure we will have it much longer.

Students/Parents: Today, you do have to be more careful of what you say to students, careful about touching them, etc. I am a hugging teacher. So far, it hasn't gotten me into trouble. In this day of lawsuits, it is quite scary. In my early years of teaching, students were more respectful of the teachers and administration. They also respected their parents more and the parents knew what their kids were doing. Today, many students are rude and disrespectful. The girls can be bold and brassy—they will release gas or burp around everyone in class and it does not bother them. Parents don't know what their kids are doing. Many times when I have called home for a discipline problem, I can hear kids in the background being rude to their parents. Many of the parents tell me they can't do anything with their kids. So what in the world are *we* supposed to do? Many also say that they never see their children because they come home and go straight to their room. Most of the mothers work. Students tell me that they sneak out all night after their parents have gone to bed, they drink and have wild parties, and they stay up all night on line and sleep in class.

Hindrance: Overcrowded classes are a big problem. I have one small room and they schedule 25 students in my Art I class. The discipline problems have increased because of this. School administrators are basically afraid of art teachers. It is a field that most of them are unfamiliar with and so they don't feel comfortable evaluating them. Likewise, they don't realize the funding necessary to equip an art room and how expensive art supplies are. I am always begging for money.

Help: Strong student and community support are among the greatest helps.

Personal: I feel that I haven't changed that much. I still try to find that creative vein in every student—stressing originality. I still feel young and fresh and excited about my job. I have developed art curriculum, worked on the Standards of Learning for Art in Virginia, increased enrollment in art programs, added course electives, built community awareness of art education, developed good rapport with most students, made new friends with faculty, staff, and administration. Most of all, I have given students a chance to express themselves and hopefully develop a personal awareness of the world around them. It is my hope that they will carry the appreciation for art and beauty with them throughout life.

Stories of Failure: Early in my teaching career, I had a wonderful student who was so talented and I was very excited about his possible art career. He was sent off to a school for wayward boys called Boys Home. He had had a lot of trouble with drugs while living in a larger city. He ran away and no one knew where he went. He was so intelligent and talented.

I met with disappointment when in my first year of teaching, I had a student who went to college to major in art—he soon changed to business. Likewise, four years ago, I had a student who would have received the art award, but decided to play in a soccer game instead of participating in a special all day art field trip. He graduated from Virginia Commonwealth University in May with a degree in graphic art and needless to say—I did not receive a graduation announcement. It was also upsetting this year when I had two Advanced Placement students who failed my class. I have to realize that I can't reach every student but I really tried with these. One was a Boys Home student who hated life but was very talented. In his senior year, he gave up. The other student had problems at home with his parents splitting up and leaving him alone. I did listen to their problems but could not get them to do their work. You can't win them all. I also feel bad when students don't take my advanced classes. I take it personally. Many say my class is too hard, that they took art for an easy credit so they will not take it again—of course, that could be a compliment too. I have also been in the same classroom for 30 years. I have been asking for a decent sink for 30 years.

Stories of Success: In one family, I have had two of the children in my art class. One went on to be an art major. One became an art teacher. That's exciting! This year, a parent of one of my students came to me and told me how much their child enjoyed art class and that it had been their favorite class too and the only one they remembered with pleasure. This year, my "outstanding art student of the year" joined a group of artists and is selling his work. Both he and his brother felt that art was one of the most important parts of their lives and are both majoring in art. Last year another of my students discovered art in his junior year of high school, could not stop painting and decided to dedicate his life to art. He painted on everything and it was dangerous to leave even a piece of cardboard lying around because it would become a painting. He now majors in art at Radford University and is winning lots of shows. I have created new courses, including photography, Advanced Placement, and Senior Art, designed for seniors who never had art before. I have increased community awareness of the arts and have built the popularity of the program allowing for the hire of another full time art teacher.

Candy Alexander: *Learning assessment is another issue of change. It may be a pain in the neck and it may be time consuming, but it's part of what* *you've got to do to prove your value. I'm glad to see it coming; I'm just anxious to see how it's going to be implemented.*

Teaching: Art teachers have always gotten a really mixed bag of students in their classes. You've got kids who like art and want to be there. You've got kids who don't like art; they have nowhere else to go so they were stuck in art. You've got kids who like the idea of art yet are too insecure to really try it, and you're spending the first contacts with them building up their courage and self-esteem to where they're willing to just try. You also have students who are wonderful artists, but in only one method or technique or media and will not leave it. You've got kids who intend to go on and have a career in art or have a hobby in art. One year I taught a middle school class that had 32 students. Eight of them were interested in art, 12 of them needed the credit and didn't mind being there, and the rest of them were pretty much from the football and basketball teams and didn't give a flip about where they were. Those things probably don't change that much for art teachers.

In the 70s and 80s, when I taught special ed. students, they were in self-contained classrooms. I had a class of cognitive impaired but educable children and a class of high ability special education students. I was able to gear the projects to what their ability levels and their interests were as a group. Now that most of these students are mainstreamed, I'm finding that I'm having to have two or maybe three lesson plans for a given class. This past year, my fifth grade included a child with severe multiple handicaps, a Downs syndrome student, and two special needs children who were rather high functioning students—all in a general classroom. The multi-handicapped child has parents who wanted him to do what everyone else was doing. That goes against my philosophy. I would far rather have projects that are congruent with his interests and ability levels—he could learn more from that. To give the parents what they wanted, the teaching assistant who was with him full time ended up doing the projects for him . . . and he didn't get a thing out of it other than to have some crayons and drawing pens in his hands. Because he was an IEP (Individual Education Plan) child with a parental mandate, I had to bite my tongue and go on with it. Currently, we have several autistic, CDC and other special needs children at my school—a small school of 360 students in a small town. I learned today that the updated IEP on one of our autistic kindergartners now calls for no pencils, crayons, paper, or scissors for him since he is adverse to using any of them. We are to teach him without these materials. I am used to modifying lessons and creating parallel activities, but....

Learning assessment is another issue of change. It may be a pain in the neck and it may be time consuming, but it's part of what you've got to do to prove your value. I'm glad to see it coming; I'm just anxious to see how it's going to be implemented.

Students/Parents: Kids' attitudes have generally changed. Discipline problems have changed and are more persistent. There is not nearly the parental support now. A letter or call home now pretty much nets you a "So what?" Sometimes a trip to the office nets a "So what?"

Hindrance: Back in the 70s, the budget was a problem and it still is, especially in teaching multicultural art and other types of art appreciation. Prints are expensive. Time and space have also been problems. Projects like papier-mâché or frescoes or ceramics are multi-lesson projects, so you have to balance the worth of the project with the time, space, and facilities they consume.

This year, I have met with several big changes. Both of my schools have new principals, I have a new music teacher to share a room with at my main school, and now share my art teaching duties at the smaller school. If I were any more flexible, I'd be a rubber band! Seriously, I don't think there is a group who is expected to be more flexible and adaptable than art teachers. Few classroom teachers could endure the constant uncertainty of where and how we will teach year to year. Music teachers are a close second, but they don't have to juggle the same kinds of supplies/materials issues that we struggle with. If it didn't feel so great when the lesson goals actually match the results, I'd be a graphic artist somewhere!

Help: In classroom management, the greatest facilitator has to be experience. When I came out of college, sure I had lots of philosophies and lots of ideas and a general knowledge of how things ought to operate. But nothing replaces experience in dealing effectively with kids. Nothing replaces experience in controlling your initial reactions in situations where the problem focuses on a student's argumentative, malicious, or destructive intent and things need to be diffused or sidetracked.

Other facilitators are having the time and the space and materials to do the lesson the way you really want to do it. I've also come to appreciate and rely on collaboration, things like NAEA conferences, or even at the local and state levels, having meetings with other art teachers and exchanging lesson plans, or discussing the handling of various problems or challenges. Having the resources of other people to draw from and lean on is one of the greatest facilitators to art-teaching effectiveness. Problematically, unlike regular classroom teachers, it's harder to find time for art teachers to get together. Art teachers, especially at the elementary and middle levels, are usually one per school and very few school systems bother to get them together for in-service meetings; you really have to go out of your way to find a way to collaborate with art colleagues.

Personal: I'm not a big earth-changing kind of teacher. Though the content of what I teach has changed, my style has not. I haven't made any major waves anywhere. My best contributions have been in imparting enthusiasm and opening the minds of children and teachers as well. I like being a resource to other teachers and showing them the relatedness of the arts.

Stories of Failure: The failures come with the challenge of being a teacher. Art has national curriculum guidelines as well as state guidelines for Tennessee, though they are not in depth. My goal with the system I am in now is that at the end of this current year, all of the students will be on grade level for the curriculum guidelines and the frameworks. The problem is that it is hard to find the time to check the students and see where they are, how much they have actually retained, what is their current level, and where I need to go from there. I can tell as a class when a lesson has flown or not and which students are consistently behind or don't get it, but one of the things I have failed to do is to find a way to get a block of time to do skill checks on the kids and to see if they are achieving the curriculum goals. When you have students only 45-50 minutes a week, you have few options.

Stories of Success: Some of the success stories come in small moments and in individual cases—things like the year I was at the elementary school on the sea islands off South Carolina and we had zero for a budget. We had our children make artwork and crafts and sold them for enough money to fund a second semester's worth of projects and activities. That was success! And there are things like the high school junior who was marvelous in art but really not interested in finishing her high school career. She was one of those small town girls who was "scared to leave the mountain" and had never taken a chance to have her work displayed. I submitted two of her works to a state-wide art contest and hers was one of the pieces chosen for display at one of the colleges outside of Nashville. She got permission from her grandmother whom she lived with to attend a reception honoring the artists. We took her to that show and watched her horizons grow. It wasn't just that her piece was on display, which she was proud of, but also to have her see the other artwork that was there and to talk to the people who had come to recruit the art students to their colleges. It was just a wonderful experience watching her at that reception that day!

I have blind students. And I have modified lessons to make them more tactile or to get them in other ways to adapt to the limitations and the abilities of the blind students. Even their coordinator has come and sat in on some of these lessons to see how we're doing this for those students. She is taking my ideas to other schools who teach blind students as well. That was a challenge to me at first—the idea that at both of my schools I would be teaching a blind child art. Now my ideas come quickly and the students are enjoying their experiences. So success stories I think are in meeting the challenges, of having something be relevant and personal to the students, in tapping some of their talents and desires and in having them leave you a little more enriched than they were when they came to you.

Marie Shack: *Through my advanced degrees, I have more of an academic awareness, but the bulk of my intuitions were formed early in my career.*

Teaching: I was teaching in Woburn when they passed Chapter 766, making it easier for special needs students to be part of the regular classroom. Luckily I was in the mist of my Masters and did a research paper on this topic since I had a Down's syndrome girl in my class. Through that early experience and research I came to the conclusion that these students want to be treated like everybody else. Inclusion is a hallmark reform that we need to be constantly prepared for.

In Massachusetts, the Ed Reform Bill has given the Commonwealth's legislature much more say in the everyday running of the classroom. Our certifications are no longer for life, we are required to have a certain number of Professional Development Points, and teachers are most often blamed for poor testing results. This bill also stated that the principals can no longer be represented by a union; their jobs are at the mercy of the superintendent. This truly impacts how they run their schools and deal with their teachers.

Concerning my own discipline, I have to give credit where credit is due and the Getty Foundation has backed art with materials, ideas and has lent credibility to the visual arts. In the beginning they were definitely ignoring the importance of play and working with materials in favor of more rigid academic issues, but they have evolved and grown and I think listened to art educators. I had always used art history as a base in my teaching, so their approach was nothing new to me. I have always given notes, written tests, believed that students need to have a foundation and need to know (although not necessarily *like*) the way different artists think and how they are influenced by who they are and where and when they live. So DBAE was not a shock for me. It was just a warning that we art teachers are going to be held accountable for students learning content and being able to put it to use in their creative products.

Students/Parents: I find the kids today take less upon themselves and expect more of me. At the smaller high school I would take the slides for their senior portfolios. Often they would come to my house and stay with me when I did it, helping me. I always received a little gift from them. Nowadays, I find that the kids just expect me to do this, often dropping off the work so that I can do it during my free period. The factors that I think have led to this sense of privilege are the fact that we tend to spoil our children. We protect them and coddle them. I do not find the students as accountable for their actions as I did when I first taught. I admire those kids that say to me that they will be going to a state university because that is what their parents can afford, or those kids who are working two or three jobs during the summer so that they can afford to go to college at all. On the whole, I see kids willing to do less and expecting more... higher grades, praise for what we would consider a mediocre job, acceptance of lateness or missed assignments with no expectations of recriminations.

After September 11th, the world of our students is very different and I do not envy their role of bringing children into the world and raising children in the future. I think it will be harder for them. I look at my own children, along with many of my students...they are a privileged group and I fear it will be harder for them to overcome adversity.

But on the whole, adolescents still amaze me with their zest, ideas and passion for what is important to them. And after all these years, they still make me laugh and luckily, I can still pull a few chuckles out of them.

Parents are more educated. They appreciate the effort we put into helping their children prepare for college; they seek our advice and respect us as professionals. On the other hand, sometimes they are also less grateful for our time, effort, and commitment. Sometimes they see the extra things we do as just part of the job and to be expected . . . but we do it for the children, not for the parents. Sadly, I find parents more willing to make excuses for their children, rather than to back up a teacher's concern. In the long run, the child loses and often when they get to college and face a harsher reality some of them are not able to cope.

Hindrance: On the whole, it is usually not the students who disappoint you. You are there for them, to teach and guide them; they are searching for answers about themselves and their world. When they are ungrateful, when they are less passionate about their work, when social- life concerns dictate actions more than academics, when they resist opening their eyes to modern or abstract art, for example, I can accept this. I keep on going, keep on trying to edge them towards maturity and aesthetic fulfillment. The disappointment is cushioned in the fact that they are young and someday they just might remember what you were trying to get across.

It is the administrators who thwart when they forget that we are there for the students. We are not there to advance careers or make our bosses happy or come away with prizes…we are in school to teach and guide our students through their childhood and young adulthood.

And it is the parents who have ideas that do not take into consideration their child's strengths and weaknesses but only their own images of what is right and wrong for the child. It is the parents who think that if you feed their child a magic pill, a teacher can make everything right. It is the parents who forfeit their own responsibility but expect the world from their child, teachers, and school.

Help: If you have administrators who respect you, value you, show concern for you and the students and their school, then the way is clear to pursue extra projects; you're willing to volunteer that extra time, work for longer hours. The same with parents. If they respect and appreciate what you are doing for their child, you are confident that you can expect more from the child…and this always involves more instructional energy and commitment on your part. Help also comes from the students who are in awe of what they learn. Whether in elementary, middle or high school, they spur you to teach more because their delight is so infectious and fulfilling.

Personal: Through my advanced degrees, I have more of an academic awareness, but the bulk of my intuitions were formed early in my career. I love art history so it was always important and I realized that the student's artwork was the result of a journey and a process, so critical thinking was always important. But it always has and still comes down to trying to help students live more human and enriching lives, become good citizens and good people. When I see a bird flying, I think of Matisse's paper cutouts. I want to give students experiences to enhance their living. I try to get them to see that sometimes it's those little joys that keep us going through large troubles and times of stress. This philosophy has never really changed through teaching different levels, in different towns, public or parochial schools, and through three decades of various art education movements. What is important in the end is the realization that students in my classroom are really learning new ideas, skills, and passions. It is reaching out to fellow faculty members, being a comrade. It is maintaining my vision of the student as my primary focus. It is supporting our program through research, community involvement, and close relationships with parents. Most importantly, I hope that the students who have passed through my classroom will lead richer, fuller, more human lives having been touched by my presence.

Stories of Failure: Tim Navage was a very talented artist, and a very sensitive one. His art teacher let him take independent art classes beginning with his freshman year. By the time I had him as a senior, he resisted any kind of direction, and he wasn't used to dealing with the dynamics of an art class. Instead of bringing him along slowly, giving him more praise and leaving him be with his way of working, I was too forceful. He didn't appreciate me, my humor, my remarks, my pressuring him to be more a part of the class. I think if I had been more patient and given him more latitude, we might have had a better year.

Stories of Success: Tony Marko is starting as an art major at a local college this September. I have taught him for four years. He is talented but always feels inferior to some of the "stars" in his classes. He is quiet and often his artwork needs to go an extra step. In his last year in high school I introduced charcoal drawing to the portfolio class and Tony found his calling. He loved the medium, did atmospheric and expressive work with it. I also have one computer with PhotoShop on it and gave Tony the option of doing a project with this rather than a ceramics piece. He chose the computer and found another medium with which he is comfortable and in which he excels. These simple lessons, coupled with a sense of independence and choice, gave him confidence in his ability. He got together his portfolio, visited colleges, applied and was accepted into Montseurrat College.

Tony's mother is an artist. She never came into the classroom flaunting this fact. She always was very interested in the lessons, the artists taught, and the visual diary assignments. She had no illusions about Tony, who could be lazy and distracted, so she tried to work at home with him too. She helped him choose a school that was right for him, helped him apply and is providing support for his study in art school. [Some parents won't pay for art school.] She understood and guided who he is, not her ideal vision of him. She also allowed me to help him from where he was at the moment; so together, we helped this boy. I consider Tony Marko one of my success stories.

Jeannie Siegler: *Bringing me full circle from my early teaching days in Sierra Leone, one of the high points in my teaching career occurred in May, 1998. My proposal to begin "Landscapes," a cross-cultural, cross-curriculum electronic exchange between classes in Ghana, West Africa, and classes in western Montana was accepted and put into place.*

Teaching: Now I have taught long enough to see a scope and sequence of not only methodology but also of students as a reflection of the changes in their families and society. One of the most important things I've seen is the change in importance of art in our lives and in the lives of our children. From an expression of a young person's growth and development, art has become an avenue for expression and self-growth for all ages in society. In keeping with this, in my early years, teaching art in the public schools was seen as both crafts and fine arts. It seems that the discipline of art has now moved more into the fine arts area. Here in Montana in the last 10 years, study in fine arts is now required for all high school students for graduation. This is a step in the right direction for our discipline.

On a more specific level, DBAE has given some teeth to the teaching of art. It incorporates the aesthetics, history, criticism, and production of art. It has really helped to give credibility to art programs.

Students/Parents: Working in K-12 classes over the years has allowed me to see changes, particularly in the younger students. As adults, we need to reclaim the childhood years so that children are experiencing and participating in growth and development rather than being entertained. It is experience that gives children ideas. More and more young people, boys and girls, seem to be pushed into adulthood way before they are ready.

There are still concerned and engaged parents, but I think for whatever the variety of reasons, many have not been. Maybe we need some courses on parenting before we have children, because it's a longer haul than many realize.

Hindrance: One of the greatest obstacles to teaching art, especially in the early years was attitude. "Why art? It's frivolous, it's an extra," was a frequent criticism, particularly here in Montana where resources were scarce and funds limited. Instead of looking at art as an important process in the growth and development of children, it was viewed as something classroom teachers could do with pre-designed assignments on Friday afternoons. In many districts, but not all yet, art is increasingly viewed as essential to the growth of our children.

Throughout the years in our mostly rural area, the voting on local bond issues and on the election of school board members who set local policy has seen ups and downs. If our children are short-changed when they are young, the consequences are devastating when they are older. I still feel very strongly that if we pour in resources when children are young and work with a small teacher-student ratio, the results can be outstanding.

Fewer children are lost in the cracks on both sides of the curve and the general population moves positively toward being productive citizens.

Help: The contact with my peers through course work at the University of Montana has been one of the greatest facilitators to my teaching. The interaction and exchange of ideas and new techniques is always stimulating and refreshing. I am presently participating in the second stage of a teacher exchange through UM and will be traveling to Hungary this summer.

Personal: My teaching philosophy is still inclusive rather than exclusive and I seek to find the value and worth of each student as an individual. Presently my classes are no larger than 18, which has allowed for more individual contact than in years past. My budget continues to be very limited, but I still try to emphasize the importance of ideas rather than merely the availability of materials.

Bringing me full circle from my early teaching days in Sierra Leone, one of the high points in my teaching career occurred in May, 1998. My proposal to begin "Landscapes," a cross-cultural, cross-curriculum electronic exchange between classes in Ghana, West Africa, and classes in western Montana was accepted and put into place. I presented the proposal at a distance learning conference in Accra, Ghana. Through an extension of our school's web site, inter-classroom electronic exchanges have occurred over the past year. Most important, the exchanges are helping to break down barriers of stereotype and misconception on both sides of the hemisphere. In looking at the big picture, I feel that the most significant contribution in my teaching has hopefully been to instill the importance of a lifetime of learning.

Stories of Failure: One of my biggest failures has been to lose students before they've given themselves the opportunity to try.

Stories of Success: I think one of my biggest success stories centers around the "I can't draw, therefore I can't do art" syndrome. Learning skills, techniques, and acquiring the confidence to try often opens a student to a variety of possibilities they never thought they could do.

Kathleen Thompson: *I'm not real conservative, I'm not real liberal. I like the middle of the road and there isn't much time that pendulum spends on the middle of the road. It's swinging toward tradition or it's swinging toward reform, and we seem to get a little too far to either side for me most of the time.*

Teaching: I'm not real conservative, I'm not real liberal. I like the middle of the road and there isn't much time that pendulum spends on the middle of the road. It's swinging toward tradition or it's swinging toward reform, and we seem to get a little too far to either side for me most of the time. When I began teaching, the open classroom was everything. It was just the other extreme from today. The academic requirements for high school graduation went way down. Ten years after that movement died totally, I was at this high school and I was doing the yearbook. I was teaching both middle school and high school and there was a scheduling glitch where I actually had a two-hour planning period in the middle of the day. Because I was doing the yearbook, I would walk around the building with my camera. And it was appalling. You would sit in classrooms that were separated by moveable room dividers. This was a physical outcome of the open class-room that could not be corrected for more than 15-20 years because of funding. I remember feeling sorry for the English teacher who could hear the two classrooms on either side of her. As far as change goes, that was the extreme: "Let's try new things and let's be very open and not have so much structure." And that was the swing of the pendulum to the far left, to the more liberal side. And it was absurd. On the other hand, I find much that is oppressive in education today.

About eight years ago, our school was involved in the Association for Supervision and Curriculum Developments' Consortium on Interdisciplinary Teaching and Learning and we were one of 13 schools from all over the US and Canada to participate. We were just into this, another new reform movement. We started this whole thing with "constructivist learning." I got books on it because I was having a hard time putting a handle on it, but I thought, I've been in education 26 years and I've heard this stuff before. I said to my assistant principal, "I still can't get a handle on constructivist learning." And she, being a very down to earth practical person, said, "Oh, it's the open classroom with computers. They couldn't do it before—remember all those individualized learning packages and all those sheets, those ditto sheets? And the teachers went crazy trying to keep up with it all? Well, now you can do it because of the computer."

I would say that there are three major movements during my time that have been important as educational reforms. One is interdisciplinarity, which I've been very involved in within my school system. Another is Discipline-Based Art Education. The third is multiculturalism and I would have to say that all of those have changed my classroom in major ways. I no longer feel guilty about the fact that I am a person who crosses disciplines, who enjoys more than one discipline. I'm now fashionable. I've added multicultural materials for years, had a tremendous selection of things that I do in the multicultural area. Of course, I added aesthetics, changed my approach to art history and added art criticism. I see a lot of change in middle and elementary schools. I see more emphasis on creative thinking, more emphasis on using art and music to teach in the regular classroom.

In the last decade, there is the middle school movement, which has been a fairly successful movement, but is now waning because teachers are tired of it. They want to change.

Students/Parents: In the 60s and 70s sometimes kids came back from lunch stoned. And we weren't very sophisticated at drug management. Today those kids would be picked up by the police, taken and tested. But we weren't prepared for that. It came as an unexpected thing in education. The 80s and 90s were much more conservative. I remember a kid…we were going through my cabinets, boxing up materials, and we came across all these brochures from the dye company on how to tie-dye. And Anthony pulled them out (he was real preppy and rich) and said, "People actually wore these! Why, that's unreal!" And of course, that's come back as fashion. In general, I don't think kids have changed since I started teaching. Some of their attributes have changed, but I find kids, whether they are elementary, middle, or high school, are very similar today.

I do, however, see an immense difference in violence and this is particularly poignant in light of what has happened in schools around the country. Kids are more violent, more accepting of violence, even those who have no violence within them have a tolerance for violence I don't have. There have always been kids at my schools that were disturbed enough that they could shoot someone. But it never happened. It never happened at other schools. I don't have an explanation as to why they can shoot now; they were just as disturbed years ago and they didn't. I find I am fearful. I had a former student that got involved in a drug thing and he hated art and hated me. I had these visions of him showing up with a gun.

For parents today, self esteem has become a mantra, the most cherished thing of all. Self-esteem has eclipsed responsibility. It is a sacred cow.

Hindrance: Administrators who limit what I can do for the children can present a major obstacle.

Help: The last eleven years I've had two marvelous, supportive principals and they've made a difference. Before that, I've never had that kind of support. They've made a difference. In addition, the Georgia Art Education Association has been a tremendous influence on me and a tremendous help.

Graduate school improved my teaching 100%. I took a great deal of art history, studio, aesthetics, and criticism. I was not allowed to take a single education course and was happy as a clam. And it did more for my teaching than anything in my entire graduate education. I swear my master's degree was a waste with its emphasis on education courses.

Personal: I'm far more confident. I'm probably the most enthusiastic I've ever been. I'm at the point where *how* and *what* to teach is not an issue. I've conquered DBAE. I'm very confident in art criticism, aesthetics, things like that. So at this point, the struggle is over. I now see myself as a manager, as an organizer. I also have more materials to organize than I've ever had. You can tell an experienced teacher by going into their resource closet. And I find discipline not to be an issue. My relationships with my students are still good. I have very close relations with kids that I really care about and that really care about art. That kind of relationship began about five or six years into my teaching. On an emotional level, I am much more realistic about how much change I can make in kids' lives. I used to think I could take them out of poverty…and yes, there are those kids that you can make a difference in their lives, but by and large, you're not going to change lives as dramatically as you thought you could. As you get older, you come to accept that what you have to give kids isn't always a life-changing experience. It may be something very small, and that's enough. I'd like to be a magician and wave a wand over them. And art happens to be my wand.

Stories of Failure: There was one child, Wilma, that I worked with in the 6th and 7th grades. Wilma's mother was mentally ill. There were six children. They lived in a horrible trailer in a very rural area. Wilma was one tough cookie. She would beat you up at the drop of a hat. She was just a real little mountain girl. She did absolutely stunning, beautiful art. When she was in the 7th grade, one of her teachers said to me, "Wilma's only hope in life is art and you." And I knew right then we were in trouble because I couldn't overcome those years of bad parenting. I've tried over the years. I can't overcome those kinds of situations. I encouraged her because she had real art abilities—she and her sister both. I took her work to the state level, an art exhibit at the Capitol in Atlanta. She was very pleased; she got her picture in the paper. I took her with me and my daughter to the High Museum during the Olympics. I took Wilma and her sister shopping one Christmas. [Her sister is 19 now and has three kids and is a single parent.] Wilma dropped out of school (may someday get her GED), got pregnant, and is working as a waitress. I wanted to lift those kids who were in foster care and were in horrible abusive homes into my middle-class world. And it didn't happen. And years ago, I would have been crushed, but I know that's the reality.

Stories of Success: I received a letter from Wilma this year, sent to me through another student. Let Wilma's letter speak for itself.

> Hey! How are you doing? I'm okay, but not as good as I could or should be doing. I moved back to Ellijay a couple of weeks ago. Angel told me that she is in your class. I told her to ask you if you remember me, and to tell you "hey." One of my purposes of writing you this letter is to let you know that I really appreciate the kindness you showed to Felicia and I. I remember the time you took us to the mall around Christmas-time, and let us pick out something we wanted. I appreciated it then, but now that I'm older, and look back, I appreciate it *even more*. You were aware of the kind of life we were having in foster care, and all that, and it was very generous of you to do the things you did for us. You complimented me on my artwork, which made me feel good about myself, and raised my spirits. You were, and what I hear from Angel, still are a great teacher, and a friend. You really did put a positive impact on the way I felt about myself. Thank you so much, Dr. Thompson, for everything!
> Sincerely Wilma

Ken Wilkie: *Sometimes you're focusing on the whole class, and you get caught up with the kids that are more demanding. Sometimes people slip through your fingers. And I'm sorry I missed them.*

Teaching: The last 15 years, the standards and the testing have pushed us toward making art appear to be more like an academic discipline to protect ourselves from being cut in funding and in the scheduling of classes. And I don't think this has necessarily been good. I think in some ways it's made us look a little more closely at what we do, to focus our teaching and learning outcomes, but I'm not sure we've done all that for all the right reasons. And I'm concerned about DBAE, which has bothered me for some time. There's certainly lots of good stuff in that, but I think it's been so omnipotent, with its funding and promotional avenues, that it has come to dominate the field. I think that's probably unhealthy. Certainly we need to take things from that instructional approach but not adopt it wholeheartedly.

Students/Parents: In some ways, changes in my students have less to do with time than with location. I went first from teaching poor, working class minority students, second, to a homogeneous middle class district, and third to Princeton, which is very diversified. In comparing the poor, middle, and wealthiest children, poor and wealthier kids are more expressive. They tell you what they want more quickly. They are less intimidated by teachers. They're more likely to speak up and say what they think and what they want. And it's interesting—I see that at the lower end of the socioeconomic scale and at the upper for different reasons. The middle group is much more conformist. That may say something.

Though it varies with location too, kids are more sophisticated in some ways than they were 25 years ago, just because of their media exposure. Some of the elementary kids I had 25 years ago were city kids so they were exposed to a lot. There are other kids the same age now who are much better protected and insulated, even with the Internet and cable television. So I think it has less to do with time than location and other personal circumstances. I've changed districts twice now. I'm working within a district with more resources, so that what I do now is very different from what I did in the first districts where I taught. I've got more latitude. The kids are more resourceful. I have fewer problems in discipline and fewer kids with learning problems.

My perceptions of parents are also influenced by location, economics, and my own age. When I was 21, in this poorer district, I had fifth graders who were 10 or 11 years old; their parents were somewhere in their 30s. So I was rather intimidated by parents because they were older and knew a lot more than I did. And, you know, there was some prejudice. I was sort of like a "hippie" in the eyes of some because I had longer hair and didn't wear a tie to school back then. Ties were still conventional. Teachers are allowed to grow facial hair? Amazing! That was 1973. Parents then weren't sure what to do with me. When I moved to Princeton in 1986, I was 35 years old, close to the age of the parents, and I finally felt comfortable talking with them. Now, 13 years later, I'm starting to be referred to as "Mr. Wilkie" by parents because some of them are ten years younger than I and I think I'm just going to have to get used to it. I'm now on the other end of the generation gap and once again, we seem to have less in common when we talk.

Hindrance: One of the greatest obstacles in my teaching has been struggling with management. Classroom management [not discipline]. There are so many things I want to do, I think would be good for kids to do, but they are things that require them to be more independent than they're used to being, or that require me to take more time to organize things to make it easier for them to do. I just think of some of those very first lessons, the first month of school in 73, you know—not being able to get the kids to clean up because we didn't have any clean-up procedures. I didn't know how to make them understand that it was time to stop and clean up. I hadn't figured out that clean-up meant picking helpers and then insisting that everybody at each table pick up under and around this table and so on. The problem with time management still lingers. You only have this one 50-minute period, once a week, and the structure of the lesson each week isn't exactly the same. It's different materials, techniques, processes, and this requires different behaviors. And you know, it's not like you can take the time to really make it clear what they can do, when they can do it. You just kind of plunge into it and kind of pull them in from the outside edges. So I find managing—setting up procedures and expectations and structuring it all within the constraints of a classroom difficult.

Help: What helps me to be more effective is my own organization ahead of time….dealing with the problems I have just talked about under "hindrances." It's having some kind of system in place so that everybody can have expectations and an understanding of what my expectations are of them. It's also my own enthusiasm. Their enthusiasm. Connections to things they already like, or know about, or are working on in their regular classrooms. It's all about making those connections between what they're doing and who they are or what their life is all about.

Personal: Those first couple of classes that I had when I first started teaching—those were so exciting. It's just so exciting; it's so new. I feel I could tell you tons of things about those first groups of kids I had back in 73 and 74. And then, of this group now, I'm nowhere near the attachment, and you can't get as attached because they keep coming and going, coming and going, and where I am now, there's a high turnover. Only half of the fifth graders are kids that start out with me in kindergarten. And so it's hard …actually I have to make an effort to focus in and spend some time talking to kids about things they like, about their families and things like that, to get to know them better because I get so caught up with what I'm trying to do with them in class that maybe the *kids* get lost. And I really need to take time while they're painting or drawing, not to take that time to wash out some cups or put things away, get things out for the next class. I get the feeling now that I have to make every second count. Sometimes I have to keep myself from being overly structured. You know—these are kids. They can only jump through so many hoops so often. And so, sometimes I have to back off and loosen up. I need to go and sit and say, "So what year is your brother in high school?" or "Tell me about the trip you took." And just try to make some connections. And I think that's what I'm missing now and I think I just really need to push myself in that direction.

Stories of Failure: I think it's the kids that I just missed the opportunity with. I didn't take the extra time. I grew impatient, or I allowed myself to be pulled over to the kids that were easier to work with. I'm thinking of one boy in particular who kept asking for help and I gave him help here and there. But it was never enough, and I realize now what I should have done is carved out time at lunch or some other place where he and I could have worked one on one. I could have had a much more satisfactory relationship with him. I think there's been a number of kids over the years who have just slipped through my fingers that way. Sometimes you're focusing on the whole class, and you get caught up with the kids that are more demanding. Sometimes people slip through your fingers. And I'm sorry I missed them.

Stories of Success: I created the idea of an art lab and have been providing this experience for teachers and their students for more than 10 years. It's a great opportunity to integrate art with other subject matter. Classroom teachers who want to integrate science or social studies with art bring their students to art class and we co-teach a lesson. I teach the art and they support the language arts, science, whatever. I think this has been a great success. Teachers have appreciated it and administration and parents as well.

Another innovation I am very proud of is the arts festival every year. This wasn't my idea; it came from the parents talking about "Let's do an art day where we get artists coming into the schools and working with the kids in the artist's own medium." It's like the artists in residence, but it's informal, kind of a little shot—it's a cheap way to do it in other words. Instead of coming up with thousands of dollars in order to pay people to come in, we take advantage of our university community and the artists here. We take a night and display all the student artwork. We also display artwork by artists who are coming to work with our kids. This gives the artists a new audience, even allowing them to sell some of their work, although we don't make a big deal out of that. So this has been very good for me and for the kids because the artists in the community come into our school, and in some cases, it's the only connection these artists have with the schools. This is something I am very proud of, something I see as a success.

Carol Wellein: *My whole art curriculum has become more global.*

Teaching: Teachers today are faced with a variety of problems we never imagined in the 60s. A more uncivil society, drugs, AIDS, school violence, and the breakup of families are just a few of the problems that plague society and make teaching more of a challenge. Art teachers have been placed in the difficult role of teaching multiple students with complex special needs, working with limited supplies, accommodating a growing number of ethnic groups, receiving little support from administrators, and having to deal with unusual scheduling problems.

Multicultural, multiethnic, multidisciplinary learning, cooperative learning, and DBAE have all come about after my college education and I have had to teach myself by reading, attending workshops, and logging on to various web sites like the Getty Institute and ordering their curriculum. I wanted my small rural school students to have all the advantages of a large one, so I ordered curriculums from various school districts. I have bought books containing an interactive, multilevel approach to art education. I was hooked. It opened up a whole new world to me as an art educator. What a difference from teaching the holidays, my vacation, and line, shape, color, and texture!

Now I am teaching much more about history, cultural context, and aesthetics than I ever did before. My teaching style is less teacher-oriented and more cooperative based. I am integrating with math, science, and social studies. My whole art curriculum has become more global. I include more contemporary issues such as saving the environment and endangered animals, the rainforest, and focus on appreciation of modern architecture. Now I have access to a computer, the computer lab, slides, posters, videos, CD and laser discs, art magazines for students, and numerous art books. Though my philosophy has not changed, my instructional approach is probably more flamboyant. We have to compete with the technology of today.

Students/Parents: Students today are more intelligent, more active, more disruptive, more creative, less-disciplined, less responsible, find excuses for everything, more well-traveled, more stressed, less polite, more knowledgeable about sex, less afraid, more social, more divergent thinkers, and more well-rounded. I have to be more creative in my teaching to hold their interest, be clear about my goals, and stay up on their culture in order to communicate with them.

Children's parents, more questioning and less supportive, find excuses for them, challenge you on grades, and want you to change a grade whether it is warranted or not. Until this year, I have never had a parent question me about a grade. Recently, I have been told that I ruined their child's weekend, or they cried all weekend just because of a 2 (above average) in their effort grade in art. The positive part is that apparently they are seeing the importance of art in the curriculum.

Hindrance: Finding myself teaching middle school art and having no training or experience with this developmental age has been an obstacle for me. It hasn't been too difficult working with a curriculum (which has actually been rewarding), but I want to be sure I'm doing age appropriate lessons—the right exemplars, materials, concepts. Teaching this age group is also very demanding and requires a totally different demeanor. Scheduling has been the second most difficult obstacle. It is very difficult teaching 6th grade, then on to first, then on to 7th which is how my schedule has been set up. Likewise, obtaining suitable facilities and materials has been a problem.

Help: Having a parent volunteer in my first grade and eighth grade classes has been one of my greatest facilitators. An extra hand is always a help in an art room. In addition, I recently received a digital kiln which is automatically timed so that I don't have to set the timer every 45 minutes to remind me to change the temperature. Now I also have my own overhead and slide projectors, and have recently acquired six tracing boxes. All have proven to be time savers for me.

Of our local museums, the Walters Art Gallery and the Baltimore Museum of Art have provided numerous workshops and opportunities for teachers and students. Both have become user friendly and have provided many hands-on activities for students.

Personal: I realize that my philosophy hasn't changed a whole lot but I as a teacher have. My teaching skills and the knowledge I have gained have improved immensely. The experiences, the many schools, and the many people I have worked with have helped to make me a better teacher. But it is still my love for children and their art that gives me the greatest thrill.

Stories of Failure: One of my biggest disappointments has been with a special needs student. I was never able to successfully reach him with art since his coordination was so poor. He never grew in his skills and I always felt my class was adding to his poor self-esteem. Though from my perspective, I have had very few failures in my career, there has been one major disappointment: the fact that I never got my masters degree.

Stories of Success: My most recent success was an evening called "Celebrate the Arts" where the art, drama, and music teachers collaborated on showcasing the visual and performing arts at our school. Students performed in skits and plays, many played musical instruments and sang, and the halls were filled with art from grades 3 to 8. It was an event that I have been trying to establish for years. Over the years, I have also had many students' works selected for the Maryland Artist traveling show, for the exhibition at the Governor's home in Annapolis, and for the Sally Foster card and paper design contest.

Coping, Contending, and Carrying Forward
In working to draw together the pages of experiences and perspectives
offered by the teachers in this chapter, I remembered a student teacher I
once supervised in a large middle school in Missouri. About half way
through his semester-long experience, in a moment of fatigue he admitted,
"You know, people are expecting things of me—lots of things— and I'm
not sure I'm ready to be expected from." In comparing and contrasting, in
searching for themes, I thought about that student teacher's words and about
the myriad expectations these 30 people had placed upon them over the past
several decades. Among their narratives are recurrent themes about the
changing emphasis from issues of social equity and reconstruction in their
early years to today's auditing outcomes, teacher accountability, and
academic standards. Prominent are worries over multifaceted accountability and expanding expectations. There are the growing concerns of adapting
instructional approach and content to escalating changes in student demo-
graphics, including economic discrepancies, diversifying ethnicities, and
proliferating populations with special needs. There is the necessity to adjust
for transitions in parenting, to be aware of changing family structures and to
work to accommodate subsequent student needs. There are the pressing
issues of school safety and the real potential for campus violence. There is
the omnipresent problem of funding. These are issues that consume the
thoughts and feelings and actions of teachers across disciplines.

The creation of standards for the assessment of student and teacher performance, and for the assessment of curriculum and learning activities at the
local, state, and national levels is a principal issue with which all of these
teachers are grappling. Teachers are torn and confused over the development and imposition of standards for schools and specifically for the visual
arts. Some see the establishment of standards as a way to create consistency
and rigor, a way to gain recognition and legitimacy for visual arts programs.
Some say standards are a way to avoid the budgetary chopping block.
Others see it with more skepticism, as just another groove worn by the
wheels of the political bandwagon as it travels to and fro on the path of
education reform.

In other talk about curriculum, there is the discomfiting sense of change for
its own sake, the push for re-vision without an initial vision. Several
teachers ask whether education changes are a result of informed analysis
and assessment of teaching and learning needs, and they wonder to what
degree economics, politics, and appearances enter into it all. In John
Skrabalak's words, "I have written and re-written my curriculum more
times in the past ten years than I did my first 20." From the viewpoints of
many of these teachers, there must be more thought before the movement to
reform.

At the heart of their discipline, so many express a reassuring sense of on-going progress in art education. They address curriculum development, the changes that have moved art education from the fundamentals of self-expression to a comprehensive approach to teaching art in context; nurturing sensitive, intelligent response to art; and addressing aesthetic issues. Commensurately, among all of them, there continues a fundamental, perhaps best put, primal commitment to the processes of creativity—of making art. They conceive of themselves as artists and pride themselves in their empathic understanding of the intricacies—the pleasures and difficulties—involved in the art making process.

According to these teachers, the field of art education is a work in progress. From their perspectives, the continuance of that progress will require academically informed, politically diplomatic, and above all, relentless advocacy on the part of every art educator.

In reading these seasoned reflections about changing times and teaching, I recalled another voice from my own past. It came from one of my college professors back in the late 60s, who in one of his more cynical, iconoclastic moods said something like, "Good teachers teach in spite of the theories imposed upon them." There is a candid (perhaps for some, distressful) truth to this statement, and I see the implications permeating the teachers' narratives throughout this book. Despite the pressures, the hurdles, and constraints, each one of them has found their own distinctive ways to cope, to contend, and carry forward their commitment to educate children through the arts. Susie Kropa provides apt summary:

> I think my best years are happening now. I don't know if it's the students or that I finally have my own room to teach in. It's probably both of these things and one more—I feel like I finally know what I'm doing. I've seen trends come and go, and after thirty years of experimenting, I know what works, and I know for myself what is important.

In the present, I think of something Elliot Eisner, Professor of Education and Art, said in reflecting on what he has learned throughout his many years in education. It is a lesson that he regards as either depressing or exciting.

> Education will not have permanent solutions to its problems, we will have no "breakthroughs," no enduring discoveries that will work forever. We are "stuck" with temporary resolutions rather than permanent solutions. What works here may not work there. What works now may not work then. We are not trying to invent radar or measure the rate of free fall in a vacuum. Our tasks are impacted by context, riddled with unpredictable contingencies,

responsive to local conditions, and shaped by those we teach and not only by those who teach. Those who want something easier to do for a career should go into medicine. (1998, p. 5)

The Flower Teachers understand intimately the uncertainty and the complexity that underlie education. It is, in fact, those qualities that keep them open to learning and amenable to change. It is, by their own accounts, a big part of what keeps them interested.

In Chapter 6, the teachers share their metaphorical stories.

Chapter 6
Experience is the Stories People Live: Teaching Metaphors

Through the poignant grip of a story and metaphor we meet ourselves and the other in our mutual quest for goodness and meaning.

Carol Witherell and Nel Noddings,
Stories Lives Tell, 1991

For those of us who seek to know and understand the experience of others, stories are the essential research tools. They draw us in—thought and feeling. They dispel indifference. They make us care. Stories suspend us in a medium of fascination, providing us glimpses of other truths, other lives. For researchers interested in deep meaning of personal experience, many believe that the story is the only way to access the experiences of real people in real circumstances, struggling with real problems (Witherell & Noddings, 1991).

Through theory and practice, teachers know the magic of a good story and are, without fail, consummate storytellers. This is why, at the very outset of their long interview, I posed to the Flower Teachers this question:

Could you share any particular stories about your real-life teaching experiences that might encapsulate or impart the essence of what it has been like to be a classroom teacher for the last quarter of a century? I am looking for a true narrative of something that you experienced within your teaching career, something that might serve as an embodiment of your teaching experiences.

From my perspective, this question would present the greatest challenge of all the items in the interview, for after a quarter of a century of teaching experiences, how could one choose just one experience that encapsulated them all? For some, the choice was easy—one student, one incident or milestone came quickly to mind and their writing began with this narrative. Others saved this task for last, waiting for insights to emerge as they completed their responses to the other interview items. Some shared a single story. Others, finding it impossible to choose, offered several. In a few of these cases, I took the prerogative to place some of their stories in other chapters where they fit strategically. A few felt that they could not chose at all and dispersed their metaphorical experiences throughout their responses to the many other interview items; because of this, not every teacher is represented in this chapter.

As it turns out, these stories offer some of the richest insights into the Flower Teachers' careers. They pored over the decades, remembered people, issues, events—a whole world of experiences. They eliminated and selected, analyzed and weighed, and finally, exposed their most cherished metaphor—the spirit of what being an art educator has meant to them. The stories they told did not disappoint me. They are heartfelt and quietly profound and they are true.

In their own words . . .
Teaching Raul
Lora McNeece Barrett, Holyoke Magnet Middle School for the Arts, Holyoke, Massachusetts

This year I taught a young man of Puerto Rican descent who was probably the most talented person I've ever taught in my life. He was a real cool kid, admired by his peers, a terrific athlete, and absolutely in love with art. We'll call him Raul, and he was in my drawing class. I had heard about Raul from friends who taught in his elementary school, and I had hoped to have Raul in the sixth grade, but there was no room in my school until the following year. As a seventh grader, he was good, but very undisciplined. His line when drawing was uncontrolled. I saved the first piece he proudly did in my room and challenged him to do better. Raul was in a race against himself. Highly competitive, he wanted to be the best. He was better than most of the others, but there was not a great enough distance between himself and the "wannabe's." The question was always there for the others, "What did Raul do?" "Which one is Raul's?" I held his first drawing up on a regular basis, and then the second to compare it with, and then the third, and so on. After his third drawing was complete, Raul hung his head every time I pulled out the first drawing where the lines were wild, the cross-hatching was crude, irregular, the composition not strong enough.

One day not long after Raul came to my class, for a still life, I put out colored blocks on white cloth. Raul went wild! He saw the reflections of the colored blocks bouncing off the fabric. He ran around to the other three tables and excitedly challenged the others to see what he saw and they did. I pulled out bottles and filled them with water; Raul immediately saw what happened to the stems of flowers when they pierced the water, and excitedly showed others. He was hooked. They were hooked. From then on, I learned from Raul. I heard him describe to other students what he saw. I found things harder and harder for him to draw. I had to think of how I would present a drawing challenge so that not only would everyone else understand, but so Raul would be challenged as well. He grew by leaps and bounds. I saved every piece he worked on, whether during school, or during my weekly office hours, or when Raul stayed through to 5:00 while I had in-service training for other teachers in my room.

His drawing ability soon exceeded mine. Raul won contest after contest, including a Gold Key in the national Scholastic Art Contest when he was in the 8th grade. I told him that I would buy his drawing for the $100 offer if, for some reason, one of the sponsors didn't pick it up. I discussed it with his father, who approved. The drawing came back from the contest unsold, and went on to be hung in the citywide art show. Raul brought his family and friends to the opening, and a proud Raul stood before his drawing and asked me to be in the photo with him. I've known enough cool eighth graders to realize that this was an unusual request. I was delighted.

Several weeks later, on Class Day, Raul received the Award for Outstanding Achievement in Drawing. In addition to the usual gold charm awarded by the school, I purchased Raul a handsome portfolio into which I placed every piece of art he had done at the school, complete with beveled mats. I spoke about Raul and about how much I had learned from him, how much everyone had learned from him, and how he had presented a challenge to me that I welcomed and enjoyed. He hugged me in front of his peers, and there were tears in his eyes. About an hour later, the guidance counselor came to my room and asked if she could talk to me. Apparently Raul had gone to her for guidance; he told her that I had given him everything and that I had even bought his drawing, the one thing that he could have given me, and now he was left not knowing what to do. He wanted to give me something for all I had done for him. What Raul didn't understand was that I didn't need a drawing to remember him, but that a student like him comes along maybe once in a lifetime, and that what I will remember him with is deep in my heart and not framed on a wall. Raul has no money to spend on a gift for me; I need nothing. I told the counselor that what Raul could do for me was to make something of himself so that I could once again recognize what an amazing person he was.

We shed a tear or two together at graduation that night, he with his two gold charms, one for the Scholastic Art Contest, the other for the Class Day Award. No one told Raul to wear his charms, but somehow he knew. I owned a piece of his artwork, a piece that he would have gladly given to me had I just asked. But more importantly, I had the experience of teaching Raul, and that will forever make a difference in the way I teach.

The Art of Healing at Columbine High
Barbara Hirokawa, Columbine High School, Littleton, Colorado
[July 6, 1999, 3 months after the Columbine shootings]

This question was a hard one for me to focus on this spring when I started this project. But now it has become simpler. Though I can't answer exactly *how* yet, there is no doubt that the event that will be most pivotal when I look back on my career will be what happened at my school, Columbine High School, on April 20, 1999. It is just starting to sink in now that none of us will ever be the same, that we have been fundamentally changed in many ways. I have been in a fog of sorts since then, and don't know yet when I will come out of it. But some realizations have already begun to make themselves known. One is there is a reason I became the kind of teacher I did, and that was so that I could survive the challenges that I have had to face and will face for the rest of my life. I have been able to see how important I am to my kids, past and present. And how important they are to me. I have received phone calls and letters from students I had 20 years ago, many of whom I had lost touch with. It has driven home how much of an influence we have on the lives of our students, often without knowing it. Many have visited since and the hugs and tears have done a lot to help the healing process begin.

Months later, the events of that day still seem like a bad dream. Each morning when I wake, sooner or later I remember that this really did happen and then adjust my brain to that reality. I would like to write not of the horror and the sorrow and the loss, but how we have begun to deal with it. There are no answers, but there are solutions. Paramount in that dealing and coping and beginning to heal has been the role of the arts.

In what is called Visual Arts Standards Based Education we have our first standard which deals with art as a language and a means for communication. The other arts subjects have similar standards in their list. As educators we have all seen the successes of students as they discover this possibility and the voice to say something they have never been able to say before. What we have discovered through our experience these past few months is the power of the arts to give us voices to express the depths of grief and horror, to give us a means to speak the unspeakable. And by doing that, to begin to heal.

Because of our commitment to and success with the Artist in Residence Program here at Columbine, the administrators and artists were determined to help us in the ways that they could. In the first few days after the shootings, they wrote a grant to NEA and began formulating a plan to use the arts to help us. They organized a workshop for the kids the second week. And when we returned to school at Chattfield, every teacher had a packet of artists, what they could do, dates available, and contact numbers. Teachers who had never paid any attention to Artists in Residence had them in their classrooms to help the kids and the faculty get through those agonizing weeks. We talked, played theater and dance games, pounded on drums, tentatively began letting some of the emotions out. The artists needed this as much as the students because they had such a strong connection with our school and felt the need to be there. Emotions were raw, but we also had some laughs. It was an amazing thing to watch other teachers discover what those of us in the arts have known all along. My colleagues and I who have struggled with this program for years are now determined to take this show on the road, to make presentations at as many conferences as possible about the capacity of the arts to reach our children. I can't help but wonder if things would have been different if Eric and Dylan had been in Art!

For me in particular, the visiting artists were a godsend. My students responded to Betsey and William more openly than they would to me because they were so respected as artists. Betsey had them writing about a place where they felt safe, and it was wonderful to see those good memories replace the awful ones for a while. Quite a few students chose to do their final project on a Safe Place, rather than their recent experience. When William came in, he had them make group sculptures dealing with catastrophe turning into opportunity. Some were beautifully abstracted representations of the idea. Most were so graphic and raw they were hard to watch, but the acting out and the discussions represented the beginnings of healing.

Both of these artists returned to my classes several times to help with the projects and talk through solutions. The final products are beautiful and wonderful and hard to look at because the kids are so honest. We will have a show at the new LoDo Guiry's next month and they are anxious to show off their work. But to them these sculptures, books, and collages are much more than a piece of art for a show. They are representations of their beginning to heal from something no one of any age should have to experience.

Look! I Found Anita!
Ken Wilkie, Riverside Elementary School, Princeton, New Jersey

In the process of school integration, in 1973, I found myself in a predominantly black school, Pinewald Elementary, four days a week, and one day a week at Beverly Road Elementary, the white school (for want of better labels). Earlier in the year, it was announced that the following year, the kids would all be integrated into the two schools, so naturally everybody in both schools was apprehensive about how this would work—the bussing, and who would go where, and whatever. And here I was in a unique position. I knew the kids in the all-white school. I knew the kids in the predominantly black school. And it occurred to me that I could be [I don't know where I got this idea], a kind of messenger between two schools. Once the students knew that the following year the third graders (then divided between Pinewald and Beverly Road) would all be together for fourth grade at Pinewald, and the fourth graders would also be together as fifth graders, I started having the third and fourth graders from each school write to pen pals at the other school. And there were many more kids at Pinewald, so we had two or three pen pals for each art student from Beverly Road. Sometimes it wasn't even a letter; it might be a little note or even a drawing. Somebody at one school would say to me, "Give this to Anita from me" and they would exchange phone numbers. They were really only living maybe three miles apart, but were in very different school situations. So, for a year, I would carry these little letters, notes, and drawings back and forth between the two schools, and it was gratifying on the first day of school when these populations came together. Black girl and white girl came up to me, all delighted, saying, "Look! I found Anita! She's the one I was writing to last year!" And I felt this was really wonderful, and it was just the simplest, easiest thing for me to do, and yet, I think it helped that transition.

This story explains my reasons for going into teaching, having the ability to make changes, to make a difference in the lives of some children. And that, I was very proud of. And I'm still talking about it 27 years later.

Meeting Peter Hurd: A Story of Tragedy and Healing
Sharon Henneborn, Ethel McKnight Elementary School,
East Windsor, New Jersey

This is a story of tragedy. It is also a story of art breaking through tragedy and it is the kind of story that, for me, encapsulates what art teaching can be about. Early in the 1960s, I taught a young boy in my fourth grade class whom I will remember all my life. We'll call him Thomas. The summer before, the family, which consisted of his father, his mother, a baby, and his father's brother and his family, prepared for their annual trip from Texas to New Mexico to spend the summer at their ranch. The sister, a teenager, decided to stay home with neighbors for the summer. The highway they traveled to reach the ranch passed along deep ravines without protective guardrails. Somehow the station wagon they were traveling in went off the road into a deep ravine. The only ones to survive the accident were

Thomas, the baby, and the mother, who remained unconscious as the car lay at the bottom of the cliff. Days went by and no one saw the overturned car in the ravine. Thomas managed to care for himself and the baby from the supplies they were taking with them to the ranch. I do not have an accurate memory of the number of days he was in the vehicle. When they were finally found, the mother was in a coma. She remained in that condition for the rest of the summer and for a good part of the second year. The community provided support for the family, and the children were living with a neighbor. Thomas spoke very little throughout the year. When his mother began to recover, he tried to speak but it was very difficult for him to form words. He was an attentive student, but it was difficult to know how much he was retaining from his class work. We studied the lives and works of many artists that year. Most were the usual artists I present in fourth grade, but for some reason that year I chose an artist that I had never before presented to my students. When school was out in the spring, Thomas's mother was determined to return to the solitude of the ranch for the summer. His favorite summer activity in their New Mexico home was to roam the desert around the ranch, and he was looking forward to it.

In the fall, Thomas rushed into my room and shouted, "I can't wait to tell you! I am so excited!" I had never heard him speak more than a few halting words, so I was amazed. "Every morning I went walking in the desert like I always do. One day at the top of the hill there was a man sitting at an easel painting. I walked over and sat and watched him and he didn't seem to mind. Every day he was there, I sat and watched him paint. One day I got a surprise! I ran over to him and said, 'I know who you are! You are Peter Hurd.' He looked at me very puzzled and asked me, 'What makes you think I am Peter Hurd?' I said, 'That's a Peter Hurd painting.' He laughed and I talked to him every day until the painting was finished."

I will never truly know whether the painter on the hill in New Mexico really was Peter Hurd. Given his meticulous tempera paintings of the arid Southwest landscape in that area, it certainly might have been him. But I wonder if that painter ever knew what he did for a boy who had not spoken for a year. I also wonder what would have happened if I had not taken out the Peter Hurd prints that particular school year.

Mixing Up the Sex Thing with the Art Thing
Sharon Henneborn, Ethel McKnight Elementary School,
East Windsor, New Jersey

When I changed schools in my district, I found that many pages in the books in my new classroom had been stapled together by the teacher before me. I realized that I must step lightly around the subject of nudity. I waited until I had a student teacher who could serve as a witness in the classroom in case a problem arose. I started with the very safe Matisse blue paper cutouts. Finally a child asked the question, "Are they naked?" We had a discussion and I asked, "What do you think?" and eventually, "Why do artists put clothes on the subjects sometimes and don't at other times?" They had very good ideas about studying clothing and people's bodies and realized that the clothes would interfere if the drawing of the human body itself were really the focus. I asked what they thought made some people comfortable with studying the pictures of the body and others uncomfortable. The most insightful answer came from a third grader who said, "I think they get the art thing mixed up with the sex thing and they don't know how to react."

Hugely Ironic
Sharon Henneborn, Ethel McKnight Elementary School,
East Windsor, New Jersey

I love telling the stories of my students and have kept in touch with many over the years. It is interesting to get their perspectives as adults looking back over their early school experiences with the arts. I remember one middle school student who attacked me. Because of my long arms, he was able to land only one blow and I was able to hold him off until he calmed down. Comically, and hugely ironic, years later he became an excellent teacher and he is currently a superior assistant superintendent. In teaching, you just never know. . . .

Donatello's Cherubs
Kathleen Thompson, Gilmer Middle School, Ellijay, Georgia

I have several anecdotes related to teaching art history and criticism, but I will share just one. So anyway, we're looking at Donatello's statue of *Judith and Holofernes*, and she's got his head in her hand, and she's just about to chop it off. And that's all I saw. So I'm focusing on the sword, and I'm also focusing on the fact that Donatello was an early artist—early in a lot of the techniques of the Renaissance. And I'm talking about the action. Then some kid raises his hand and says, "Why are there cherubs, little cherubs down there at the foot of Judith?" Well, I don't know! I've never seen those cherubs before. I did not know they were there. I did not see them. You cannot imagine how many times these kids have pointed out to me—6th, 7th, 8th graders—things in those paintings! It doesn't matter if you are teaching art history or art criticism, they have taught me so much about works of art. I have understood them from perspectives and points of view that I would have never gotten on my own. They have enriched my knowledge of art through art criticism and art history, and it's been so much fun.

Take Richard
Suzanne Greene, Spring Branch Middle School, Houston, Texas

Each year I have taught students who have made a difference in my life. Take Richard. He hated school and refused to attend. In sixth grade, he missed over 89 days and in the seventh, 75. I met him as an eighth grader. He slunk into my class, threw himself on a chair and looked at me as if to say, "Lady, I'm not here for long." As I walked around the room after giving the first assignment (create a self-logo using the letters of your name), I noticed that he was drawing with a very fine ink pen. I asked him if he liked pen and ink and he mumbled out a "yes." I handed him a book that contained very detailed ink drawings created by an artist from Japan. I lent him the book and gave him different ways to use the ink pens. I noticed he wasn't absent much, and his drawings became more detailed and complex. He had a wonderful way of drawing trees, so I asked him if he could paint trees like he drew them. He did and the results were so good that he and another student, who was a master at drawing bears, painted a mural of bears outside the front entrance of our school. One day his counselor called him into the office to talk to him about how well he was doing that school year. Richard said he came to school only to take my class. He is now in high school in advanced art classes and is planning to attend art school.

Even Small Triumphs
Carolyn S. Skeen, Linden Elementary, Oak Ridge, Tennessee

I keep a picture by a student named Les taped behind the door in the art storeroom. It is old and faded now. It's a still life featuring wobbly vases, an attempt at texture, a stick lizard, a sort-of-plaid background, and lots of ants unaccountably and inaccurately portrayed. It's an unskilled piece of work by a child whose fine motor coordination was almost as poor as his social and academic skills. If he had a gift, it was for appearing to be busy as he wasted time. But his work remains on my wall. Why? It's complete. The whole page is covered and designed. And most importantly, it was finished with a joyous flair and admired lavishly by the other students at Les' table. It was one of those special moments given to us as art teachers, a time when a child forgets to be self-conscious, angry, and frustrated and enjoys creating, enjoys the process and finds himself caught up in it. Les gave me the picture. He had taken it home but his parents didn't want it. It is mine now. I've written the word "remember" on the back to remind myself that art is a joy for all children not just for the talented few, that every child can create. Even if it is a struggle to reach a particular child, a teacher should never give up. And I remember that even small triumphs are worthy of respect and praise.

On Easter Sunday, the School Burned to the Ground.
Sonia Pratt, Southern Garrett High School, Oakland, Maryland

[Sonia's story about the school that burned on Easter Sunday was a good fit for two different chapters in this book. So, I made the difficult choice of including her story in Chapter 3, *Pray for Absences: The Early Classroom Years*. I hope you will return to her story and read it in a metaphorical light.]

Bird Lice and Rats
Carrol Morgan, King George Middle School, King George, Virginia

In 1974-75, my art room was an old industrial shop, which had a ceiling open to the rafters. Each spring a pair of birds built their nest and raised their young overhead, and students noticed little black moving spots dropping on their artwork—the bird lice were falling from the nest. It lasted for a few weeks out of the year, and after I explained the spots, the students accepted them without complaining.

The same students, however, were sent into a panic when a rat ran across the floor under their tables. There were numerous holes in the walls where old pipes had been removed and there were openings that led to spaces under an old adjoining building. I had a team of rattrap setters—boys who thought it was fun to crawl under the old building to set traps. I seldom thought of liability back then. One day a particularly large rat ran between the feet of a girl whose father was on the local school board. I specifically told her to go home and tell her father about the problem. Within weeks, the maintenance men appeared and plugged the holes in the outside walls. But before long a big gnawed hole appeared at the bottom of my adjacent art office door—the hole was still there twenty years later when another art teacher was assigned to the room.

Michelangelo and the Ceiling
Carrol Morgan, King George Middle School, King George, Virginia

During my first years as a middle school art teacher, I began teaching a unit on Renaissance painting that included perspective and Michelangelo's Sistine Chapel. As a culminating activity, I had each student paint a "looking up" picture on a 24" x 24" ceiling tile. It is a tradition that I have continued. Back in the 1970s, my school superintendent noticed the paintings on the ceiling and told me to remove them because they were a fire hazard! I did not remove them and no fire inspector has ever mentioned them. When our building began to leak profusely in other rooms, I collected many of the cast-off stained ceiling tiles and recycled them into paintings. Many of the older paintings are still on the ceiling—some students or their parents have taken some of them home, but I look forward to having a student whose parent created one. The ceiling is a wonderful growing album of my former students' work, and it is a great conversation piece for new students each year.

Was It a Record?
John Skrabalak, Altoona Area Senior High School, Altoona, Pennsylvania

In my new art room early in my career, some of my students were in the back ceramics area pugging clay. I noticed the grouping of students got bigger as they were trying to make a continuous coil of clay without breaking it. The experience became maddening as the students kept throwing clay into the pug mill. Even projects in construction were sacrificed for this continuous coil of clay. The coil extended out into the hallway and down the hall. Each student held and supported a section of the coil. I was somewhere in the middle. Finally it ended as we had no more clay or students. We figured the coil was about 40 feet long. Was it a record? I don't know. But for us it was.

Lolli-pop, Lolli-pop
John Skrabalak, Altoona Area Senior High School, Altoona, Pennsylvania

I promised my students one time that if they would improve their clean-up routine drastically, I would tap dance for them on one of the workbenches. Well, guess what! They did. As I was performing my tap dance routine to the song "Lolli-pop, Lolli-pop," the principal walked in unaware of what was going on. Shocked and embarrassed, I quickly turned the event around to a complaint. I told the principal that "the lights up here are incredibly dirty and no wonder the students are having difficulty drawing." His response to me was to fill out a work order immediately. He had no clue. Needless to say, my students and I doubled over in riotous laughter. I had kept my promise.

Water Wands
Candy Alexander, Church Hill Elementary, Church Hill, Tennessee

Our regular fourth grade classes do a unit on oceans, so I did a project with them last year where the students made water wands using plastic blank tubes that are extruded into two-liter bottles. We talked about what happens in the various layers of the ocean and we added real ocean sand and shells and we colored the water and the oil to make the ocean and the sky areas, and we added confetti fish. We did a lot of study on the science aspects of the project. For most kids, it was fun just putting it together, but for my multiple handicapped child, this was probably the favorite project of the year. He gripped that water wand in his hand for a week non-stop—I am not exaggerating! When he looked through the water and wand, it would slightly distort things and he loved looking at everything. Everywhere he went he looked though it to see what the distortions were doing to the colors and the images he saw. Even the special education teacher said, "I can't believe how this has really piqued his curiosity and has gotten him interested in his environment again."

So Many Stories
Marie Shack, Wilmington High School, Wilmington, Massachusetts

There are so many stories. There is Brett Kastle who moved from Kentucky and lived for football. He took all my art classes, was my pal, and still sends me Kentucky Derby souvenirs each May. Loung Nwin who wasn't even going to take an art class and ended up compiling an impressive A. P. portfolio on which he received a Four Rating. Linda Small who wasn't very academic but managed to graduate from college because of her art abilities and interests—she babysat and worked as a waitress and married her high-school sweetheart. We keep in touch. Aron Mathews who was brilliant and talented and recovering from his sister's suicide… art class kept him sane and I still have the pin that he gave me as a present. There's my pal Amory, who isn't academic or talented but appreciates his artwork, took everything home and loved my class. There is Lynn Donner whom I had in ceramics class in the late 70s and when I saw her a few years ago she told me she still has her ceramic dish she made in high school. There is a former student—a "guy genius" whom I meet sometimes at a restaurant who tells me I was his favorite teacher. There is Bethany Billings, another "genius," who took art classes as a release from her academic studies, appreciated what she learned and became more human in the process.

The Day the Gulf War Grabbed the Headlines

Phyllis Bosco, Florida State University Elementary School, Tallahassee, Florida

The day the Gulf War grabbed the headlines, I stopped and bought newspapers on my way to school. My first class, third graders, came in with long faces. I knew several students had relatives overseas. I posted the headline and asked if anyone wanted to say anything. A floodgate was opened. The day's lesson plan was abandoned. Children spoke of their feelings concerning their fathers, older siblings, and friends who were now in a war. I gave each child a large card and told them to express themselves any way they felt appropriate to the discussion we were having. They created beautiful collage portraits, symbols of war and peace, and poems. Before school that morning, I was advised not to bring up the war because it would be too upsetting. The collage was rejected at the county elementary art show because it was "inappropriate."

Years later, one of those former third grade students was working on a college project about censorship. She came to me and asked if I would be in a panel discussion with the FSU library director and a state prosecuting attorney. She said her dad had been in the Gulf War and she had been thankful for the opportunity I gave her to express her feelings that scary day long ago when she was nine.

He Was a Wild Kid.

Mark Phillips, George A. Smith Middle School, Quarryville, Pennsylvania

One student comes to mind when I think of what it's been like to be a teacher—not only an art teacher. It was a boy who had lost his father through death. I really hit it off with this boy and, wanting to help in the best way I knew how, I became his self appointed "Big Brother." All the time I tried to keep him on the right track. He was a wild kid when I had him in the 7th and 8th grades. I tried to guide his interests and later get him into tech school, but sadly, after a couple of years, I lost touch and he continued to have troubles. For quite a few years, I did not hear from him. Then, much later, he called and said things had really gotten bad. He had even been in jail. He said he was at his lowest point when he remembered his "time with Mark," and he wanted that back. So he tried to pull himself up, to regain those good times and that's what he was doing. He called to ask me to be his best man at his wedding. I wouldn't have had that kind of experience if I hadn't been a teacher.

Crisis Management
Lurline Lapolla, Saxe Middle School, New Canaan, Connecticut

Early in my teaching career, I took some aptitude tests which indicated I should be in crisis management. I laughed and said, "I teach adolescents. What do you think I do every day?"

Green Condoms and a Bag of Manure
Martyna Bellessis, University Elementary School, Bloomington, Indiana

I will probably write a novella when I retire. After 33 years of teaching, I have many stories to tell. The title of my book will probably be "Don't Bring Green Condoms into the Art Room," because that's exactly what a 5th grade boy did some years ago. He wanted to share this small package with the class. And, as a new teacher in my second year, I asked my third graders to bring something "special" from home for a collage. One boy brought a lunch bag full of manure. Yes, this was in a country school. I also remember the parent that the docents asked me *not* to bring back to the art museum for our next visit. Whether these are stories that embody my teaching career is questionable, but they are the kinds of funny things that happen along the way.

Hardly Proficient
Carol Wellein, St. James' Academy, Baltimore, Maryland

I would like to tell a story about Judith who was a student of mine for at least six years. She came from a home where Mom and Dad were divorced; there was always fighting going on for custody of Judith and her sister. Mom was out of work and no one seemed to be the head of the household. Judith loved to draw. She drew all the time, even in other classes, much to the dismay of her teachers. She was very kind to her classmates and they to her. If Judith had any free time, she would come to the art room to visit or to bring me drawings, which I would always put on the wall. When Judith reached 8th grade, she decided she wanted to try out for a magnet school that was outstanding in art. So we got the information about the requirements for admission. She was not only to design her own portfolio, but had to include at least 10 different assignments. This is where my nightmare began. This was the first 8th grade class that I had ever taught and I had never been required to prepare anyone for a portfolio. I was an elementary art teacher! I looked at the requirements and realized she had hardly experienced any of the media nor had she received instructions in some of the techniques. She was also required to write a paper and to attend an interview and a two-hour drawing class. So Judith began to meet me after school to begin her assignments. I would get out my teaching books to make sure I was giving her the right information and try to demonstrate the use of materials that I was hardly proficient in. We worked for weeks. She was so diligent about showing up, working at home, and doing her best. In the meantime, I was getting really nervous as the time got closer. The big day arrived and Judith was off to her interview. I made her call me when she got home to hear how it went. She was confident about the drawing class but was a little nervous about the interview. Now we had to wait for the results. To make a long story short, she made it into the school. I cannot tell you what a thrill it was for me to have a student get into a school where art was the criteria! After high school, she received acceptances from Chicago Institute, Rhode Island School of Design, and Yale Art School. I was hoping she would go far away for her college years to escape her dysfunctional home, but she chose, of all places, the Maryland Institute, College of Art, my alma mater! This story encapsulates the way I look back on my career…mostly highs. It also validates my decision to be an art teacher. The rewards and challenges are many.

Peace Corps at Kamabai
Jeannie Siegler, Loyola High School, Missoula, Montana

[Jeannie's story about her work in the Peace Corps at Kamabai in Sierra Leone, like Sona Pratt's, was a good fit for two chapters in this book. Because it was most appropriate for Chapter 2, you will find it there.]

"I don't think I could live without art!"
Gerald Vilenski, Starr Elementary, Plainwell, Michigan

One story comes to mind that seems to pull together the essence of what being an art teacher means to me and the importance students attach to art. In a way, this is an extremely simple story. I had one student for six years— kindergarten through fifth grade. She was a quiet, rather odd little girl, who was somewhat of a loner, somewhat of a misfit with her peers. She was also an extremely bright child, which was apparent even at the kindergarten level. I realized early on that this girl had extraordinary art skills and tried to help her cultivate her talents. What struck me as odd was that even though she had obvious talent, she really didn't seem to enjoy art all that much. She participated in art activities, worked well above grade level, but didn't demonstrate an unusual passion for the subject. I continued to teach this child year after year, watching her mature in her individual artistic expression, observing her progress in relation to that of her peers, and helping her with more complex activities. At no time was there much of an indication of *liking*, let alone loving art or of being an artist. By fifth grade, she was handling work that was more typically mastered at the middle school level; still there was no demonstration of a love of art.

One day, near the end of the school year, I was talking to the class about their up-coming move to middle school, and there were many questions about what to expect in art classes. I reluctantly informed the class that they would receive no art until eighth grade because only a part-time art teacher covered that age level. Out of the blue, the girl that I have been speaking about started tearing up and declared so candidly, "Oh, my god! I don't think I could live without art!" It took six years of working with this student for her to indicate anything about her love for art and what it meant to her. This simple declaration from this young girl affected me profoundly because it struck me that I had influenced this child far more than I had known.

She wrote me a sweet letter when she left school, thanking me for being her teacher and helping her to love art. I have received many letters like that one over the years, but this student helped set the direction I have tried to follow throughout my career. I have come to the conclusion that as a teacher, I can influence many, many children in a positive way through art. It also taught me the importance of building a solid program for all the future generations of students who can attain feelings of self-worth and confidence through their visual arts experiences.

Why I Call Myself a "Saint"
Cherie St. Pierre, Charles A. Lindbergh Elementary School,
Kenmore, New York

One incident happened this year which tickled my funny bone. In this elementary school, we must write report cards for art, music, and physical education. For one student I wrote that when things did not go his way, he would "go on strike" and refuse to work. The next day after the report cards went home, his classroom teacher came to my room and handed me a business envelop, saying it was from William's father. When I opened the envelop and saw a computer generated letter, the hair on the back of my neck stood on end as I thought of the possible ugly confrontation with a parent that lay ahead. But to me it was the funniest letter I have ever received from a parent. Apparently there was an intense discussion between William and his father on why I was a "hard" teacher, why I called myself a "Saint" and why I called myself a "Doctor." I have enclosed the text of the letter below:

> Dear Dr. St. Pierre,
> I am writing to inform you of William's and my discussion of the report on his performance in art class. Thank you for bringing this

problem to our attention; please know you are not alone and we have been talking to William about this kind of behavior. There are three things that William mentioned in his "argument" in his defense:

1. William said you were a "hard" teacher. I explained that I pay taxes to have teachers challenge my kids and that Dr. St. Pierre is doing that. I pointed out a piece of artwork that William has hanging on our wall. I told him that he probably never thought he could make such a great piece of art until his teacher got him to do it. I also added that I am impressed with what he brings home and he should look forward to the compliments.

2. He didn't understand why you were called a "Doctor." I explained that people can go through college and get advanced degrees, Ph. D., for example. I told him that when people work hard to gain the status of "Dr.," they deserve to be called that. It shows accomplishment. I used his aunt who is a dentist as an example. Her patients call her Dr., not Mrs.

3. He couldn't fathom why you called yourself a Saint! By using the telephone book, I showed him a number of names that begin with St. and explained that all these people were either born with last names that began with St., or married into the names. I hope our discussion helps out. Please feel free to contact me if William continues to "pout." Our home number is ⸺⸺⸺⸺.
Again, thank you for the report.

Sincerely,
Terry B. Biliaro

Showing Out
Jane Hollingsworth, Gainesville Middle School, Gainesville, Georgia

Many years ago, our school system had an instructional fair which involved a competition. In front of parents and judges, teachers would teach a lesson to a class. First, second, and third place ribbons were to be awarded. I developed a printmaking lesson that I was particularly proud of that taught the concepts of "motif" and "pattern." Students had to volunteer to return to school the night of the competition to participate in class in front of the judges. A particularly difficult student, whom I'll call Jeb, was one of the first volunteers. The other students who said they would come were a mixture of good students and problems. How was I going to look in front of the parents and judges with Jeb and some of the others "showing out?" When my turn arrived, I began with a class discussion. Jeb's hand shot up whenever I asked a question. Amazingly, his answers were correct and insightful. Other students whom I feared would be disruptive sat quietly and followed directions—they were performing in front of an audience. My lesson won a first place ribbon that night, and I learned another kind of valuable lesson. Preconceived attitudes about students are not necessarily correct. In fact, if the attitudes are negative, they can be detrimental and need to be changed. After that night, I viewed Jeb as a good student and he lived up to my expectations.

Art-On-A-Cart a la Winslow Homer
Yvonne Greene, West Ward Elementary School, Slaton, Texas

In Belding, Michigan, I drove from town school to country school and back through the beautiful and sometimes treacherous changing seasons, carrying with me most of the supplies I needed to teach my lessons. It was from this experience that I learned that pails of liquid wheat paste smell horrible in a car after a few days of springtime weather. Fortunately, I discovered the wonders of adding a few drops of oil of clove or peppermint, purchased at the local pharmacy, to any liquid product such as tempera paint or wheat paste to keep noxious odors at bay.

One cold, winter day I arrived at my favorite, turn-of-the-century country school at Smyrna (housing two combined classrooms of grades 1-2 and 3-4), running a little behind schedule. Holding a cardboard box full of watercolor paints and brushes in my arms, I stepped out onto the packed snow of the small parking lot. Promptly, I slipped, fell, and spewed paint, boxes, and brushes in all directions. Within seconds, I was rescued by a crowd of winter-bundled, rosy-cheeked children and their teacher out for recess on the snowy playground—a la a Winslow Homer painting. They swept me up, scurried under parked cars and into snow banks to retrieve paint, boxes, and most of the brushes. I taught my lessons in the two classrooms, ate a wonderful butter-laden meal, complete with slabs of homemade bread in the best lunchroom in the district and traveled on to the next country school on my schedule. One spring day when I was back for Smyrna's rotation on my teaching schedule, the children presented me with the remainder of my brushes, which they had picked up in the school yard after the Michigan snow had melted.

A SENSATional Collection
Lloyd Sensat, Jr., Hahnville High School, Boutte, Louisiana

When I started teaching in St. Charles Parish at the newly opened R. J. Vial School, I found an old teacher's desk. It was painted white and covered with graffiti. All the other teachers ignored it because they thought that it was old and ugly. They all wanted the new shiny furniture which the dynamic new principal had ordered for the new school. How that old desk had gotten to that new school building was a real mystery. Of course, I claimed it and moved it with me from school to school in my long teaching career in the Parish. Everything was always in a state of flux in the St. Charles Parish system. The desk and I moved from R. J. Vial, to A. A. Songy, to Lakewood, and finally to Hahnville High. It was at Hahnville that I finally got one of my students who needed extra credit to spend his nine weeks in shop refinishing it. He made an A in Art and Shop for that nine-week stretch! The desk was now lovely with its original oak wood exposed and handsome panel details. It was what I always knew it to be: a beautiful antique. Last year, when I retired from teaching, I took that old desk home to Sun Oak, for no one else ever saw it for what it really is—a metaphor for life. So often, it takes a look beneath the surface to see real value. Through the years, I have been privileged to have taught scores of wonderfully talented students, many of whom have kept up with me throughout the years with Christmas cards, letters, and visits. To honor these faithful and special people, I have started framing their old photos. It is how I remember them when they were my student-artists. I display the photos on my old teaching desk and I call it my SENSATional student-artist collection.

Artists at Work
Susie Kropa, Lincoln/Salem Elementary Schools, Mt. Pleasant, Iowa

As a child, from second grade through high school, I attended Saturday morning art classes at the Dayton Art Institute. Many memories of those Saturday mornings are forever imprinted on my mind. The Art Institute was like a second home. I loved the kids and teachers, the smell of linseed oil and turpentine, kneaded erasers, the caged birds and monkeys, the statues, the courtyards, and even the bushes out in front that were big enough to crawl under. Even now, I try to recreate that atmosphere for my students who will never have access to a place like that and this is what my story is all about.

After 28 years of teaching, I finally got my own room in an old K-2 building whose dwindling numbers had left a first grade classroom empty. I was new to the building and anxious to make the room a wonderful place to be. I spent a good part of the summer getting it organized. Luckily, the walls were painted a nice clean white, and the whole west side was windows. An acquaintance from a local greenhouse gave me some plants. I outfitted a small bookshelf with geodes, shells, acorns, feathers, pine cones, and a magnifying glass, along with spent spark plugs, spools, and other assorted small man-made items with visual interest. Unclaimed student projects of past years became a mini sculpture gallery in a built-in book-shelf. On another shelf, I lined up a row of empty honey bears and two peanut butter jars full of lids I had saved from dried up markers; one with warm colored lids, the other with cool. The Presbyterian rummage sale yielded great finds, like a metal bird-in-a-cage music box, carved sculptures, and a small, red enamelware teapot. A friend gave me a large bouquet of peacock feathers, and I retrieved a slightly bedraggled stuffed pheasant from the furnace room. On the walls, I hung reproductions, masks, and a rack draped with colored necklaces, a yellow baseball cap and a shocking pink tutu. On one windowsill, I placed six plastic jars filled with water in the primary and secondary colors. The sign on the door read "SAUNDERS' ART STUDIO," and beneath that a yellow, imitation road sign: "ARTISTS AT WORK." The first day of art class, a second grader whose homeroom had been in the art studio the year before said, "I liked it better when it was a first grade room." Well . . . . That's the way we started.

Over the year, I tried to teach the kids how to use the studio. There was one shelf where all the regular supplies were available to them to use when they finished their assigned projects. I encouraged them to draw things they found on the shelves and around the room and showed them how to prop a drawing board on the back of a chair, so they could move away from their tables. The shelf with the natural and man-made objects was *extremely* popular. You'd have thought the kids had never seen stuff like that before. They were often enthusiastic to the point of boisterousness. My favorite line was, "You don't have to shout!" It took a while to figure out how to use some of the things on the shelves, the jars of colored marker lids for instance. I had envisioned children emptying them on the table and recombining them in different color combinations, like primary and secondary, shades of blue, darkest to lightest. I was surprised one day to find Joe and Billy crawling around on the floor, marker lids on their fingertips, playing monster, with the coolest claws they'd ever imagined! I explained that although that was a creative use of the marker lids, the activity wasn't exactly suited to an art studio. I don't know how they explained their marker-stained fingertips to their parents.

At the beginning of the next school year, it was decided that the old building would have to be closed the following year. I met a new group of kinder-gartners and welcomed back the veteran first and second graders. By now, they were accustomed to the art studio. Every time I brought something new into the room, they noticed it right away. We continued our art making through fall, winter, and spring—painting, drawing, sculpting, cutting, and pasting. All the while, I was having tiny pangs of grief over our soon-to-be empty, wonderful art studio. Halfway through one of the last second grade classes, there was time for open studio. The two years I had known the second graders seemed like an instant, but that day I discovered that during that time, these seven year olds had learned exactly what an art studio is for. As I looked around the room, I saw two boys sitting backwards on their chairs, boards propped up, drawing each other; several girls, sprawled on the floor, baskets of markers and crayons scattered among them, were happily drawing, each engrossed in her own creation. Five boys had arranged the plastic dinosaur collection on a chair and were grouped around it drawing. Other children were sitting in their assigned seats, coloring, cutting, and pasting. One girl was moving around the room, making drawings of pieces of our studio, to remember it by. Everybody was busy, and instead of the usual uproar, there was a quiet hum. We could even hear music on the CD player. I must say, the whole scene got to me. At that moment I felt I had taught those children something important.

Not Much Was Easy in His Life.
Judy Williams, Thomas Intermediate School, Shelbyville, Tennessee

Roland was a minority student who had struggled economically and academically to attend and graduate from high school. His accomplishments in class were not standout. He entered the nearby university, working to pay his way. One day he told me, eyes sparkling, that he had enrolled in an art class. He was delighted to find that some of the students didn't know what he knew and the art class was "easy" for him. Not much was easy in his life.

"Do it!"
Judy Williams, Thomas Intermediate School, Shelbyville, Tennessee

Tim was the son of educators and considered extremely talented. He accepted my suggestions to improve his work more out of politeness and respect than from a belief in their validity. He struggled when I suggested new materials, subject matter, or approaches, and pretty much dragged his feet, wanting to continue doing what he did well. Years later, after he became a successful illustrator, I asked him to speak to my high school class about his career. I can't remember what all he said that day, but I vividly recall this: "When Mrs. Williams asks you to do something in your work, do it! She knows what she's talking about."

Another Fiddler on the Roof
Joan Newcomer, McDonogh Elementary School,
Owings Mills, Maryland

There is a picture in my photo album of a green faced woman with a painted mustache and beard. There are life-sized paintings of a girl and boy that seem to be floating on both sides of her head. She is wearing one light shoe and one dark shoe, a purple jacket, and a single green glove on her right hand. One of her feet is on the roof of a dollhouse and it looks like she is floating above it all. She is playing a violin and wearing a prayer shawl. It's a very odd photo, but when you look more closely, you see small copies of paintings by Marc Chagall in the background. She is a living reproduction of Marc Chagall's painting *The Green Violinist* (1918).

I'm the woman in the photo and it was taken during "Adventure Day" at our school. Every other year our school has an Adventure Day when the entire faculty devotes itself to one theme, which might be taken from any discipline. The theme for the year the photo was taken was "Art." I was in my glory with the prospect of having all the teachers in the school sharing artists and artworks with our students. My goal is to inspire my students, but I found the events of that day to be inspiring to me as well. It was wonderful having all the teachers share their ideas about their artists and their Adventure Day presentations with me. It was exciting to see the support and enthusiasm that could be generated for the visual arts. My goal of inspiring a creative spirit within students seems always to have an interesting reciprocity: so often, they, in turn, awaken the spirit in me. In this case my fellow colleagues were part of it too. I felt especially fortunate to teach in a school with such dedicated professionals who willingly gave of themselves to make my discipline come alive to our student body. I think that everyone went home that day feeling more excited, enthusiastic, and enriched by the role that the arts can play in the curriculum of our school, and ultimately, in our daily lives.

. . . and one more
As I did once before, I have exercised authorial privilege and have included a teaching metaphor of my own. It happened in St. Louis, Missouri, in the spring of 1984. For our annual field trip for my two high school humanities classes, I decided to top off our study of Byzantine architecture with a tour of the Cathedral Basilica of St. Louis. This massive cathedral, whose construction began in 1907, was modeled after Hagia Sophia, the Church of Holy Wisdom, built during the reign of Justinian in Constantinople. Like its predecessor, the Cathedral Basilica of St. Louis is one of the architectural masterpieces of its era. Here's a snippet of what happened that warm May

day with my teenagers and me in the wondrous Byzantine interior of this church.

Bill in the St. Louis Cathedral
Candace Stout, Hickman High School, Columbia, Missouri

As a part of the program of formal tours of the Cathedral Basilica of St. Louis, my classes were provided with a very competent, albeit very formal, docent. To begin our tour, she guided us around the cathedral's exterior like an art historian, pointing out the many classically Romanesque features. Throughout our 30 minute walk around the building, I brought up the rear, gently rounding up and prodding the stragglers among my 42 students. Although everyone was pleased to be on a field trip some 90 miles away from their school, there were those who were easily distracted and whose interest in architecture was understatedly scant. At the very fringes, I would always find Bill Thalley, disinterested, lethargic, and ever bored. No matter how I tried, I could never get a rise from him, never a modicum of interest. After our exterior study, it was time to learn about the wondrous Byzantine interior, with the largest mosaic collection in the world, covering 83,000 square feet and including 41.5 million pieces of glass tesserae. The docent proceeded through the doors, up the nave and stopped in the basilica's core, right under the massive dome ringed with colored mosaics and Romanesque style windows. The sun was shining through one side of the dome, the golden mosaics were sparkling, and even the most secular among us felt something of the spiritual in the air. So there were my students, what I thought were *all* of them, gathered and very quiet in the heart of this old church, waiting for the lecture to begin. As I was taking one last look around to make sure everyone was there, ready, and listening, all of a sudden the enormous wooden doors at the back of the cathedral swung open and in walked Bill Thalley. Everyone was so surprised, and so still, he had no idea we were there. He stepped inside the door and stopped, mouth open, eyes sweeping heavenward to the golden, gleaming dome. In the hush of the colossal room, we all heard Bill's candid evaluation of his experience: "HOLY SHIT!" There were no giggles from his classmates. There was no reproach from his teacher, no motion of shock or disapproval from the grave docent. Bill had taken in the full effect of the magnificent cathedral. He had been moved. Everyone knew it and despite the indelicacy of expression, everyone agreed.

In Chapter 7, teachers identify major issues looming on the education horizon, make recommendations for reform, and offer advice for a new generation of art teachers.

Chapter 7
Looking Backward and Forward: Advice for a New Generation

Increasingly, the big question that teachers will have to grapple with will be this: If we continue our strong focus on plurality, on the maintenance of ethnic distinction and diversity, how do we promote community and, on a more grand scale, global unity?
                Candy Alexander, Church Hill/McPheeter's Bend Elementary,
                                                Church Hill, Tennessee

Among the Romans, there was a god named Janus who presided over doors and entranceways and, thus, over the beginnings of things. His temples, having two portals, would always run east and west, just as the days begin and end. The statue of Janus had two faces, one young and one old. The eyes of the young looked through the door to the future; the old looked back through the portal of the past. Throughout the writing of this book, I have been thinking of Janus and how like him the Flower Teachers are. As one century comes to an end, and a new one begins, they too find themselves looking backward and forward through portals of time. Like Janus, they have a view of what has passed and a vision of what is beginning. And in this instance of simultaneity, there comes a special kind of wisdom, one that combines experience with foresight.

This chapter is written for the new generation of art teachers. The intent is to provide some enlightened foresight of what might lay ahead. From their seasoned vantage points, the Flower Teachers identify some of the issues and problems that loom on the education horizon, make recommendations for reform, and ultimately offer advice for coping with the demands of the job that stretches before us. Responses have been arranged into two categories: *Issues and Recommendations* and *Advice*. Teachers delineated issues and problems, outlined recommendations, and offered advice with more profusion and facility than on any other item in their interview. It is as if they have lain in wait for the opportunity. In fact, I believe they had, for these are the very matters that teachers reflect upon, wrestle with, and talk about every day of their teaching lives. The pity is, their perspectives are seldom sought by those outside the confines of the school. When issues of education come to the forefront and decisions are to be made, it is the administrators, the lawmakers, the taxpayers whose views are most often heard.

With few exceptions, teachers' thoughts in these matters came in rapid lists—there was no need for narrative. Their thoughts were crafted and complete, queued with the efficiency of an assembly line.

Carolyn Skeen

Issues and Recommendations: Like Jonathan Kozol, I assert that we must put an end to unequal education in this country. We cannot pretend that all of our students have the same facilities and the same opportunities. They do not. This is the major challenge for the new century. Do children from a school system with a broad tax base deserve art in their schools, while children from the ghetto do without art? Is art education only for the daughters and sons of parents who are educated and financially comfortable? Is education in the arts a luxury? I believe that the answer to these questions is a resounding NO! All children deserve the best education that we can give them and that education must include the visual arts.

The trend toward privatizing education to cure the ills of teaching and learning is my pet peeve. Not everything is or should be modeled after business. What our schools don't need are temporary fixes by those who do not really understand that education requires more than an impressive balance sheet. In a documentary on the ills of our education system, Jonathan Kozol said that cheap vouchers for private schools would not help and that the day each child gets a $25,000 voucher to go to Exeter, he would become a Republican!

Most of the problems facing the next generation of teachers are societal problems which keep our students from learning, for instance, drugs, violence, the dissolution of the family, greed, and attempts to solve disputes, no matter how petty, through litigation. If elected officials do not start dealing pragmatically with some of these issues instead of just whining and sighing over them, society is going to evolve in a frightening direction.

Advice: Remember that there is no one perfect way to teach art. New trends come and go. Take the best from the reform movements and integrate the new information into your teaching to help your students in their own context. There will always be art teachers who have taken other paths, teachers who use other methods, those who think differently. Respect this!

Be aware of kindergartners with scissors, especially if they are sitting near someone with long hair!

Candy Alexander

Issues and Recommendations: Right now, we have large numbers of teachers retiring. I wonder who will mentor the new generation of teachers who will take over their classrooms in the coming fall. Further, because of alternatives in professional opportunities and the lure of better salaries, there is a drain on highly qualified young people going into education. People with business expertise and those who are competent in math and science are lured away by paychecks way out of scale with teaching.

With the massive influx of culturally diverse immigrants, the interests in multicultural education will continue to grow. Increasingly, the big question that teachers will have to grapple with will be this: If we continue our strong focus on plurality, on the maintenance of ethnic distinction and diversity, how do we promote community and, on a more grand scale, global unity? For the teacher, you have to consider each child's back-ground—the whole context and his/her individual capabilities. How do you integrate all of this, both in managing your classroom and in building an art program that is effective for all of the students? These are problems of grand scale concern.

As for the art teachers, we will have some of the same-old/same-old. The perpetual idea that art is a "frill" is probably going to continue. The interest in enhancing art education with technology will probably be thwarted because of lack of funding. Technology is expensive and money for technology in education will most likely be committed to other academic areas. More generally, in these times of budgetary shortfalls, the gains we've made and the jobs that we've generated in art are probably going to be in jeopardy. Perhaps it would help if we would quit defining or justify-ing art education in the two extremes. One group asserts that it's just a frill, a time to have fun. At the other extreme are the people who say, "You've got to have art and music because study in these areas promotes better scholastics, improving math and other disciplines." It's the "chicken or the egg" puzzle. Is it because kids who do well in art naturally are the ones who are better students and who have higher cognitive abilities and me-chanical skills? Or, is it the other way around? No one that I know in any of the research has been able to prove that being in art or music made them better students in other academic areas. It's more likely the other way around. Some believe that if we can't justify that study in art boosts learning in other areas, then art on its own has no value. This is a fallacy that art teachers will have to continue to combat. They will have to be advocates for the innovative and critical thinking, the initiative, the organi-zation, and the sense of independence and responsibility . . . and joy that education in the arts nurtures.

Advice: New teachers need to come into the classroom with more on-task or hands on experience with classroom management. Many new teachers, not just art teachers, come with the belief that 90% of the class will be wonderful, that there are only a few problem students. They need to realize that this is not reality. New teachers should also be prepared to deal with the administrative "stuff," the attendance and various state forms like special education documentation. They often think they will come in and spend X amount of time teaching and are totally frustrated about how much time gets spent doing paperwork. They should also be aware of the ways in which formal lesson plans need to be adapted to classroom reality and yet maintain a solid curriculum.

Another point of advice is really for the experienced teachers. You are the people who could compile the best handbook of tips and topics for incoming teachers: Where are the school and community resources? Where can I find freebie materials? What are some good student management strategies? What are some methods to cope with space and storage problems? In a situation where I have next to nothing, what would work here? Experienced teachers could act as a tremendous resource for new teachers. In cases where young teachers replace seasoned professionals and where valued mentors are scarce, such a compilation of all this wonderful knowledge would certainly help.

Carrol Morgan

Issues and Recommendations: Teaching has become a battle against the elements of time, responsibilities, emotions, and change. It is a struggle that, increasingly, takes an unacceptable toll on new as well as experienced teachers, and it results in the loss of many good professional educators. To indulge in a popular industrial metaphor, no matter how hard teachers work to educate their students, the thought of producing potentially "defective products" is disheartening. Placing disproportionate responsibility on teachers for creating final "products" that are by and large beyond their quality control is a mistake. Our schools and classrooms are not part of a factory complex that makes widgets. Unlike the precision of an assembly line, we cannot sort, and pick and choose for perfection, we cannot discard the imperfect. We need a reality check in education. Teachers are not the only educators of our children. We must create a better balance of responsibility and accountability among teachers, parents, administrators, and communities. Future teachers must not be expected to accomplish the impossible, or they will exit public education.

There is a proliferation of problems that will have an impact on future art teachers. In general, costs are increasing for a college education. After graduation, teacher salaries are not competitive. There are increasing undergraduate course requirements in art education pedagogy, taken at the expense of studio art experiences. There is a lack of public respect for the teaching profession, overcrowded schools and over-extended teachers; consequently, there is job-hopping and relocation. There is the escalating controversy over instruction in character and moral values. There is the vast deficiency in meeting the technology needs of future art teachers. Art educators will continue to wrestle with whether or not to adopt or adapt DBAE to their own classroom setting. They will also grapple with the issues of promoting or not promoting art education as an auxiliary to learning in other subject areas, and whether or not to form a closer association between visual arts education and education in the other arts.

Advice: I would tell young teachers to learn all you can about the community in which you teach. Live there if possible and make an effort to know the families and local history. Be sensitive to the socio-economic assets and deficiencies of your students. Be active in youth organizations that represent the interests and activities of your students. Know your local resources, including professional artists, businesses, libraries, and agencies that can be enlisted to support art education. Display your students' artwork at every opportunity—in hospitals, businesses, and libraries. Make these exhibits attractive and supply additional information on the purpose or techniques of the artwork. Take pictures of your students' work. Provide your students with real life art experiences via visiting artists, field trips to college art departments, museums, and local galleries and artists' studios. Don't forget to include out-of-the-ordinary areas of the visual arts like local architecture, landscape design, welding projects, and more.

More specifically, my own friends and family experiences with mental illness have made me extremely sensitive to the particular needs of my students who live with these special circumstances, who must deal with the stigma and misunderstanding of mental illness. I have had and will continue to have students who must face the facts of their own or of a family member's mental illness and the devastation it can bring. I approach their needs with empathy and a commitment to helping them find success in their own way in the art room. For new art teachers, please know that these special students' needs for acceptance and approval cannot be underestimated. Be aware of your limitations as a teacher, but know that awareness and understanding of mental illness lessens the fear of dealing with it with those children in your classroom. I hope that future pre-service teacher training will include reading at least one good autobiography by a person who has lived with such illness, such as Patti Duke, Kate Jamison, and many others.

Broadly, love what you do and do what you love. Be prepared for the most exciting and challenging experience of your life, but if you are not suited to the task of being a dedicated art teacher, please leave the profession. You can do more damage than good to yourself and your students. If you are enthralled by teaching, don't give up. Keep a positive attitude towards change and develop long-range plans, then take one step at a time towards your goals. Refresh your enthusiasm with continuing education, both in and out of your discipline. Take every opportunity to expand your technology skills that will translate into more effective teaching. Attend art conferences, read professional journals, share ideas with other art educators. Join an art organization for opportunities to develop your personal art skills. Make time to travel and take a break from teaching to renew your energy. Develop cooperative working relationships with your school guidance department and other faculty in your school. Be really nice to secretaries, custodians, and aides who are the unsung heroes of your school. Don't overextend yourself by assuming responsibilities that do not benefit your art program. Plant seeds of positive attitude at every opportunity; avoid negative people, they will pull you down. Always say "thank you," and a written note is best.

Susie Kropa

Issues and Recommendations: All of society's problems affect the schools. The next generation of teachers will need enormous coping skills. Art teachers will need to be prepared to teach children with a wide range of abilities and exposure to art. Patience and a sense of humor will help. As art is part discipline and part self-expression, teachers will need to walk the line between control and chaos. I think this balance will be harder to maintain than it was in the past.

In my view, the best way to improve education is to hire smart, well-educated, enthusiastic, and energetic teachers. Art teachers need these qualities, plus artistic ability. There are many practicing teachers who have few skills or little talent. I would almost rather not have art than have children exposed to ill-conceived ideas. Finally, art teachers have to be passionate.

Advice: My advice to the next generation of art teachers is to join the NAEA (National Art Education Association) and read the journals. Keep up with the latest theories. Read articles on both sides of an issue and form your own opinion. Work with classroom teachers, but don't let them dictate your curriculum. Be a storyteller. Don't be afraid to ham it up to capture the students' interest. Most children naturally love art—nurture that. Know that you'll never reach every child. Don't dwell on your failures. Be nice to the custodian.

Gerald Vilenski

Issues and Recommendations: Many of the issues, problems, and difficulties
facing art educators are not all that different from those faced by others in
education. Dwindling resources, lack of administrative support, aging
infrastructures, increasing micro-management by state lawmakers, quick-fix
educational fads, overcrowded classrooms, among others, are all contribut-
ing to the problems we have to face. Art teachers, particularly, have to learn
and put into practice the skills of advocacy, a situation which other teachers
may never have to face. Political advocacy is becoming increasingly
important as a way of effecting meaningful change and progress in art
education. The days of art teachers working in isolation are over.

There are three keys to improving education in general and art education in
particular: Leadership! Leadership! Leadership! Schools have lost their
sense of independence and innovation, becoming a reactive rather than a
proactive force in education. Without competent leadership, art educators
will accomplish little more than maintaining the programs they have now,
which are, in too many cases, meager. If art teachers are serious about
changing the way we are perceived by the public, then it is up to them to
become more involved. If we sit around waiting for others to come to our
aid, it simply won't happen. When I talk to student teachers about art
education, I always admonish them to prepare themselves to define, justify,
and promote the value of their visual arts program with colleagues and
administrators. I also feel that art education associations at the state and
national levels have to provide more aggressive leadership towards improving working conditions for art teachers in the field. All the research in the
world will do no good if real-life situations prevent theory from becoming
practice.

Advice: My advice for the new generation of art teachers is focused in two
areas: the mechanics of being an art educator and the importance of being
an art advocate. First, successful art teachers need to be experts in multiple
media. Take time to educate yourself in as many art experiences as you can
as you continue to teach. I cannot over emphasize the importance of
knowing the content and skills within your subject area. That knowledge
base assists teachers in preparing art activities that are developmentally
appropriate; it also enables you to offer a wide variety of art experiences to
your students. Further, make your expectations clear. Set a high level of
standards for both the behavior in your room as well as the quality of the
products created in it. Process is important, but so is the product. Possess
and show a passion for your subject. You have to love teaching art and be
an active artist yourself in order to inspire children to love art. Develop
activities you are interested in and have fun making; this will translate to

your students. If your students know you are an active artist, you will gain credibility. Intertwined with all of this, have and use a sense of humor. Relax and have fun with your students! Humor goes a long way towards diffusing conflicts in the classroom and results in students being more willing to do their best if they think you are learning and having fun right along with them.

The second area of advice concerns learning to be an advocate for art, both within your school environment and the community. Think of yourself as a leader and take the initiative to lead for your department. You will find that few of your colleagues will do this for you. Your department will not flourish without good leadership to guide its progress. If you are going to be an advocate, you must keep up with current theory and practice, attend conferences, learn about DBAE, brain research, technology, all of the instructional trends and reforms that are being bandied about. Importantly, practice art yourself. The most effective art teachers I know maintain a second professional presence in their communities by exhibiting their art and being active members in professional art organizations. Learn the skills of advocacy by attending seminars at your state and national organizations' conventions. Finally, apply leadership strategies to build cooperation with other arts professionals in your schools and community. Serve on local arts councils, coordinate art shows in the community, and build a relationship with business and government officials who can lend support and credibility to your program.

Above all, I have learned in my many years of teaching art that it is essential that you keep focused on the most important thing: children. If you don't particularly like working with children, don't see the inherent value in art education for yourself, don't take yourself seriously as an artist/educator, then leave the profession.

Suzanne Greene
Issues and Recommendations: As our world becomes more visual and symbols more universal, keeping up with computer technology will be an on-going issue, especially for the visual arts teachers. Teachers must be well trained in the computer arts and in how the brain works so that they can understand that every kid is his/her own person. They cannot be lumped together and treated alike. Equally, multicultural issues will be a factor in how art and all other subject areas should be taught.

Teacher pay must be increased so that the younger, brighter students will want to go into education. Consider, for example, that a teacher in the 10th year in Texas is paid thousands of dollars below the national average.

The one thing that really scares me is the rising violence in our schools. We had a 6th grader threaten to blow up our school, and one of my district's high schools was under police protection after a hit list and bomb plans were found. After Littleton, we take all threats for real. I also see more of our kids bringing guns and knives to school. Most will tell you that this is for after school protection. When I first started teaching, it was tobacco and Scotch in tea bottles. Now it's drugs and weapons. Our kids today are growing up too fast—dating too early, having sex too early. I have had many pregnant girls, mothers and fathers in my 7th and 8th grade classes. Too many come from broken homes and are without any supervision after school. I have one boy who is locked out of his apartment every day, so he roams the streets. I can't help but worry about my students. Are they going to make it? Have I given them reason to?

Advice: It is difficult to teach if you don't have a supportive faculty. You need to reach out and work together to make your school a better place. In my school, we have that. When my mother died, I was helped in so many ways; shortly afterwards when I started to cry because she was gone, I turned to another teacher who also lost a family member and we comforted each other. Sometimes even the kids will comfort me if I'm down or upset. Today a girl brought me a flower just to say, "Thanks!" I'm a big believer in hugs, but only if the student is OK with one. Perhaps it is because I'm an older teacher or a mom, but my students come to me for comfort when they are upset. Be honest and open with your students. If you say you are going to do something, then follow through; otherwise, your students will learn quickly that you don't mean what you say and you will lose credibility. Keep humor in your life. Don't be afraid to tell jokes, smile, or have fun with your students. My students tell me my class is best because they are allowed to be themselves. Stay current in your field, take classes, visit art shows. Become a friend to your head custodian and the principal's secretary. They have a lot to give and to teach you.

Carol Wellein

Issues and Recommendations: Teachers today are faced with a variety of societal problems, many of which were unforeseeable in the 60s. The issue of accountability is very important and is slowly being resolved. Money will always be an issue, especially with the rising cost of art supplies. Class size continues to be problematic. Class enrollments should be smaller, more manageable. The focus must be on training well-qualified teachers who can create a well-rounded educational program for all age levels. We need more interdisciplinary approaches with adequate planning time to create these curricular structures. In addition, teachers in our age bracket need more training in computers and ways to implement computers into the art curriculum.

Just because parents feel their children are more safe in an independent school, it is not necessarily so. Teachers in private schools face many of the same problems as those in public schools and they too need to be prepared for the Twenty-first Century. All teachers are going to have to learn how to help students living in difficult situations. We are going to need training in how to better handle problem students, how to deal with unexpected acts of violence and how to teach life-long coping skills to our students.

Advice: As an art teacher in the 21st Century, you need to be well prepared to teach art, to be flexible, have a sense of humor, be well-organized and innovative, and to learn from your students as well as from more experienced teachers. You will need more content knowledge. There is so much more information available than when I first started to teach and that should make lesson planning easier. There are outstanding videos, CD's, art packets, and Internet web sites to supplement your lessons. Take advantage of the variety of resources for all grade levels. It is so important for new art teachers to watch for changing trends, to evaluate lessons, teach students to "talk" art, make changes according to class dynamics, drop the lessons that don't work, and bring back the tried and true skill-building lessons.

Joan Newcomer
Issues and Recommendations: I have been disturbed by the amount of shootings that have taken place in our schools recently. It is frightening that someone with distorted thinking can bring guns to a school and shoot innocent students and teachers. There is no reason that guns should be so readily available and this continues to be an issue that is largely ignored. Powerful members of the NRA who care more about profit than the future of our children exert tremendous control over policies of gun control. When I was in school, if someone became disturbed by something, they might use their fists rather than guns when they felt an aggressive need to fight. We need much more strict gun regulation laws. England is a country that does not allow guns and consequently has a lower homicide rate. We might learn something from them.

I think that our art teachers need to be weary of some of the latest pedagogical trends. Should students working on computers with Kid Pix, for example, by-pass the tactility of real paint and clay? Are rubrics appropriate for lower school art just because it is the hot approach today? Do very young children need to feel the pressure of being graded on their artwork?

The teachers and classrooms of today have proliferating needs. For disruptive students, we need an effective system of dealing with their problems to prevent them from impairing the learning of others. We need smaller class sizes and class periods long enough to develop a coherent, sequenced lesson. We need dedicated teachers in our field and administrators who have a healthy respect for the importance of art education. Likewise, we need positive and supportive parent involvement. We need funds for appropriate art supplies, guided tours of local art museums, and programs like visiting artists. More attention should be paid to celebrations and exhibitions of children's artwork. Effective art education programs on the graduate level and more in-service teacher workshops in the visual arts would help to keep teachers up to date and motivated. Equally, the development of professional networks for art teachers to share ideas and support each other would be a great facilitator.

Advice: Art teachers must be sure that administrators and other people who have the power to make decisions about their teaching environment are aware of the best ways to facilitate quality art education. Young teachers just entering classrooms should be filled with energy, enthusiasm, and excitement about dealing with children. Most importantly, new art educators should care about their students, love their subject matter and want to inspire their charges to be passionate about art. Those new to the profession should realize that they are never too old to learn. They need to be inquisitive and have the desire to read materials and attend conferences and workshops that are relevant to their field. Art teachers must realize that the visual arts is an awe-inspiring subject to teach; the possibilities are limitless. They should appreciate the idea that art often reflects humankind's spiritual side and provides meaning to our daily existence.

As for some short nuggets of advice, try to find humor in what you do. Try to be relaxed. Speak up and let it be heard when too much work is being pushed on you. It's hard to provide quality art education (no matter how experienced the teacher is) when classes are too large or there are too many classes to teach. Realize that college doesn't teach you *how* to teach. The only way to really learn is by experiencing the classroom. Little children have a natural love and enthusiasm for doing artwork, and motivation and demonstrations make them even more excited. Keep lots of picture files and examples of artwork. Organization will make or break you. Positive reinforcement really works. Not everyone loves art and children as much as you do. Never lose these loves. Each student is unique in the way they express themselves and in how much time it takes them to create. Effort is more important than the end product. If the child's heart is in it, it is an A+. Children would much rather do artwork than listen to you talk. Most importantly, bring lollypops.

Yvonne Greene

Issues and Recommendations: Teachers are facing a continued devaluing of the arts. Technology, academic testing, and athletics are squeezing out the arts in our schools. School vouchers are presenting another formidable threat.

Art should be required at all levels for students, at the least, kindergarten through seventh or eighth grade. Art should be taught by art specialists in adequately equipped art rooms. An art elective should be required to complete high school. Art resource centers in regional education service centers, like in the 1970s and early 80s, should be established to provide on-going staff development for educators. As part of their principal's and superintendent's certification, all administrators should be required to take at least one course in the value of arts education, just as they do for reading and math. Administrators should come with an understanding of the inherent value of arts education, as opposed to the perception of art as a handmaiden to boost reading and math scores.

Advice: Be proactive in your advocacy of art in the schools. Keep your program visible in the community through exhibits, billboards, presentations. Continue to impart love of art to students. Encourage creative problem solving. Plan meaningful art activities that stretch students' capabilities to respond, to grow and express themselves in an articulate manner through the visual arts. Avoid teaching art as a disjointed group of unrelated "projects." Constantly draw connections between art and other fields of study without letting art become a mere handmaiden to the other disciplines.

Kathleen Thompson

Issues and Recommendations: I don't know what the future holds. You can't predict some of the changes in society. I never thought the walls would come down between here and the communist countries—never thought I would see the Berlin wall literally come down. There are all kinds of things I never thought I'd have to deal with, like the prospect of a kid coming and shooting me or my students in my classroom. So I can only wonder what the next century will be like.

Advice: In the end, it doesn't matter what your wand of enchantment is, you can't change everybody as a "magicator." You do the best you can. You try the best you can. Some children you'll help in small ways; some you'll just put enormous energy into and you won't help at all. A few you'll make a lot of difference in their lives. On the whole, you will know that at least they will have been touched by kindness. At least they'll have a moment when they did something well and they knew it and they could be proud of their art, whether it was an exhibit at the airport in Atlanta, an art show in the capitol's legislature, or just a small, local exhibit. You know, I have kids, now adults, who still have the art they created in my classes. They don't save their science papers. They don't save those tests from math, even if they become mathematicians. But they still have their art and I'm talking about 10, 15 years later I've come across kids who will say, "I still have that!" So, I've become more realistic in the amount of change I can make in people's lives, and though it's less than I thought it was going to be, I still feel really good about it. I still think that even if I have helped in just a small way to make human lives better, I have accomplished a lot. Even if you have to lower your standards to move your students forward, you should still feel good about the progress you've made, about being a teacher.

Jane Hollingsworth

Issues and Recommendations: The information glut from the media often portrays public schools and teachers as being grossly ineffective; consequently, the public has lost confidence in our system of education. An increase in legislative and community support for our schools is a must. The teaching profession must be elevated to a level where classroom teachers are viewed with respect and rewarded financially for their efforts. As it is, the present pay structure rewards those who come in contact least with the students. Neither parents nor students seem to have a sense of ownership of their schools. Decisions seem to be coming from remote, unknown sources. Smaller, community based schools with site based management involving teachers, parents, and community leaders would embrace all those involved in the decision-making process. Furthermore, curriculum, particularly at secondary levels, needs to be less fragmented along content lines. Students should be presented with information in a way that enables them to see the interconnectedness of learning. Art and other "exploratory" subjects should not be seen as an addendum to more important subjects, but instead, as an integral part of all learning. Art teachers should be educated with a strong background in language and the humanities. Pre-service courses should provide information to potential art teachers about the ways in which art relates to other content areas.

Advice: Love your subject. Continue to create art—teaching art without creating it is an artificial experience. Don't fall into the trap of saying, "There is no time." Make time. In addition, find out what your students are learning in other classes. Learn as much about those subjects as you can. Colleagues tend to respect those with a broad education. Become a good role model in your school; become known for your quality teaching and your willingness to learn. Continue your growth through classes, travel, reading, and technology. Learn all you can about computers, software, video and photography equipment. Join your professional organizations; befriend other art teachers. Volunteer for committees that might improve the school environment. Call parents to let them know when their children are doing well, as well as when they're having a problem.

Cherie St. Pierre

Issues and Recommendations: Equipping schools with contemporary and sufficient technological tools continues to be a major problem. I have long fought for a computer with a CD-ROM for the art room. It should be standard equipment to have a large TV screen hooked up to a computer so that, with the touch of a finger, each child can see art galleries around the world. Moreover, learning assessment and assessment reports continue to be problems in the visual arts area.

Advice: Remember to evaluate each child on individual merit. Do your best to motivate all children to have a positive experience in art.

Martyna Bellessis

Issues and Recommendations: Funding will be cut if we don't become stronger advocates for art. The parents and the general public need to know all the terrific things that happen in the art room. Art educators must "brag" a little and share mucho! Young art teachers must recognize that they need to become an integral component of the school environment. They need to be communal participants and generously offer their expertise.

Advice: Be involved in your school's activities. Attend pizza suppers and other fund-raisers. Share in your students' lives. Learn their names, be aware of their circumstances, and hear their stories. I teach at a school with 600 students and I learn everyone's name every year. We have an ethnically diverse student body with many international students—one-third of our population returns to their home country each year. Know that even if students don't speak English, they can achieve success in the art class. Remember, you are teaching a universal language. Finally, all art teachers should join the National Art Education Association, state and local arts organizations, and attend conferences. They should exchange knowledge, give workshops.

Lurline Lapolla

Issues and Recommendations: Improving human relations and understanding are vital needs. The key to bettering education in the future is nurturing a basic concern and consideration for each other. As for art education, the focus is on diversity. All people offer enrichment in an ever-shrinking world.

Advice: Love what you do. Like people. Seek support from your family, especially significant others. Take time for yourself.

Mark Phillips

Issues and Recommendations: I'm not sure where we are headed. I wonder what technology will do to learning. Will there be a time when students do all their learning on computers, perhaps from home through distance learning? Where will that put the arts which are all about getting hands dirty in real materials and which are steeped in human interaction? I hope the arts as we know them will continue to exist in a technological age.

Advice: Be prepared. Learn all you can learn and keep current. Remember that teaching is dealing with people, so be a good listener, get involved. Know that kids are undergoing lots of changes and pressures, so try to be sympathetic. Keep everything in perspective and live your own life—don't let your job eat up your entire life. I say that but I have not done that; nevertheless, I want to pass those thoughts on to the next generation of art teachers.

Phyllis Bosco

Issues and Recommendations: There are many educational issues to be considered for the future, including vocational training programs, pre-kindergarten availability, continuation and enrichment of elective choices, and equal opportunities for children with special needs. After elementary and high school, the open door policy for community college enrollment will become even more important in our rapidly growing and changing society. What my list of issues boils down to is this one message: The future vitality of our nation rests directly on the importance every citizen places on education. Community-based commitment in making education one of its highest priorities should be a major public goal.

Advice: I recently asked my teenage son and some of his friends what they think a teacher should know. A usually witty and vociferous bunch, they became unusually quiet and contemplative. "A teacher should know and teach her stuff but have the patience to learn something with her students too," said one boy. "Some teachers get bad deals and get burned and make mistakes, so I think all they have to do is be able to admit their mistakes, especially to their students, and move on," added another. "Thanks, I couldn't have put it better myself," I told them.

Marie Shack

Issues and Recommendations: If we are not careful, the art programs will be immersed in interdisciplinary studies. We will lose our identity and our own self worth as a discipline with its own integrity.

The national testing trend is once again going to "streamline" American education and allow standardized testing to dictate all levels of education policy, even at the local levels.

Societal problems including alcohol, drugs, teen pregnancies, peer pressure will become more problematic. Teachers are by tradition a voice of reason in the wilderness of adolescent blues and one that students will often listen to over their parents. We have to be there for these students, a foundation for them with good advice and ways to achieve valued and worthwhile goals.

What is needed is cohesiveness among art educators. One of the most important organizations I belong to is the Massachusetts Directors of Art Education, including music and visual arts educators. Teachers belonging to groups like this are inspiring, dedicated, and well informed. Such forums and organizations facilitate the sharing of ideas and information and give teachers confidence in dealing with the system and its administrators.

Advice: Thirty years ago, one of my teachers gave me a pencil. This simple act left an indelible memory of how a little kindness can be so appreciated. Kindness to your students is invaluable. Likewise, once I told a third grade teacher how nice she was to her classes and complemented her on a special lesson she was teaching. She was in tears that someone valued her work. Kindness to fellow teachers is invaluable. When I send students back to their work areas to improve their technical form, put passion and feeling into their work to better their composition, from first through twelfth graders, they recognize that the added effort produces a more aesthetically meaningful artwork. Be aware always of your responsibility to your students.

John Skrabalak

Issues and Recommendations: Budgetary cutbacks in the arts will continue as a top issue. The employment of uncertified teachers in arts education is also a threat. Because of both of these, arts advocacy will have to remain a major priority to art teachers. Increases in class size, the possibility of over-dominance of technology, and a growing imbalance between cognitive standards versus performance standards (the former dominating) loom large on the horizon.

What is needed are federal and state mandates requiring art in K-12 in all school districts, as well as setting reasonable quotas for class size. In addition, funding should be increased at the federal and state levels. In the high schools, eliminating class ranking of students and removing the weighting system for courses would help in more areas than just the arts. Further, art classrooms, like all others, should be better equipped with computers. Learning assessments appropriate for the arts should be developed and approved in order to further credibility of art as a discipline. For the purposes of public relations, art teachers will need to exploit the avenues of multiple media and encourage the NAEA to lend stronger advocacy and support. In the big picture, the whole idea of vouchers for education should be eliminated.

Advice: Advocate. Advocate. Advocate. I advise future teachers to hold their ground and never sacrifice their personal integrity. Take as many skill-orientated art courses as you can and keep up to date with current trends, research, and instructional methodologies. Read professional research journals and familiarize yourself with new materials. Join your professional organizations and be active in them. Learn how to create and use a variety of forms of learning assessments. Be computer literate. Become skilled in grant writing and fund raising.

Sonia Pratt

Issues and Recommendations: One of the key problems which continues to grow is teaching time versus time spent on "other" duties. Pressure for accountability increases. Threats of violence proliferate. To counter a sense of alienation, we need to make all students feel that they are a part of the school; we must work to ensure that every student finds some success. For art education, there is growing apprehension over standardized tests, the potential of diminishing, devaluing the creative process.

Advice: My advice to the next generation of art teachers is be prepared to learn as much as you can. Develop organizational skills and focus on classroom management. Know that you are an important part of the whole educational process, but focus on the art classroom. It is not your job to make all the school posters or provide the materials for everyone else to create them. Stay out of the teachers' lounge where many teachers are venting their frustrations. Venting is important for their wellbeing but it is easy to get caught up in the negativity and you will carry it back to your own classroom. Learn to make a silk purse out of a sow's ear. It will be good practice, for if there is a budget cut or your school burns down like mine did in West Virginia, you will be expected to teach art without materials. Work with other teachers. There is much to learn from them and vice versa. Blended instruction is great! Join the NAEA. You will remain professional and up to date. Go to conventions. Be patient. Treat every student with dignity and respect. The parents have sent you the best that they have. Communicate with parents. Allow them to be involved whenever you can. Pay attention to what you have learned in your human development courses; you will be less reactionary. Take classes and travel for stimulation and broadened horizons. Get in shape. Teaching art takes a lot of physical energy and stamina. Have a life outside the classroom. Teaching can be draining and can consume you.

Ken Wilkie

Issues and Recommendations: In the future, will we still need teachers with certifications in the visual arts? Will the future require more integration of curriculum so that instead of specialization in art, teachers will need an interdisciplinary degree? Will we return to an earlier sweep of the pendulum where general knowledge at the elementary level is more desirable than specialization? It's hard to say whether the next generation of college students focused in art will be able to follow the paths toward content expertise that we have been recommending. Getting the art education certificate and keeping the "art job" may not be the end-all. It may be that new teachers at the elementary level might have to have more general, interdisciplinary knowledge. For budgetary and/or curricular reasons, the pendulum may swing back to the times when the art specialist was a "resource" person, a planner and a source of expertise with whom the classroom teacher could consult.

In shaping art education for the future, we must pay attention to developments within the world of art and visual arts learning. We must also focus on the learner and what research can tell us about learning capabilities. We must pay closer attention to society—what is it that our society wants and needs from their children? And that's something that is hard to weed out because there are certain outspoken sectors of society that drown out the others and so we must listen carefully and take input from a variety of voices.

Advice: Get all the education you can. You may not have the autonomy that art teachers have had nor the freedom to focus so strongly in your content area. You may have to be more flexible. Tune in to what's going on in other disciplines; understand what it means to teach in an integrative way. Keep current in team teaching trends. Throughout this past century, there has been a growing sense that teachers have to do more and more. There isn't enough time, so you are going to have to pick and choose what is most important to attend to in the short time you have with your students. Lastly, it's really necessary to make changes. It's hard to do fundamentally the same job for 26 years. I was fortunate enough to change districts, so my focus has changed, the kind of students and teachers with whom I'm working are different and these new challenges help you learn, expand your horizons.

Anita Winfrey

Issues and Recommendations: Teachers are going to face increasing rigors in accountability in many arenas. School financing will become more problematic. Multiculturalism, standardized testing, and significant numbers of students with special needs are all impacting and effecting changes in art programs.

Advice: Be open, positive, willing to change and grow. Be ready to try something new. Continue to expand your technological expertise. Nurture fellowship with other art teachers, sharing knowledge, problems, and experiences. Keep in touch with the PTO and with the community. Know that sometimes you have to wing it!

Sudee Sanders

Issues and Recommendations: Respect for the teaching profession must be nurtured. The lack of it diminishes the individual and ultimately the system itself. Scheduling for visual arts classes is another issue that impacts both the students and the teachers. Art teachers continue to be shuffled from school to school, often relegated to an itinerant's schedule, having to work with limited materials within limited instructional time. Teachers working within the arts should be allotted professional rights and conditions equivalent to those of all other faculty.

Advice: Share what you know. At every opportunity, attend National Endowment for the Humanities seminars and institutes and your local, state and national art education conferences. Continue to learn all that you can. Understand the importance of modeling higher level thinking and creativity. Philosophically, remember the old Chinese proverb that goes something like this: "He who asks a question is a fool for five minutes. He who never asks is a fool forever."

Nancy Zadra

Issues and Recommendations: We can't know what the future holds for our students. What we must do is promote the arts as one of the greatest resources in developing the mind and in preparing students to be creative, inventive, in short, to handle change.

More specifically, I believe that the big issue will continue to be education funding, especially in the arts where there is a constant threat of program cuts. We will have to deal with this so that we can jump over and beyond this limiting and perennial theme.

Advice: Be an art advocate, constantly searching for ways to reinforce the public's understanding of the value of art programs. Be sturdy and strong. Observe, learn, and do. Keep your mind and senses open. When I am tired and worn with the demands of my job, I look directly into the eyes and faces of my young students, I reconnect with them, and I become renewed and re-energized.

Bonnie Keyser

Issues and Recommendations: Drawing good people into art education, well qualified teachers who like working with children, who are sincere, fun-loving, and caring must be a priority. Art teachers will need to have interdisciplinary knowledge, plan and teach interdisciplinary units with other teachers. We must push even harder to bring art education into the core curriculum of all of our schools. As it is, students must take more and more "essential" or "required" courses, which infringes on their chances to take art as an elective.

Advice: Try to remember that all of your students will not become artists. Many teachers forget this. Keep up with technology, of course. Join your art associations and become an active member. Be a practicing artist. Try to attend all conferences so you can keep fresh in your teaching and planning. Keep art fun. Develop a good rapport with your students by taking an interest in them and getting to know them as individuals. Encourage their originality and creativity.

Jeannie Siegler

Issues and Recommendations: Among the major issues I see on the horizon for the next generation of teachers are tolerance and respect. Teachers must have tolerance for the varying ideas and individual differences among their students. They must respect them. Likewise, students must learn to respect their teachers. Globally, there must be respect for our earth and all of its inhabitants. All of the issues the next generation will be facing are subsumed under the need for tolerance and respect.

The key to improving art education in the 21st Century is to continue to value its importance in the growth and development of our students. Art has been one of the defining factors of most cultures all over the world. Oftentimes as teachers and curricula become compartmentalized, we lose sight of the fact that art is everywhere. It's in scientific illustration, literature, history, math, and inseparable from popular culture. We should notice it and be aware of its integrative nature. Art needs therefore to be taught across the curriculum. We need to keep art in the forefront of education.

Advice: Stay engaged. Don't stagnate. Keep aware and grow along with your students.

Judy Williams
Issues and Recommendations: The difficulties I see in the future are the increasing special needs of our students. Behavioral problems, abuse in the child's background, poor nutrition, and scores of other difficulties interfere more and more with teaching and with student learning. Another growing issue is the expectation that teachers should try to please everybody— students, parents, principals, the public. The stress of job security and lawsuits is ever present. Teachers are expected to cover more, discuss more, and do more in the same amount of time. In keeping with this, the computer and Internet access in the art classroom are exciting, but I wonder if technology will take us away from the thoughtful time intensity that goes into the hand-making of art objects or will it send students to seek more knowledge and experience to enhance these things made by the heart and hand?

I believe we need to re-inject content, basic facts and concepts before we spend so much of our time making instruction *fun*. Educators, particularly art educators, must be advocates, and continually talk about the knowledge, the thinking, the understanding and skills that we are teaching our students. I believe choices about education should be in the hands of educators. I believe educators must refuse to be bashed and belittled. We must find ways to counteract the negativism of national media.

Advice: Do whatever you need to do such as exercise, paint during your weekends, travel, to keep your enthusiasm and energy fresh.

Lloyd Sensat
Issues and Recommendations: The job of an art teacher is somewhat like that of a gourmet chef who creates beautiful gourmet meals, providing the aesthetics of a culinary experience for so many others, but when he goes home, he is too tired to replicate the experience for himself. As an art teacher constantly working with kids in the making of art, when I get home, I am burned out. I find it hard to keep much more than a sketchbook. It's all about the issue of time, being pulled in so many different directions, being accountable to so many different people for so many different responsibilities. This is what our future teachers will be facing.

Advice: Join, and equally important, be active in your local, state, and national art education associations. Be an incessant advocate for the arts, capitalizing on every opportunity to promote the cause with administrators, parents, fellow faculty, and the community. Collaborate with your colleagues, form networks and support one another. Be active in community organizations and services. Don't forget that you are both an artist and a teacher, but be aware that the artist in you will often get neglected. Remember that teaching is an art, intense and personal. It takes enthusiasm, commitment, well-balanced content knowledge, and the ability to empathize.

Barbara Hirokawa
Issues and Recommendations: The biggest problem for the coming generation of teachers in all disciplines is the continued lack of support for education. I think we are going to have a harder and harder time attracting the best people to a field that doesn't pay a decent living or receive much respect. To get an idea of how under-appreciated we are, you can look at the events at Columbine. According to the media, that school consisted of 1,950 students, the teacher who died, and the teacher who made the 911 call. The presence and perspectives of the rest of us have been ignored.

Art teachers in Colorado will have the same challenges of holding onto their programs in times of money crises. Since Colorado is a local control state, even standards decreed by the legislature can be ignored or by-passed; the most this legislation has accomplished in our state is to make the arts slightly harder to cut.

Despite the negative circumstances, I am optimistic that things can improve if people will come to recognize the importance of the arts and the role they can play in our schools. This is happening in some states, and has been for years, but not yet in my own state of Colorado.

Advice: My advice to new teachers is to stick with it! It's all worth it because you have the opportunity to teach students about beauty, controversy, heritage, about how to express themselves and how to think deeply about the life that they live. You will have an influence on the rest of their lives. And you may even be responsible for the awakening of an artist or two.

Lora Barrett
Issues and Recommendations: State and national art standards have been established. Where is the financial and physical support to implement them? In society in general, there is a growing disparity between the

"haves" and "have-nots." With their low salaries, art teachers will have fewer and fewer hours to keep their craft alive when they will have to work part-time jobs to feed their families. Relatedly, the cost of personal art supplies is outrageous, so fewer art teachers will be able to afford materials for their continued artistic growth. Re-certification is another problem. For those of us who would like to get an MFA, there are few schools where we can take courses part-time, and those that are affordable are even fewer.

Advice: Avoid the isolation that can come with the teaching profession. We are constantly surrounded by "little people," and so rarely have the opportunity to interact with our peer group. Become active in your union. Interact with your arts colleagues to nurture personal development and leadership skills. Find time for your own art, seek a mentor, and then be a mentor.

Know that it will be difficult to set goals on a daily basis when you don't know how the administration will tinker around with the schedule. Know that it's difficult to stick to a schedule in the classroom when student discipline or emotional issues arise that take precedence over the teaching of art. Teaching about life and how to be a better human being takes so much effort and energy, but it is vital.

Above all, understand that it's difficult to let go, to know when you can't do any more to help a student. It's sometimes hard not to get too involved. It's hard to try and push outside the limited socio-economic and cultural box that each of us is in so that we don't impose our (often) middle class norms/values on the kids.

Chapter 8
In the Long Run

There's bloom on these old flowers yet.
Yvonne Greene, West Ward Elementary School, Slaton, Texas

Without formal declaration, without pomp and the conferring of special awards, the Flower Teachers find themselves now in a position of privilege. But it is not the kind of privilege bestowed gratuitously, of frivolous favor. It is a costly one gained through time and exertion, through study, contemplation, human interaction, success, failure, sorrow, fear, beauty, and joy. The privilege that they have earned is the right to speak from the vantagepoint of experience. In Katherine Anne Porter's words, "Experience is what really happens to you in the long run; the truth that finally overtakes you" (1955, p. 229).

It has been three years since I first collected the stories of these 30 teachers. As I explain in the Epilogue, I was unable to conduct live interviews, so teachers either wrote or audiotaped their responses. Because of this, I have not met all of the participants. Several of us have come together at the National Art Education Association conferences over the past three years. I have talked to many on the phone and, thanks to the indispensable e-mail, have exchanged reams of questions and ideas via the Internet. Throughout the writing of this book, there have been many changes, both positive and not, in the professional and personal circumstances of the participants. There were the tragic events at Columbine, where Barbara Hirokawa had been teaching. Several of the teachers have been struggling with health problems; one from New Jersey is recovering from a life-threatening injury sustained at her school. Some have lost loved ones. In one way or another, all have been deeply affected by the horrific events of September 11. There have been more joyous and welcomed changes too. Over the past two years, seven have retired, excited to return to their artwork, to travel, and to some much deserved leisure time. Several of the retirees are beginning new careers as part-time university instructors. One has opened a pizza parlor in Virginia. Another has become a New Orleans tour guide, nurturing his appreciation for the cultural richness of the Big Easy. A few, including myself, have moved and are now in different schools. In the past two years, several have won lifetime achievement awards and have been nationally and locally honored. We have exchanged cards, letters, and e-mails at holidays, especially with each New Year. All of the participants have good-naturedly permitted me to prod them for additional information. The times when I was tired and bogged down with the enormity of the project, they bolstered me, especially toward the end. We have become friends.

During these many months I have read and re-read hundreds of pages of text. I have probed and sorted through these people's thoughts and feelings in an effort to reconstruct as much as possible of their teaching wisdom and experience. In looking back over their years in the schools, at where they have been, what they have done, where things have flourished or faltered, the Flower Teachers have found their own truths. Whether they are your truths or whether they represent the truths of the majority of the teachers of this generation, we do not know. What is important is that they are truths gained from the most authentic means, living a life in the classroom. Certainly, they are truths worthy of consideration.

In reflecting on the whole of the Flower Teachers' stories, I return to the poetic lines of T. S. Eliot, the sympathetic refrain with which I opened this book. On his visit to the historical village of Little Gidding, the poet pondered the patterns of past and present and the achievement of moments of insight:

> We shall not cease from exploration
> And the end of all our exploring
> Will be to arrive where we started
> And know the place for the first time. (1942, p. 1500)

In their sojourns in the lives of so many students, parents, administrators, and colleagues, in their travels through the myriad days in the schools, it seems true now that they have arrived where they started and they know the true nature of the job that they do.

Chapter 9
Epilogue
Cultivating the Project

I have come a long way but it has not been a lonely journey. I can look back and see the many individuals who have pointed the way, walked along with me, offered a helping hand, and brought some outstanding refreshments for my mind. I hope I can do the same for new and future art teachers.
Carrol Morgan, King George Middle School, King George, Virginia

Between Buzzers and Bells
Somewhere in the skinny time between the changing of classes and the quick chats in the lunchroom, the idea for The Flower Teachers' Project began. As an art education professor, a significant part of my university teaching responsibilities has entailed spending many hours each week in elementary, middle, and secondary classrooms supervising student teachers. Over the past fifteen years, I have visited scores of schools and hundreds of classes in several different states. Integral to my visits are consultations with the art teachers who accept these pre-professionals into their classrooms. Most of the time our talks are about the progress of the student teachers, their knowledge of art, proficiency in planning, and the way they conduct a class. But sometimes, after the farewells of chattering children, in between buzzers and bells, or during the quick minutes of a teacher's lunchtime, these conversations change; they move away from the pragmatics at hand toward things more philosophical, more enduring and indicative of teaching and learning as a whole. In listening to the stories about teaching, of schools and children, of dejection and delight, I came to realize the mother lode of knowledge and real life experience that was so generously laid before me. And so it was within these brief but frequent occasions of informal talk, in hallways, lunchrooms, or over an after-school soda in the faculty lounge that I decided to undertake a search and write this book.

As teacher, researcher, and writer, I found myself in the midst of a field of research riches that promised a payoff of critical insights into the world of art teachers and their schools. From the conversations I had been having, I realized that I was learning things that, despite my own experience, had not occurred to me before, new perceptions about teachers, students, administrators, parents, and about changes that have occurred in our schools.

All of this would have provided enough incentive to undertake this research project. But there was something more that was driving my desire to delve into these teachers' stories. Early in my classroom visits, I noticed that the time I was spending with some teachers was expanding beyond what was necessary to monitor my student teachers' progress and it didn't take long for me to realize why these particular teachers piqued my interest and provoked me to extend my stays. They were the senior teachers, a little gray in the temples, dependent on reading glasses, and a little different in their outlook on what teaching is all about. I was drawn to them because of their peculiar mixture of confidence and humility, because of the things they knew, and because of their intriguing anecdotes, which stretched from sometime "back then," to now. I was also drawn to them because of a personal tie. For a time, I was one of them, a Flower Teacher, part of that same generation, and if I had stayed beyond my fifteen years in the high school classroom, rather than moving into higher education, I would have been their teacher-colleague. And so, part of the intrigue I had with these veteran teachers emerged from my own quest to sort things out, to make sense of, and to find the significance that defined my own early years in the classroom.

During those years from the 1960s through today, there have been myriad changes in education, and likewise, in art education. Some of these changes have been subtle, barely nuances evoking, over the years, the well-worn idea that the more things change, the more they stay the same, and in the world of education, that sameness may itself be significant. Many of the changes, however, have been revolutionary. There have been progress and regression, growth and decay, and in the midst of it all, the Flower Teachers have been there day after day and year following year and, in my thinking, they are the ones who know something about how and why these things are so.

Finding the Participants

Sorry if I rambled on through this interview, but I guess another function of my participation has been to get me to actually sit down and organize my thoughts around all that has happened here at Columbine. What we have discovered through our experiences these past few months is the power of the arts to give us voices to express the depths of grief and horror, to give us a means to speak the unspeakable. And by doing that, to begin to heal.
                    Barbara Hirokawa, July 1999, Columbine High
                                        School, Littleton, Colorado

From among all the teachers comprising the many disciplines in the curriculum of a school, there are several reasons why I chose art teachers as the primary participants in the Flower Teachers' Project. Perhaps the following authentic anecdote will serve to animate my rationale. As tour guide for a student new to her school, one twelve year old pointed to the art room and emphatically announced, "This is art! The big room at the center!" Though the room was situated at the end of a hall, at the back of the building, and was not very big at all, this middle schooler was right. The art classroom does have a big central presence. The visual arts are inextricably intertwined with all other subjects. In many indispensable ways, they are also interconnected with the community of school, that collective spirit that brings and keeps teachers, students, parents, staff, and administrators working together toward a common end. From among all the teachers with whom I have worked over the past 30 years, I have discovered qualities that are distinctive among art teachers. This is not to say that these are comparative qualities for better or for worse. From my perspective, however, they are qualities that allow art teachers access to a breadth and depth of insights about school life to which many other teachers are not privy. More than most, art teachers see the school's big picture. At the elementary level, during the course of a week, nearly every classroom teacher brings his/her children to the art room or, when art is "on a cart," the art teacher brings art to them. In preparation for these visits, the art teacher enters into a collaboration with the classroom teacher, forging interdisciplinary ties, sharing content and methods, and exchanging perceptions about individual children, their special talents, needs, and even the personal conditions of those children's lives. Through such frequent and close contact, art teachers learn a great deal about the students, and equally, about fellow teachers, how they think and work, what they value and teach, and how they relate to the children and their school. At the elementary level, art teachers teach more students, often more than 400 in one week (some more than 600), thus observing and coming to understand the diversity that defines a student body. More than most others, the art classroom, at all levels, is inclusive; teachers learn to appreciate and work with children whose learning needs and capacities are as diverse and as changing as their individual personalities.

At the secondary level, contact with other faculty is not as well defined and student numbers are not as large, but the art teachers there have something else in common with the elementary art specialists: school-wide involvement. Whether voluntary or not, the art teacher is called upon to participate in a breadth of curricular and extra-curricular activities. When individual students have problems with social adjustment in school, when they lack motivation and/or skills and fall by the wayside in their daily studies, the art teacher is often asked to take that student into their classroom to remediate in some creative way. Everything from the aesthetics of the hallways and administrative offices, to creating stage scenery, hand-lettered signs for the PTA, covers for yearbooks, and prom-night fantasia, falls within the purveyance of art teachers and their students. In this way, the art teacher becomes involved with the school as community, coming to know the web of people, activities, and even the economics and politics that bring a school to life.

Elementary through high school, art teachers tend to maintain ties with students, often teaching the same pupils over several years, frequently mentoring students passionate about art through years of personal development. In these not uncommon instances, art teachers come to know students more intimately, following and guiding their artistic growth and maturation over time. Because of the very nature of visual arts learning, in many respects, art teachers see students in a different light. In the art room, the focus is on potentials; performance in the present is important, but what is foremost is the search for possibilities, the opening up of creative thinking, feeling, sensing, and acting, summoning the vitality that art can contribute to a lifetime. There is an indispensable synergism among all of these qualities, and in working toward their nurturance, an art teacher discovers layers within each student that may otherwise remain hidden, unexamined and ultimately in neglect.

It is for all of these reasons and one more that I have chosen to delve into the experience of art teachers, and that last reason centers around their abiding enthusiasm and unmitigated faith in the potential of education through art. There is among these teachers an almost dogged adherence to what I call an art teacher adage: Life without art is unimaginable. As made plain in their interviews for this project, these teachers' lives are inseparable from their content areas. Simply—they live and love art. They are committed to making art, understanding and appreciating it, promoting it, and, emphatically, impelling others to do the same. With a mixture of humor and honesty, high school teacher John Skrabalak put it best:

> I couldn't see myself doing anything else. As a kid I always liked to construct things and decorate the house during all the holidays. I salivated like a Pavlov dog when I heard the sound of construction paper being cut over the TV on one of those kid shows. Simply put, I loved ART and continue to adore it.

The Flower Teachers

It's the parent who stops me in the hall to say I have made a difference in their child's life.
It's the non-English speaking student who begins to smile more often and learns to say my name.

*And it's the student who brings me weed flowers that he gathered while
drawing trees outside.*
                    Suzanne Greene, Spring Branch Middle School, Houston, Texas

The stories that brought the Flower Teachers' Project and this book to life
come from 30 art teachers working in rural, suburban, and urban centers,
elementary through high school, in 17 states from all parts of the nation.
Through phone, fax, letter, and largely e-mail, they came to me in the spring
and summer of 1999. After thinking about the project for nearly two years
and finally deciding to begin the research, I posted advertisements for art
teacher participants in the most prominent place I could think of— the
newsletter of the National Art Education Association. The ad was simple
and direct, describing the nature of the project and soliciting the participation of K-12 classroom art teachers who were educated in the 1960s and
who began their teaching careers in the 1960s and early 1970s.

In order for these art teachers to participate in the Flower Teachers' Project,
they had to meet three qualifications. First, participants had to be part of the
"flower teacher" generation, that is, they must have begun their careers in
the 1960s or early 70s. Essential too, their careers must be continuous,
having been absent from the classroom a minimum amount of time, and
continuing to teach as the new millennium unfolded. Finally, they must
come to the project of their own accord. It was important for me that these
people be volunteers, teachers who had something to say, wanted to share
their experiences, and who would be as passionate about the project as I.

I specifically sought participants through a professional forum for several
reasons. First, it was the most accessible way to reach teachers at all grade
levels, in a variety of teaching settings, widely distributed throughout the U.
S. In choosing to acquire participants in this way, I knew at the outset that
the perspectives I was seeking would be, in some ways, biased. But for my
project, these were precisely the kinds of biases I was looking for. I wanted
to learn from teachers who have remained actively engaged with their
professional organization, who regularly read the professional literature,
keep abreast of changes in education issues and reform, and who maintain
collegial ties with art educators in a larger venue. In this regard, I wish to
be clear about two things. First, there is no superior claim for the quality of
teachers who are members of a professional art teachers' association.
Second, whether or not their professional insights and experiences represent
the majority of art educators is not known, but for all of the reasons I have
mentioned, these are the teachers for whom I created the Flower Teachers'
Project. These are the individuals I have asked to reflect upon and share
their classrooms, their lives, and times.

From talking with so many art teachers, my researcher's intuition told me there would be some enthusiasm for the project. My pragmatic self, however, was skeptical. I thought about the job of an art teacher, the packed teaching schedules, the extra-curricular activities, their own drive to create art, and their on-going quest for more coursework and degrees. In reality, the most I expected were a few e-mails or letters of inquiry, and if luck were with me, I might get 10 or so participants. The response that I actually received was far beyond what I anticipated. Only two days after calling for participants, the e-mails began to arrive and a few days later came the letters, faxes, and phone calls. After about two weeks, I had received inquiries from teachers all over the United States. What was heartening about these inquiries, other than their numbers, their varied geographical distribution, and their immediacy, was the nature of these initial contacts. Even before I had posed a single question, their chatty e-mails and informal letters were providing samples of precisely the kinds of information and stories that I had hoped to collect. Many of them expressed surprise and appreciation that someone, in the words of one participant, was "finally offering a forum" for them to relate the experiences and insights they had gathered over their decades of teaching. In the words of another, "I read your call for K-12 art teachers and commend your efforts to put together the personal reflections of teachers from my era. We have seen and done so much." Another said, "I would like to participate in the Flower Teachers' Project. I sometimes feel like a forgotten soul—an unsung hero." In the end, the majority of the teachers who initially inquired, signed on and dedicated hours of reflection and energy in writing and taping responses to complete an interview for this project. The participating teachers are listed and pictured in the introductory pages of the book.

Among the wealth of information collected from the participants was a curriculum vitae. Over the past four and five decades, from the 1960s through today, the teachers in this study have evolved from what some themselves call "do-good neophytes" into professionals whose credentials and accomplishments in the world of education stand disproportionate to what anyone would expect. As I read through their curriculum vitae, I felt both respect and surprise at the experiences and achievements of these people who so readily volunteered for my study. There are among them enough honors, awards, and accomplishments to fill a chapter in itself. There is, for example, a National Trust for Historic Preservation in the United States, awarded by First Lady Barbara Bush; the George Washington Medal of Honor from the Freedom Foundation; the American Federation of Teachers' John Dewey Award for Excellence in Education; and multiple awards from the National Art Education Association for Art Educator of the Year. There is even an Award for Excellence in Educational Broadcasting.

Scores of honors have been bestowed upon these teachers' personal artworks. However, from their perspectives, most noteworthy are the hundreds of distinctions that have gone to their students, including the Foreign Minister's Award from the 29th International Children's Art Exhibition, a feature on CBS Sunday Morning, exhibitions in the busiest international airport in the world—Hartsfield in Atlanta—and two students' paintings that were accepted as New York and Iowa Christmas Seal Stamps. These teachers have published articles and have written and illustrated books. Among them, they are global travelers, perpetual learners, and perennial volunteers. [See abbreviated autobiographies in Chapter 10.]

The Interview
Thoughts that went through my mind as I answered these interview questions came in a deluge! They were complicated, nostalgic, and I was amazed to recall such diverse memories from so long ago . . . and I was startled to realize that I have actually been in this business so long.
Yvonne Greene, West Ward Elementary School, Slaton, Texas

In constructing the interview, I directed my inquiry in four different, yet synergistically related directions. First, there were inner-directed questions, those requiring reflection on personal metaphors, inspiration, philosophy, successes, obstacles, and disappointments. Second, there were questions about everyday actions or outward circumstances, such as instructional conditions and settings, curricular approaches, trends, issues, and education reform. Embedded within these were questions looking backward and forward, seeking insights about students, parents, administrators, teachers, and about methods, theories, progress and transformation.

My original idea was to conduct each interview in person, but the lack of travel funding prevented this. Rather than abandoning the project, however, I formulated a body of seed questions that I thought, from my research and professional experience, would open up possibilities, jogging memory, stimulating reflection, and allowing ample latitude for personal narrative. Participants were invited to respond in writing or through audio-tapes. Twenty-four teachers wrote their responses; six taped theirs. The interview was long and inclusive, and in the words of respondents, "challenging," "evocative," and "time-intensive." The truth is, I got a little greedy in my questioning; after all, there was so much these people could tell. In its final form, the interview contained 43 open-ended items. Given this large body of inquiry, I decided to subdivide the interview into four prioritized categories. In the first were 24 "Essential Questions." Participants were instructed to make these questions their priority, focusing the bulk of their energies there. The "Essential" category dealt largely with teacher philosophy; personal background, education, and formative experiences; actual classroom events and practice; inspiration and professional motivation; reflections on education trends and issues; perspectives on the future of art education; and advice for a new generation of teachers. For those respondents who had spent their energy and exhausted their available time for the project, the next category, "Secondary Questions," was labeled "Optional." It consisted of 11 items more specifically focused on academic information, such as opinions on specific curricular innovations, issues of diversity, assessment, standards, and education funding. The third category, labeled "Odds & Ends," was also optional and contained five more personally oriented questions.

The last category "Participants' Questions," came not from the interviewer but from the teachers themselves. When asked whether there were other experiences that were left untapped by this interview, teachers made three suggestions. First, they thought there should be inquiry about the degree and importance of their own involvement in professional organizations at local, state, and national levels, in organizations such as NEA (National Education Association), AFT (American Federation of Teachers), and NAEA (National Art Education Association). In addition, one teacher broached the issue of toxic materials and hazardous conditions in early art classrooms and the potential long-term effects on teachers' and students' health. The last of their suggestions pertained to the interview itself. Several teachers wanted to talk about their involvement in the Flower Teachers' Project, what it meant to them, the thoughts and feelings they experienced as they responded to the questions and reflected on their careers. Each of these three suggestions was formed into a question and posed to the participants after the initial interview.

Surprisingly, the majority of the participants responded to all of the questions in the first three categories. The tapes and written responses were personal and comprehensive, the majority totaling 20-30 pages of text, a few exceeding 50. From these teachers' abundant outpourings, I have gathered a thick body of data from which, as discussed earlier, I have culled out the spirit, the sum and substance of their professional ventures.

Chapter 10
Autobiographies

Then

Now

Candace Elizabeth Cummings Alexander (Candy)

Current Position: Elementary Art Teacher, Church Hill Elementary & McPheeter's Bend Elementary, Church Hill, Tennessee
Education: M.Ed. Elementary Education, Tusculum College, 1999; B.S. Art Education, Georgia Southern, 1973; continued graduate studies
Studio Interests: textiles
Years in Teaching: 27

I was born in Massachusetts and drifted south. I began teaching in Charleston, South Carolina, moved to and taught in the Columbia, SC area, then relocated to northeast Tennessee where I am still teaching. Moves required me to "get in line" for an art teaching position, so interim jobs have ranged from photographer to publication lay-out artist, needlecrafts designer, substitute teacher, and even kindergarten teaching assistant. The one constant through these years has been my involvement with children and keeping my hand in various teaching venues. I have been a foster parent, Council on Child Abuse Intervention Volunteer of the Year, United Way Volunteer of the Year nominee, and craft director for several summer enrichment programs. I started Just Say No and CHARACTER COUNTS! programs in three schools. I have also illustrated two children's books. My teaching experience has included grades K-12 (including one small rural school that was itself K-12). My professional activities have included being a model teacher in South Carolina's Program for Effective Teaching, a pilot participant in the National Board for Professional Teaching Standards in Early Childhood through Middle Childhood Art, and an NAEA and state affiliate member in SC and TN. My students have exhibited their work in many local, state and regional shows. My areas of interest in art have drifted over the years; my current passion—and therapy—is basket making. How ironic to be nearing the end of my teaching career as a "basket case"!

Then

Now

Lora McNeece Barrett

Current Position: Arts Resource Teacher, Art Department Head, Holyoke Magnet Middle School for the Arts, Holyoke, Massachusetts; Assistant Professor, University of Massachusetts-Amherst
Education: Ed.D. Cultural Diversity/Curriculum Reform, University of Massachusetts-Amherst, 1993; M.Ed. Multicultural Education, University of Massachusetts-Amherst, 1987; B. A. Art, minor Secondary Education, College of Our Lady of the Elms, 1972
Studio Interests: oil painting, pastels,
Years in Teaching: 30

I knew since childhood that the art room was where I wanted to be. I loved working with my hands, seeing things that others didn't notice and being recognized for those abilities, and I loved interacting with people. My undergraduate degree is in Art from Elms College in Chicopee, MA. After teaching for 14 years in the Holyoke Public Schools, I entered a doctoral program in multicultural education and curriculum reform at UMass, Amherst. Politics had always been one of my passions, and my dissertation was on the impact of politics on parental involvement in schools. I have been president of the local affiliate of the Massachusetts Teachers Association (MTA); served on the MTA Executive Committee, chaired their Human & Civil Rights Council and Communications Committee. In 2001, the Massachusetts Alliance for Arts in Education selected me as the Distinguished Visual Arts Educator for Massachusetts. I paint in oils and pastels and exhibit on a regular basis. I have worked in the same urban district for 30 years, both as an art teacher and department head, and as a central office administrator. To my surprise, this year I have been awarded the Massachusetts Middle School Art Educator of 2002. My happiest moments are when I'm wrapped up with the students, moving from easel to easel, engaging in evaluation and critique. They are wonderful, so resilient, and they *love* thinking about and creating art.

What we share, what we say to each other will have a positive, permanent impact on their lives, as well as mine.

Then

Martyna Bellessis

Current Position: Elementary Art Teacher, University Elementary School, Bloomington, Indiana
(Retired 2001)
Education: Ed.D. Art Education, Indiana University, 1986; M.S. Education, Indiana University, 1973; B.A. Art, Cardinal Stritch University, 1963
Studio Interests: ceramics
Years in Teaching: 37

Now

Over these many years I have loved teaching elementary art students who were happy to enter the magical atmosphere of the art room where there are no rigidly "right" answers and where children know that hard work and creativity go hand in hand to produce wonderful art. I have had a wonderful career and have received many honors. In 1991, I was named Elementary Art Teacher of the year in Indiana. In 1994 and 1996 respectively, I was awarded a fellowship to study art in France and Italy and another to study at the National Gallery in Washington, D.C. I was a Disney Teacher finalist in 1996 and a Christa McAuliffe Fellowship finalist in 1998, 1999, and 2000. In 2002, I was nominated for a Cardinal Stritch University Alumni Award. I have also co-authored a series of art activity books for elementary students and have served as adjunct professor at Indiana University-Bloomington. After 37 years of teaching elementary art, I retired to be with my husband and help him grapple with difficulties in his health. I plan to do research and write articles in my retirement. As a wonderful career culmination, this year I received the Alumni Award for Professional Distinction from Cardinal Stritch University.

Then

Phyllis Bosco

Current Position: Elementary Art Teacher, Florida State University School, Tallahassee, Florida
(Retired for reasons of health)
Education: M.F.A. Sculpture & Painting, Florida State University, 1976; B.S. Art Education, Florida State University, 1968; A.A. Art, Miami Dade Community College, 1965; continued graduate studies

Now

Studio Interests: painting, photography, mixed media, sculpture
Years in Teaching: 30

I believe that when one has a passion for anything in life, the energy from that passion cannot be contained. My passion is art and music. My expertise is in the visual arts, but all forms of expression fascinate me. I dabble in music, dance, drama, and all forms of writing. I greatly appreciate architecture, cultural and religious ceremony, beautiful gardens, anything in which a positive sensorial expression of humanity is demonstrated with passion and skill. I began my teaching career in northern Florida in the late 1960s. I taught humanities, studio art, art therapy, and various other courses in art education to students whose ages range from 5 to 105 in elementary school, community colleges, nursing homes, in rural and urban environments. I have earned grants, received numerous distinctions for my teaching as well as my artwork, including winning the Kodak International Snapshot Competition. Membership in a wide range of professional organizations, including the NAEA and the Florida Art Education Association, has been an important part of my career. In 1992, I was fortunate to receive a fellowship to work with Faith Ringgold at the Atlantic Center for the Arts in New Symrna Beach, Florida. In 1997, I was chosen District Florida Teacher of the year. I am most proud of the scores of honors won by my students. I have a love for this profession which allows me to learn *with* my students, which is its own reward. I believe continued learning is the essence of vitality, no matter what the age of the student.

Then

Mary Suzanne Goodrich Greene (Suzy)

Current Position: Middle School Art Teacher, Spring Branch Middle School, Houston, Texas
Education: B.F.A. Art Education, Southern Methodist University, 1971; continued graduate studies
Studio Interests: sculpture, fibers, photography
Years in Teaching: 31

I was born in Texas, am married to William Greene and have two extraordinary sons, Will and Michael. During my childhood, we moved a lot. It was a great experience seeing the USA in the 50s and 60s before life changed forever. I started school in Port Washington, New York, on Long Island. I graduated from LaJolla High in California; you might say I had a coast-to-coast education. The years in between were in Texas, Oklahoma, and Colorado.

Now

Whenever we moved, we explored, touring in our '49 Ford or '57 Dodge. On these trips, I started my love affair with museums, history, and art. When I entered SMU in 1967, I majored in drama, but quickly switched to art. My father told me that I had to get a teaching certificate if I planned on majoring in art so I did. The first time I worked with kids at the SMU experimental art program, I was hooked. I have now been teaching 31 years; 30 in Houston with Spring Branch ISD. Awards? Well just lasting 30 years in a middle school classroom is a *major* achievement. What I can remember is Who's Who Among America's Teachers, my school's Teacher of the Year Award, Crystal Apple nominee, Outstanding Teacher Recognition Award, and PTA Life Member. I am an officer for Texas Art Teachers Association, Department Chair for the Electives, a member of the SMU Alumni Club, Pi Beta Phi Alumni, DAR, and the University of Texas Parents Association. This year I had the honor of being nominated for the Texas Middle School Art Teacher of the Year.

Then

Yvonne Greene

Current Position: Elementary Art Teacher, West Ward Elementary School, Slaton, Texas
Education: M.F.A. Printmaking, Texas Tech University, 1978; B.A. Art Education & English, Central Michigan University, 1965; continued graduate studies
Studio Interests: drawing, printmaking
Years in Teaching: 25

Now

My husband Wayne and I have two children and a grandson. I have taught kindergarten through college in Michigan, Oregon and Texas. For the past 17 years, I have been teaching elementary art in the small, West Texas town of Slaton. Early in my career, I taught high school English, then served as an itinerant elementary art teacher, pushing a cart between classrooms in rural Western Michigan schools. I taught elementary art in Eugene, Oregon as a "radio art teacher," a "helping art teacher," and an art consultant. For my radio series, *Art on the Air* , I received an award from the National Association of Educational Broadcasters. During graduate school, I was a teaching assistant in drawing and art history. In another capacity, I worked six years as a journalist for a small town newspaper prior to my current teaching position. For the past nine years, I have been Chair of Slaton's annual Youth Art Month celebration and have received awards of excellence for this work from the Texas Art Education Association. I have served as a TAEA Regional Representative, given presentations at TAEA conferences and written articles for *Arts & Activities* magazine. I have been President of the Slaton Classroom Teachers Association. In 2000, I was privileged to be a Fulbright Memorial Fund Scholar, taking a three week trip to Japan, along with 599 other American educators. A Lubbock Area Foundation mini grant has made it possible to continue a student art exchange with an elementary school in Japan for a second year. In 2000, I was selected as Regional Texas Elementary Teacher of the Year.

Sharon Henneborn

Then

Current Position: Middle School Art Teacher, Ethel McKnight Middle School, East Windsor, New Jersey [currently on health leave]
Education: B.S. Elementary Education, Oklahoma Baptist University, 1962; continued graduate studies
Studio Interests: drawing, papermaking, watercolor
Years in Teaching: 40

Now

My family lineage reads like the history of the West. Some were cowboys and some were Indians. I am, in fact, proud of my Native American heritage. Many members of my family have been educators or ministers or have held public office. They are people of action and strong conviction, so it was no surprise that I too became a teacher after my graduation from Oklahoma Baptist University in 1962. My first teaching position was in the regular elementary classroom in Wichita Falls, Texas, where I taught from 1962-69. In 1969, I moved to New Jersey where I did graduate work at Trenton State College and began teaching elementary art. I have been active in the National Art Education Association, having served as a conference delegate. I have also been actively involved in the local and state art education associations, having served on the executive board, chairing conference programs, acting as Elementary Division Chair, among others. I have been fortunate to receive several awards, including the New Jersey Governor's Award in Arts Education in 2001 and the NAEA Eastern Division Elementary Teacher of the year in 2000. I have also published articles in various arts publications. Most rewarding, so many of my students' artworks have been selected for international traveling exhibits, as well as for the 1996 Olympics Art Exhibit in Trenton. I have had the professional satisfaction of mentoring student teachers and first year teachers. Intermixed with all of these professional endeavors, I have had the pleasure and the educative benefit of studying and traveling in Scotland, Mexico, Iceland, Canada and Europe.

Barbara Hirokawa

Then

Now

Current Position: High School Art Teacher, Columbine High School, Littleton, Colorado (Retired 2001)
Education: M.A. Art Education, University of Colorado-Boulder, 1973; B.S. Art Education, Butler University, 1968; continued graduate studies
Studio Interests: photography, bookmaking
Years in Teaching: 31

From kindergarten through eighth grade, I had a wonderful art teacher named Miss Corey. Her classes were delightful, and because of her I always knew what I wanted to be when I grew up. I majored in Art Education at Saint Mary-of-the-Woods College in Indiana, where my art education professor had been a student of Victor Lowenfeld. I taught elementary art in a huge school in Indiana for four years, then moved to Colorado in 1971. In 1973 I completed a masters at the University of Colorado and taught elementary art for another year. In 1974, I began teaching at Columbine High School, where I remained until my retirement in 2001. I went from ceramics to printmaking and fibers and finally to photography. In addition to going through media, I went through many teaching fads and movements, so many I can't name them all! But the most important "philosophy" for me has always been teaching kids to love art. Last summer, when I began sorting through all the stuff that I brought home, I put everything that will someday go into a scrapbook into a large box. Then I sorted through the thousands of slides of student work, kept some, and gave the rest away to art teachers who would use them. The whole experience gave me a chance to review my career in a very visual way, to see how my teaching has evolved, and to remember kids and adults I was privileged to work with. Now I am enjoying a well earned rest, organizing all my stuff, and planning for the next half of my life. I plan to keep working with the Colorado Art Education Association and ArtSource, giving workshops and in-services, photographing weddings and my own work, making artist books, sewing, gardening, playing with grandkids, traveling, and whatever else comes up. Now I actually have time and energy to do these things. I don't know how I ever found time to go to work! In 2002, I was honored to receive the National Art Education Association's Pacific Region Award.

Then

Now

Jane Hollingsworth

Current Position: Middle School Art Teacher, Gainesville Middle School, Gainesville, Georgia
Education: Ed.S. Art Education, University of Georgia, 1997; M.A.Ed. Art Education, University of Georgia, 1978; B.F.A. Art Education, University of Georgia, 1968
Studio Interests: oil, watercolor
Years in Teaching: 30

My artistic talent was recognized early. In the Baltimore schools, as a fifth grader, I enjoyed a TV appearance with a book illustrator; the two of us drew pictures for live television. I moved around a lot during secondary school and graduated from a high school having no art program. I attended the University of Georgia because of its art education major. My advisor was the well-known Frank Wachowiak. His enthusiasm for the profession was immeasurable and had a profound influence on my teaching. I married my college sweetheart; we've been married for 33 years and our children are both teachers. I'm proud of them. I've always been somewhat of an overachiever and like recognition for my work. I've earned grants and awards enabling me to buy a kiln and three computers. Since the 1980s, I've been involved in the Georgia Art Education Association. I've held offices and won the Middle Grades Art Educator of the Year Award. My teaching has benefited immensely from the contact I've had with colleagues in art education. My Masters and Specialists degrees were timed to coincide with my pregnancies (1974 and 1976) and my "empty nest syndrome" (1995). The last few years have included for me political involvement in professional issues, in particular, the negative impact misguided reform movements are having on arts education. I am active in the Georgia Association of Educators and the National Education Association. Until recently, I have never wanted to teach any level but middle grades, and I've *lasted* at that level for over 20 years. However, it's becoming apparent that art as an exploratory subject limits instruction by sending students through the program in an assembly-line manner. I would like to alter the middle school philosophy to allow students to *elect* exploratory classes.

Bonnie Keyser

Then

Current Position: High School Art Teacher, Alleghany High School, Covington, Virginia (Retired 2001)
Education: B.S. Art Education, James Madison University, 1970; continued graduate studies
Studio Interests: silk screening, drypoint, handmade paper, batik, digital photography
Years in Teaching: 31

Now

Having known since first grade that I would be an art teacher, it was very easy for me to focus on my career. My high school art teacher loved me and taught for four additional years before retiring so that I could take her place. I taught at my rural alma mater in that same classroom for over 30 years! Having recently retired and then brought out of retirement after a year to teach at a new boy's home school, I am now concentrating on exhibiting and marketing my own art work, which is made up of silk-screens and wearable art. My husband and I are also opening a pizzeria and I plan to have monthly art shows for local artists and students at the restaurant. My achievements include building a strong art program in our county; turning students "on" to art and having many students become successful artists; being honored as Secondary Art Teacher of the Year in my region; serving as a member of the Virginia Standards of Learning Writing and Steering Team for the Arts; presenting workshops for the Virginia Art Education Association; and raising an arty and wonderful son.

Susan Kropa (Susie)

Then

Current Position: Elementary Art Teacher, Mt. Pleasant Community Schools, Mt. Pleasant, Iowa (Retired 2001)
Education: B.S. Art Education, Ohio State University, 1967; continued graduate studies
Studio Interests: drawing, painting
Years in Teaching: 33

I graduated from Ohio State University in 1967 with a B.S. in Education. I took post-graduate courses for pleasure but with no intention of getting a higher degree. I taught in Sidney, Ohio for one year after graduating, then married and moved to Mt. Pleasant, Iowa, where I've taught since. After 33 years in

Now

the classroom, I retired in June, 2001. Many of my teaching years have been part time, so that I could spend time with my children and do art. I've had the best of both worlds. I began illustrating for publication in the mid-70s and have also published articles in forums like *Arts and Activities* and *School Arts*. I have written and illustrated three books on teaching art to children: *Faces, Legs, and Bellybuttons; Sky Blue, Grass Green*; and *A Nose Is A Nose* (Good Apple, Inc.). I know I was a better teacher for having lead a "double" life. I honed my artistic skills through the free-lance work and was more effective in the classroom because I had more energy to do those challenging projects with my students. I've organized and taught Saturday art classes, spoken to service clubs and at conferences on teaching art and on publishing and illustrating. I've helped write grants for visiting artists in the schools and participated in a USA/USSR art exchange. Though I do pen and ink drawing for publication, I consider myself a painter and have exhibited throughout my teaching career. Now I am going to pursue painting with more deliberation—for myself! I don't see myself so much as a retiree, but as a born-again artist!

Lurline McLaughlin Lapolla

Then

Current Position: Middle School Art Teacher, Saxe Middle School, New Canaan, Connecticut
Education: M.S. Art Education, University of Bridgeport, 1967; B.S. Art, Skidmore College, 1964; continued graduate studies
Studio Interests: watercolor, oil pastels, colored pencil, hand built ceramics
Years in Teaching: 38

Now

I was born in Hammond, Indiana. I received my undergraduate degree from Skidmore College in 1964, my M.A. from the University of Bridgeport in 1967, and have earned more than 60 credits beyond those degrees. I have long been committed to teaching middle school and to entering my middle school students' art work in a wide variety of international exhibitions, which allows children to be ambassadors for global understanding. I have enjoyed membership in many organizations, including the National Art Education Association, the Connecticut Art Education Association, the International Society for Education through Art, the National Education

Association, the Connecticut Education Association, Delta Kappa Gamma, the Rowayton Arts Center, and the New Canaan Society for the Arts, within which I have been a member of the Board of Trustees. I have also been an active advocate for art education, having served as a National Standards Candidate (field trials) and having worked with student teachers and the B.E.S.T program. I see myself as both teacher and artist. I have exhibited in numerous solo and group shows and have illustrated and published a book: *Flowers of the Table*. I am currently working in oil pastel and colored pencil (landscapes and botanicals), as well as in home design.

Carrol Elmira Keys Morgan

Then

Now

Current Position: Middle School Art Teacher, King George Middle School, King George, Virginia
Education: M.A. Liberal Studies, Mary Washington College, 1994; B.F.A. Commercial Design, Richmond Professional Institute, 1963; continued graduate studies
Studio Interests: watercolor, portraiture, sculpture, printmaking
Years in Teaching: 34

My teaching career was a natural outgrowth of my earlier experiences in 4-H Club activities, camps and competitions. I just started out in a different direction. In August 1962, I completed the requirements for my B.F.A. in Commercial Design at the Richmond Professional Institute of the College of William and Mary and received my degree in June 1963. I married James Rollin Morgan in 1962. We have one son, two daughters, and currently three grandchildren. I began teaching elementary art in 1968 and moved to middle school art in 1976. Along the way I earned my professional art teaching certification and a masters degree in Liberal Studies from Mary Washington College. I have spent my entire teaching career in rural King George County, located halfway between Richmond, Virginia and Washington, DC. I still love the excitement and challenges of working with adolescents. My greatest teaching rewards are the visits and letters from former students. Their successes in the arts and other fields have made my teaching career meaningful. Teaching is the greatest learning experience in the world, and I look forward to putting that experience to use when I retire next year and finally commit to being a full-time artist.

Then

Now

Joan Newcomer

Current Position: Elementary Art Teacher, McDonogh School, Owings Mills, Maryland
Education: M.F.A. Art Teacher Education, The Maryland Institute, College of Art, 1975; B.A. Secondary Art Education, University of Maryland, 1970; A.A. Education, Art minor, Baltimore Jr. College; continued graduate studies
Studio Interests: watercolor, ceramics, fabric
Years in Teaching: 32, but I'm just getting started.

I grew up in Baltimore City and was educated through the Baltimore City Public School system. I received an A.A. degree in Education with a minor in Art at Baltimore Jr. College, and went on to the University of Maryland where I received a B.A. degree in Secondary Art Education. Upon graduation, I began my teaching career at the elementary level in the Baltimore City Public Schools. I was an art resource teacher and traveled to a variety of schools teaching art from a cart. I spent four years there and feel fortunate that I was trained by some of the best art educators in Maryland. Every Wednesday afternoon our art department would get together for meetings and workshops. In February 1974, with Baltimore City Public Schools closed because of a teacher strike, I was invited for an interview for a position to teach art at the Lower School level at McDonogh School, which is a private school in Baltimore County. I have been teaching there ever since. I received an MFA degree in Art Teacher Education from The Maryland Institute, College of Art. I used my summers for travel throughout the United States and to places like Greece, Italy, Mexico, Canada, Spain, Morocco, England and Scotland. I received a grant to study art during some of my travels. My artwork has been exhibited locally, including the Baltimore Museum of Art. My students have received many honors for their work, including having artwork exhibited in the State House in Annapolis. I have a supportive husband and two wonderful teenagers who are currently attending the high school where I teach. Last summer I was featured in *McDonogh Magazine* with an article entitled "Celebrating Imaginations: Joan Newcomer."

Then

Now

Mark W. Phillips

Current Position: Middle School Art Teacher, George A. Smith Middle School, Quarryville, Pennsylvania
Education: B.S. Art Education, Millersville University, 1972; continued graduate studies
Studio Interests: photography, interior design
Years in Teaching: 30

I am a third generation teacher, born and raised along the Susquehanna River in eastern and south-central Pennsylvania. I attended high school in suburban Harrisburg and, having an interest in the arts, pursued an Art Education degree from Millersville State College, now Millersville University, in Lancaster County. I have done additional graduate work at the University of Delaware and at Millersville. Part of my student teaching took place in the Solanco District, where I was hired and have remained a teacher for the last 30 years. I do love the Amish country! After ten years of teaching in an aging school building, I was able to contribute ideas to the design of my own art room at the George A. Smith Middle School, where I teach today. Some of the design features were used in an NAEA publication on art room design. I have also run an after-school art program for gifted & talented children for the past 28 years. I am very proud of many of my former students who have taken up careers in the arts. Besides art instruction, I have worked in theater design doing stage sets. I have put my interest in photography to use preparing yearbooks for school, and I have even coached middle school wrestling. During my summers, I have served as an interior decorator and painter for the school district. I am called upon to judge local parades and currently am a member of my community's zoning hearing board. I am active in my church and share my abilities as a public speaker by emceeing many programs and ceremonies. I am a recipient of the Millersville University Alumni Award for Outstanding Service. All of this has made the last 30 years exciting, challenging, productive, rewarding and certainly fleeting. It's been quite a life!

Then

Sonia L. Pratt

Current Position: High School Art Teacher, Southern Garrett High School, Oakland, Maryland
Education: B.A. Art Education, English Education, Fairmont State College, 1972; continued graduate studies

Now

Studio Interests: charcoal, oils, mixed media
Years in Teaching: 30

I graduated from Fairmont State College, Fairmont West Virginia, in 1972, with a B.A. in Art Education. I started teaching art, 9-12, in Oakland, Maryland, in 1973 after working one year as a traveling art teacher in West Virginia. I have continued in that position where my duties include Department Chair, National Art Honor Society sponsor, and teaching AP Studio, and levels I-IV of Art. I have a wonderful job in an exceptional rural community. I received the John Dewey Award for Excellence in Education in 1980 and the Maryland Art Education Association Award for Outstanding Service in the field of Art Education in 1982, 1984, 1999 and 2000. I was nominated for Who's Who of American Women in 1994, Who's Who in American Education 1995, and Who's Who in Education 1996 and 1998. In 2001, I was nominated for American Heroes in Education. In 2002, I was selected as Teacher of the Year by the Elks Lodge of Oakland, Maryland. As an artist, I work in charcoal, oils and mixed media. I exhibit regularly, most recently at the International Symposium on Art, Culture and Nature in Flagstaff Arizona. In 1994, I received an Individual Artist Award granted through the New Forms Regional Grant Program, funded by the Pennsylvania Council on the Arts-Interdisciplinary Arts Program, the National Endowment for the Arts/Inter-arts program, the Rockefeller Foundation and the Andy Warhol Foundation for the Visual Arts Inc.

Then

Sudee Sanders

Current Position: Elementary Art Teacher, Cherry Hill Schools, Cherry Hill, New Jersey
Education: M.S. Museum Education, University of Pennsylvania, 1983; B. S. Art/Art Education, Skidmore College, 1967; continued graduate studies
Studio Interests: graphics, line drawings
Years in Teaching: 34

Now

After Skidmore, I flew for Pan Am, then taught for a year in Moorestown, New Jersey. After that, I joined the Cherry Hill School District where I have been ever since. Assignments have shifted me from school to school, where new ideas were often met with misunderstanding. The 2000-01 year was personally disastrous; professionally I saw 450 students in two schools, but an art room allowed space for dance. A sad return to the cart followed. In addition to supervising student teachers, preparing exhibits, and organizing trips, I have attended classes in Philadelphia, New York, Washington, and Savannah, GA. Summer distinctions include a Fallingwater Fellowship, two NEH Fellowships and being named a Geraldine R. Dodge Fellow. Summer 2001, I attended the NAEA Distinguished Fellow Research Institute, was gifted with a fellowship at the Maine College of Art and attended annual classes at the Lincoln Center. The preceding school year, I was funded to study weekly at the Barnes Foundation. For the Campbell Soup Company, I have been a guest curator and a lecturer. I have lectured on Folk Art at AENJ and NAEA conventions and have taught at colleges, museums, and art centers. After completing a masters at Penn in 1983, I became active in Phi Delta Kappa, Pi Lambda Theta, and served on the Education Alumni Board, the Skidmore Leadership Council and as an evaluator for NBPTS and ETS. I am further from retirement than most my age because of several leaves, but I hope to return to graduate school and continue learning and teaching.

Lloyd L. Sensat, Jr.

Then

Now

Current Position: High School Art Teacher, Hahnville High School, St. Charles Parish, Boutte, Louisiana (Retired 2001)
Education: M.A. Educational Supervision, Louisiana State University (LSU), 1975; B.A. Advertising Design & Commercial Art, University of Southwestern Louisiana, 1967; continued graduate studies
Studio Interests: photography, architectural drawing, travel sketchbook/journals
Years in Teaching: 29

The truth is I never intended to be a teacher. With a degree in Advertising Design & Commercial Art, I hoped for a high powered job in arts and publishing. The reality of the times was Vietnam, so I ended up a Squadron Illustrator for the Air Force in Korea. Upon discharge, I accepted the job of establishing an art program at Iota High, a small rural school near my hometown of Crowley, LA. I was hooked! I loved teaching and working with student artists. In 1975, I moved from the Cajun Country of South Louisiana to New Orleans and started working in the St. Charles Parish Public Schools teaching elementary, then junior high, and finally high school Art. Living here with the history and architecture is innately southern and I soon realized that the kind of teaching which has a lasting impact on students stems from educators who use insights from their own living experiences. Given my passion for old buildings and historic preservation, in 1977, I wrote and received a Teacher Incentive Grant. Dr. Eugene Cizek, Tulane School of Architecture, and I implemented "Education through Historic Preservation." Through this program and my pioneering work in Louisiana Talented Art Education, I was fortunate to garner accolades, including: 1980 Louisiana Art Educator of the Year, 1987 Southeastern Region Art Educator of the Year, 1988 National Art Educator of the Year, 1996 Walt Disney and McDonald's American Teacher Award Honoree, and 1998 Arts Council of New Orleans' Mayor's Arts Award. I taught for 29 years and during that time my most important award came from the students themselves—their accomplishments validated my teaching. I retired in 2000 and am currently enjoying my new career as a licensed tour guide and innkeeper at my historic home, Sun Oak.

Then

Now

Marie Sayegh Shack

Current Position: High School Art Teacher, Wilmington High School, Wilmington, Massachusetts
Education: C.A.G.S. Education Leadership, Fitchburg State College, 1997; M.S. Art Education, Massachusetts College of Art, 1981; B.A. Art, minors English, Philosophy, College of New Rochelle, 1968
Studio Interests: photography, paper and book making
Years in Teaching: 30

Raised in Brooklyn, New York, I was exposed early to the culture of the borough and city. Married in 1969 to a "Boston boy," John and I have made our home in the Boston area with our two adopted children, Ameena and John, both from Lebanon. Although I received my B.A. in Art, it was never my intention to teach. However, on the same day I got a job offer on Madison Avenue, I also interviewed for a teaching position at an all girls Catholic high school in Queens. I took the job and never looked back! Lucky to have a visionary mentor in Sister Marie Fidelis SSJ, I have loved being a teacher for the past thirty two years. I taught both at public and parochial schools and at all grade levels. Although I specialized in photography, I have taught a wide range of two and three-dimensional classes, including jewelry and leather. This road has led me to continue taking courses, broadening and sharpening my skills and those of my students. I am currently a full time art teacher at Wilmington H. S. and the district Art Director. In addition, I teach education courses at Tufts and at the School of the Boston Museum of Fine Arts. In my high school program, I was able to introduce bookmaking/printing which allows me to indulge in one of my favorite activities of making paper and books. In our field, where our "clients" give us hugs and forever remember our times together, I feel blessed to have side-stepped into this profession. I continue to feel wonder and awe over my students; they still make me laugh and our time together is both precious and a mutual learning experience.

Jeannie Siegler

Then

Current Position: High School Art Teacher, Loyola High School, Missoula, Montana
Education: B.A. Art, Meredith College, 1968; continued graduate studies
Studio Interests: photography
Years in Teaching: 26

Now

After completing a BA in Art and getting teacher certification at Meredith College in Raleigh, North Carolina, I began teaching math and art at Kamabai Secondary School for Girls for the Peace Corps in Sierra Leone. Art was an aside and math was primary, as the students had to complete a West African Examination to graduate from secondary school. The experience was fantastic and life-changing. Even after returning to a classroom in The Gambia, West Africa this November 2001, my reaction was that every student and most especially every teacher should spend some time in a classroom like that—minimal resources except the students, your surroundings, and your own imagination. In 1973 my husband and I moved to the Rosebud Reservation in South Dakota. I taught art and language arts in the middle school. Our art classes were a combination of traditional Lakota crafts and contemporary Native American arts. The Rosebud teachers were a fantastic and dedicated group. After the birth of our second son, we moved to Montana in 1978. Since then, I have taught art at area public and private schools, K-12, as well as starting the first education outreach program at the Art Museum of Missoula. I am presently teaching art for grades 9-12 at Loyola High School in Missoula.

Then

Now

Carolyn S. Skeen

Current Position: Elementary Art Teacher, Linden Elementary, Oak Ridge, Tennessee
Education: M.S. Art Education, University of Tennessee-Knoxville, 1998; B.A. English, minor Painting & Design, University of Tennessee-Knoxville, 1965; continued graduate studies
Studio Interests: drawing, painting
Years in Teaching: 22

I began teaching in 1965, primarily in grades 6-8, at Farragut Elementary near Knoxville, Tennessee. Since then my workplace has moved about twenty miles away to Linden Elementary in Oak Ridge, a small city with a large population of engineers, scientists, and their children. I now teach K-4 and I am more convinced every day of the importance of art education at the elementary level. My credits include TAEA Elementary Art Educator of the Year, Oak Ridge Teacher of the Year, Tennessee Governor's School for the Arts Outstanding Teacher Award, and the Tennessee Arts Commission Arts Honors School and Grant. Recent Linden students have received 16 Crayola Dream-Makers Awards, two honorable mentions from Sakura for oil pastels, and have created work that appears in two issues of *School Arts Magazine*. I am proud of my students and the distinctions they have earned.

Then

Now

John Skrabalak (Skrab)

Current Position: High School Art Teacher, Altoona Area School District, Altoona, Pennsylvania
Education: M.Ed. Art Education, Penn State University, 1978; B.S. Art Education, Indiana University of Pennsylvania, 1972; continued graduate studies in art therapy
Studio Interests: painting, jewelry, sculpture, glass
Years in Teaching: 30

Teaching art started as a dream for me and became a passion. I love art and I love children—a perfect combination. I know that when I retire I will continue to teach in some capacity. It is in my heart and soul. I have received many blessings in my life: my daughter, the chemist, who will be graduating from college this year; a creative, loving, and supportive mother; a generous father; close caring friends; and some special awards—Outstanding Art Educator of Pennsylvania (PAEA), Outstanding K-12 Art Teacher in Sculpture (ISC), the Educator CARE Award from my school district, and the Outstanding Regional Representative and Co-Sponsor of the National Art Honor Society Awards from PAEA. I am a member of Kappa Delta Pi Honor Society. Right now I am the Secondary Division Director of the Pennsylvania Art Education Association. Upon retirement, I plan to pursue the artist in me, to teach, to learn, to travel, as well as to visit many art museums and arts festivals. My teaching philosophy is that a "sense of humor and an ounce of praise go a long way."

Cherie St. Pierre

Then

Now

Current Position: Elementary Art Teacher, Charles A. Lindbergh Elementary School, Kenmore, New York (Retired 2000)
Education: Ph.D. Humanities, New York University, 1992; M.A. Italian Language, Middlebury College, 1976; M.S. Art Education, Suny College, Buffalo, 1970; B.S. Art Education, Suny College, Buffalo, 1967
Studio Interests: photography, stained glass, printmaking
Years in Teaching: 35

I earned my B. S. in Art Education at Buffalo State College in 1967. As a junior, I participated in the Experiment in International Living Program where I spent a semester in Siena, Italy. This gave me the Marco Polo fever for traveling. After obtaining my M.S. at Buffalo State in Art Education (1970), I earned an M.A. in Italian Language and Literature (1976) at Middlebury College in Vermont. In 1992, I earned my Ph.D. in the Department of Culture and Communication at New York University. My fieldwork required study in Shanghai, China; Kyoto, Japan; Paris, France; and New York City. After completing my B. S., I accepted a teaching position in Kenmore-Town of Tonawanda. Throughout my 33 year career, I taught every grade level from K-12 in six elementary schools, two middle schools, and one high school. I taught in my own art room as well as on a cart, having worked with children whose abilities ranged from profoundly impaired to gifted. I was a cooperating teacher for many student teachers and from 1995-1998, served as a full time mentor to new teachers. The highlights of my career focus on the students' achievements whose awards include the New York State Christmas Seal Stamp for the American Lung Association; the first Jay Harry

Rubenstein Scholarship at the Albright-Knox Art Gallery (for financially handi-capped students who evidenced great potential in visual art); the Foreign Minister's Award in the Pentel International Children's Art Exhibition in 1999. I have volunteered as a regional co-chair and the State Secretary for the New York State Art Teachers Association. I just received the regional Outstanding Service Award from NYSATA (2001). I retired from teaching in 2000 and now work part time as a college supervisor for student teachers. I feel ful-filled in that I have completed the full circle of educational enlightenment.

Kathleen Thompson (Kathy)

Then

Current Position: Middle School Art Teacher, Gilmer Middle School, Ellijay, Georgia
Education: Ed.D. Art Education, University of Georgia, 1994; M.Ed. Curriculum & Supervision, University of Georgia, 1974; B.F.A. Printmaking and Painting, Wayne State University, Detroit, 1966
Studio Interests: writing, painting, drawing, fibers
Years in Teaching: 31

Now

When I was 17, I said that I would never get mar-ried, have children, live in a small town or be a teacher. A husband of 30 years, two grown children, a house in the mountains of rural North Georgia, and 31 years in teaching attest to the wisdom of the old adage "Never say Never!" My years in art edu-cation have been divided between high school and middle school teaching. Additionally, I have taught undergraduate and graduate college classes as an adjunct faculty member during the last 22 years. My most rewarding accom-plishments involve the Georgia Art Education Association and permanent youth art galleries. I have initiated youth art galleries at the Atlanta Hartsfield Air-port, the Georgia Department of Education, the Federal Reserve Bank of At-lanta, and an annual show at the High Museum of Art. In a single year, 725 students have their art displayed. The other accomplishment that gives me pleasure is my writing, over 95 articles in state and national magazines. Awards include GAEA's Middle School Educator (1991) and Georgia Art Educator of the Year (2002). Community involvement has been equally rewarding and has included two books of local history (researched, written, and photographed by my high school art students), community mural, photography, and quilt projects, the establishment of what is now a 23 year old art festival, and ser-vice to two local arts associations. I have received more than I have given. Art can truly be a powerful force in children's and adult's lives.

Then

Now

Gerald Donald Vilenski (Jerry)

Current Position: Elementary Art Teacher, Starr and Cooper Elementary Schools, Plainwell, Michigan
Education: B.S. Art Education, minor Journalism Education, Central Michigan University, 1973; continued graduate studies
Studio Interests: watercolor
Years in Teaching: 29

I was born in Sioux City, Iowa, but was raised in the northern Michigan town of Cheboygan. I attended Catholic schools until eighth grade, then public high school. None of the schools I attended offered art, which was my one true passion. I resolved to become an art teacher, in part because I believed there needed to be more art teachers in the world. My first teaching job was in the Upper Peninsula of Michigan, for the Rudyard Schools. In 1978, I obtained a job teaching elementary art for the Plainwell Schools. During my tenure as an art educator, I have maintained a parallel career as an artist, having shown my watercolors in several galleries throughout the state and winning numerous awards at the local and state levels. I have conducted workshops and lectures throughout the state for art associations and classes. Throughout my career, I have worked hard to establish the arts as an educational priority for both the schools and community. I am known as a forceful advocate for the arts in my community, having helped found the local arts council and serving as its President for twenty years. By serving on city boards, task forces and cultural committees representing the arts, I have made the presence of the arts known in the community. I have also provided leadership in shaping the curriculum in my district, as well as helping develop the arts in education in the region. Being a passionate advocate for both children and teachers, I have served as a negotiator, labor mediator and grievance chair for the teachers' association. I have been described by administrators as opinionated, frustrating, and demanding, but also as talented, progressive, and most of all, an advocate for children. I claim credit for all of these! I have been married to the same woman (Barb) for 30 years and have a wonderful daughter, Allison. And finally, this year I have been nominated for the Disney American Teacher Award.

Then

Carol Ashley Wellein

Current Position: Middle School Art and Social Studies Teacher, St. James Academy, Monkton, Maryland
Education: B.F.A. Art, Maryland Institute of Art, 1967; continued graduate studies
Studio Interests: pastels
Years in Teaching: 29 years

Now

I began my teaching career on the elementary level from 1967 to 1973. For the next six years I stayed home to raise two boys but continued to teach private painting lessons to adults and children. I resumed teaching art on the pre-school level to three nursery schools for the next 10 years. Seeing a need for art ideas for pre-school teachers, I collaborated with a colleague to write a bi-monthly newsletter which eventually resulted in a book published by Dale Seymour titled *Little Fingers*. During the 80s, I continued to give workshops at Early Childhood conferences on teaching art to preschoolers. In 1986, I began teaching at St. James Academy, this time kindergarten through grade six. I served on the Teacher's Advisory Committee for the Walters Art Museum. Eventually, we added seventh and eighth grades which I also taught. I was asked to give a workshop for the AIMS conference and to teach a graduate course on integrating the arts into the early childhood curriculum at Towson University. I continued teaching this class this past summer but with other experts in the field of performing arts. It was one of the most rewarding experiences of my career. This year I began teaching sixth grade social studies, a natural subject for integration with art. Currently, I am working on my master's equivalency at Towson University. My favorite day is when I get to teach my sixth graders a double period of art and social studies, but it is very difficult not to make it a double art session.

Then

Kenneth E. Wilkie (Ken)

Current Position: Elementary Art Teacher, Riverside Elementary School, Princeton, New Jersey
Education: M.A. Creative Arts Education, Rutgers University, 1996; B. A. History, B. A. Art, Rutgers University, 1973; continued graduate studies
Studio Interests: cartooning
Years in Teaching: 29

Now

I started teaching in Burlington Township, New Jersey in 1973. Since then, I moved on to Mount Laurel and finally to Princeton where I work with K-5 students. I spent sometime in community theatre: acting, directing, writing, designing props and scenery. Later I became interested in cartooning and have published cartoons in a wide variety of magazines including *Good Housekeeping*, *Saturday Evening Post*, and *New Woman*. Along the way, I did a master's degree in Creative Arts Education at Rutgers and did additional graduate work in elementary education.

Then

Now

Judith Bills Williams (Judy)

Current Position: Elementary Art Teacher & Media Specialist, Southside Primary School, Shelbyville, Tennessee
Education: M.Ed. Learning Resources, Middle Tennessee State University, 1977; B.A. Elementary Education, Art, David Lipscomb University, 1966
Studio Interests: fibers
Years in Teaching: 31

As a native of Tennessee, I attended David Lipscomb University, from which I received my undergraduate degree in Elementary Education. In 1977, I completed my M.Ed. in Learning Resources from Middle Tennessee State University. My first teaching position was at Central High School in Shelbyville where I taught art and served as Fine Arts Department Chair for 11 years. Since then, I have taught elementary art in several settings. For over 15 years, I have been a staff member of the Tennessee Arts Academy and recently, School Administration Director. I have enjoyed presenting in the following professional forums: Tennessee and National Staff Development conferences; Tennessee and National Art Education Association conferences; Tennessee Department of Education conferences for grades K, 1, and gifted and talented; and Delta Kappa Gamma State conferences. I have been active in grant writing and have managed grants for my local school district, library, and arts councils. My distinctions include the Tennessee Delta Kappa Gamma Bradley Staff Development Fellowship; President, Publications Chair and Middle Tennessee Chair of the Tennessee Art Education Association; Board Representative at Large of the Tennessee Association of Craft Artists; and President, Bedford County, Tennessee Arts Council. In addition, I was pleased to be chosen as the Tennessee Art Educator of the Year. As an artist, I exhibit batiks and other fabric works in one person and group shows in Tennessee.

Anita M. Winfrey

Then

Current Position: Elementary Art Teacher, Irisburg Elementary/Stanleytown Elementary, Henry County, Virginia
Education: M.Ed. Administration and Curriculum, Xavier University, 1979; B.A. Art Education, Edgecliff College, 1974
Studio Interests: watercolor, woodcuts
Years in Teaching: 25

Now

I graduated from high school in Cincinnati, Ohio, in 1970, then attended Ohio Edgecliff College where I received my Bachelor of Arts degree in 1974. I got my first teaching job at Deer Park High, in Cincinnati, teaching art in grades 7-12. I was the first black teacher to work in that district. That same year, I began my graduate work in education and finished my M.Ed. in August 1979 from Xavier University in Cincinnati. Most of my career, I have taught middle and elementary school art. At the same time, I have taught part time at the college level. In 1988, I moved to Virginia where I taught at Axton Middle School for two years, then returned to Cincinnati where I accepted a position teaching art at Bethany, a private school. I taught in that private setting for ten years. To better my salary, I returned to the public schools only to have my art position dissolved due to district cutbacks. At that point, I returned to the job security available to me in Virginia, where I am currently teaching grades K-5. Though I have no children of my own, I have always considered my classrooms full of children to be "my kids."

Nancy Zadra

Current Position: Elementary Art Teacher, Missoula County Public Schools, Missoula, Montana
Education: Ed.D. Educational Leadership, University of Montana, 1998; M.A. Art/Art Education, California State University-Sacramento, 1982; B.A. Art, Minor in History, Univer-

Then

Now

sity of California-Davis, 1964
Studio Interests: watercolor, acrylic painting,
drawing, photography
Years in Teaching: 38

My career in education spans more than 30 years of
highly diversified teaching situations. I have taught
students in grades K through adult and I have worked
in three states, as well as overseas. I believe that all
students have the potential to learn and can do so in a school environment that
is safe from harm and fear, a place that fosters, sustains, and nurtures the love
of learning and positive self-esteem. When my students ask me when did I
begin to "do" art, I tell them that I have always loved to draw and to paint,
from the time when I was very young. I grew up in San Francisco, and my
father brought me to Saturday morning art classes at the "Leg Museum" before I was even old enough for school. I saw myself as an artist and viewed
the artworks on the gallery walls as the works of my compatriots. I always
knew that I would like to teach, and my selection of art as a college major
(after an inspirational first semester Art IA class) led me to become an art
teacher. I have never regretted this choice, as it was "of the heart." However,
the constant threat to art's position in the curriculum has been very wearing.
This threat has moved me to become a strong and outspoken advocate of the
role of art in education. My personal challenge has been working to ensure
the continuation of art studies now and into the future. While teaching, I have
pursued my own professional growth by earning my doctoral degree in Educational Leadership at the University of Montana in 1998. The research for
my dissertation on teaching teams took me to school settings in Washington,
Idaho, and Montana.

References

Bach, R. (1970). *Jonathan Livingston Seagull.* New York: Macmillan.

Barone, T., & Eisner, E. (1997). Arts-based educational research. In R. M. Jaeger (Ed.), *Complementary methods for research in education* (2nd ed., pp. 73-116). Washington, DC: American Educational Research Association.

Barrie, J. M. (1956). *Peter Pan: A fantasy in five acts.* New York: S. French. Original published in 1928.

Brown vs. Board of Education of Topeka, Kansas (1954, 347 U. S. 483).

Brown, D. A. (1970). *Bury my heart at Wounded Knee: An Indian history of the American West.* New York: Holt, Rinehart & Winston.

Carroll, L. (1953). *Alice in Wonderland.* New York: Peter Pauper Press. Original published 1865.

Carson, R. (1962). *Silent spring.* New York: Fawcett Crest.

Chapman, L. (1985). *Discover art.* Worcester, Mass. : Davis Publications.

Clandinin, D. J., & Connelly, F. M. (1994). Personal experience methods. In N. Denzin & Y. Lincoln (Eds.), *Handbook of qualitative research* (pp. 413-427). Thousand Oaks, London: Sage Publications.

Cleaver, E. (1968). *Soul on ice.* New York: Dell.

Dylan, Bob. (1963). The times they are a-changin. In J. Bartlett & J. Kaplan (Eds.), *Bartlett's familiar quotations* (16th ed.). (p. 771). Boston: Little, Brown and Company.

Eisner, E. (1998). *The kind of schools we need.* Portsmouth, NH: Heinemann.

Eliot, T. S. (1942). Four quartets: Little Gidding. In M. H. Abrams (Ed.), *The Norton anthology of English literature* (pp. 1494-1500). New York: W. W. Norton & Company.

Frank, A. (1952). *Anne Frank: The diary of a young girl.* (B. M. Mooyaart-Doubleday, Trans.). New York: Doubleday.

Giovanni, N. (1971). *Spin a soft Black song: Poems for children.* New York: Hill and Wang.

Heller, J. (1961). *Catch-22.* New York: Dell.

Hesse, H. (1951). *Siddhartha.* New York: New Directions. Original published in German 1922.

Hubbard, G. & Rouse, M. (1972). *Art: Meaning, methods, and media.* Westchester, IL: Benefic Press.

Kaufman, Bel. (1965). *Up the down staircase.* Englewood Cliffs, N.J., Prentice-Hall.

Kismaric, C. & Heiferman, M. (1996). *Growing up with Dick and Jane: Learning & living the American dream.* San Francisco, CA: Collins Publishers.

Lowenfeld, V. (1957). *Creative and mental growth.* New York: Macmillan Publishing.

Macaulay, D. (1973). *Cathedral: The story of its construction.* Boston: Houghton Mifflin.

Macaulay, D. (1977). *Castle.* Boston: Houghton Mifflin.

Marwick, A. (1998). *The sixties: Cultural revolution in Britain, France, Italy, and the United States, c. 1958-c.1974.* New York: Oxford University Press.

McLean, D. (1971). American Pie. Don McLean Music Corporation of America, Inc./Benny Bird Music (BMI).

Mitchell, J. (1969). Woodstock. In J. Bartlett & J. Kaplan (Eds.), *Bartlett's familiar quotations* (16th ed.). (p. 773). Boston: Little, Brown and Company.

Neill, A. S. (1960). *Summerhill: A radical approach to child rearing.* New York: Hart Publishing.

Porter, E. (1913). *Pollyanna.* New York : A. L. Burt Company.

Porter, K. A. (1955). St. Augustine and the bullfight. *The collected essays and occasional writings of Katherine Anne Porter* (1970). In R. Maggio (Ed.), *The new Beacon book of quotations by women* (1996). (p. 229). Boston: Beacon Press.

Postman, N., & Weingartner, C. (1969). *Teaching as a subversive activity.* New York: Dell Publishing.

Ryan, G., & Bernard, R. (2000). Data management and analysis methods. In N. Denzin & Y. Lincoln (Eds.), *Handbook of qualitative research* (2nd ed.). (pp. 769-802). Thousand Oaks, CA: Sage Publications

Saint-Exupéry, A. (1943). *The little prince.* (K. Woods, Trans.). New York: Harcourt, Brace & World.

Silberman, C. (1964). *Crisis in black and white.* New York: Random House.

Silverstein, S. (1964). *The giving tree.* New York: Harper & Row.

Spock, B. (1946). *The common sense book of baby and child care.* New York: Duell, Sloan and Pearce.

Toffler, A. (1971). *Future shock.* New York: Bantam Books.

Witherell, C., & Noddings, N. (1991). *Stories lives tell: Narrative and dialogue in education.* New York: Teachers College Press.

Wolfe, T. (1965). *The kandy-kolored tangerine-flake streamline baby.* New York: Farrar, Straus and Giroux.

X, Malcolm. (1965). *The autobiography of Malcolm X.* With the assistance of Alex Haley. New York: Grove Press.

About the Author

Then

Now

Candace Jesse Stout received her doctorate in 1989 from the University of Missouri-Columbia. Prior to her graduate studies, she taught Language Arts and Allied Arts in elementary through high school. Currently she is an Associate Professor in the Department of Art Education at The Ohio State University. She has authored a college level text, *Critical Thinking and Writing in Art.* She has published in *Studies in Art Education*, the *Journal of Art Education*, *Visual Arts Research*, the *Elementary School Journal*, the *Journal of Multicultural and Cross-cultural Research in Art Education*, the *Journal of Teacher Education*, and the *Journal of Thought.* She has also written a chapter for Portelli and Hare's *Philosophy of Education: Introductory Readings.*